Liberty and Locality

Liberty and Locality

Parliament,
Permissive Legislation,
and Ratepayers' Democracies
in the Nineteenth Century

John Prest

CLARENDON PRESS · OXFORD
1990

Oxford University Press, Walton Street, Oxford OX2 6DP

Oxford New York Toronto
Delhi Bombay Calcutta Madras Karachi
Petaling Jaya Singapore Hong Kong Tokyo
Nairobi Dar es Salaam Cape Town
Melbourne Auckland
and associated companies in
Berlin Ibadan

Oxford is a trade mark of Oxford University Press

Published in the United States
by Oxford University Press, New York

British Library Cataloguing in Publication Data
ISBN 0 19 820175-3
(data available)

Library of Congress Cataloging in Publication Data
(data available)

Typeset by Downdell Limited, Oxford
Printed in Great Britain by
Courier International Ltd
Tiptree, Essex

Acknowledgements

I AM grateful to Professor Keith Robbins, to Dr Charles Esdaile, and to Professor John Clive for the invitations which enabled me to try out early versions of the arguments advanced in this book in the James Tumelty Memorial Lecture at Glasgow University in February 1983, during the Duke of Wellington Congress at Southampton University in July 1987, and at Harvard University in October 1987.

I want to thank Charles Prest and Mrs Donald Greig for having me to stay, and to say how much I owe to Mr C. D. Webster and Mr J. O'Donnell of the County Record Office at Newport, Isle of Wight, and to Miss J. Helliwell of the Huddersfield Local History Library and Miss Janet Burhouse, District Archivist of the Kirklees Libraries, Museums and Arts, for their help in pointing me towards the materials needed for this study.

Mr R. M. Smart, Keeper of Manuscripts and University Muniments in the University Library at St Andrews, kindly put me in touch with Mr R. M. Urquhart, a fellow enthusiast for permissive or adoptive legislation. From the beginning Mr Urquhart was generous to me of his learning, and kindness itself with his advice. Since our discussions began, he has completed two works, upon 'The Burghs of Scotland and the Burgh Police (Scotland) Act 1833 (3 & 4 Will. IV c. 46)' (1985) and 'The Burghs of Scotland and the Police of Towns (Scotland) Act 1850 (13 & 14 Vict. c. 33)' and placed copies of them in the Scottish Record Office, all the Scottish Universities, the National Library of Scotland, the Advocates Library, the Signet Library, and the Lyon Office. These are now to be published by the Scottish Library Association. Future generations of Scottish historians will benefit beyond measure from the comprehensive and exhaustive nature of the studies which Mr Urquhart has undertaken and carried through to a conclusion.

Contents

Abbreviations

CRO	County Record Office
EFR	*East Fife Record*
FH	*Fife Herald*
FJ	*Fife Journal*
HC	*Huddersfield Chronicle*
HE	*Huddersfield Examiner*
HPL	Huddersfield Public Library
ICMB	Improvement Commissioners Minute Book
IND	*Hampshire Independent*
IWO	*Isle of Wight Observer*
LB	Local Board
LBMB	Local Board Minute Book
LM	*Leeds Mercury*
MLBMB	Moldgreen Local Board Minute Book
MPPI	Minutes of Proceedings at a Preliminary Inquiry
NBR	Newport Borough Records
PD	*Parliamentary Debates*, third series
PP	*Parliamentary Papers*
RSC1	*First Report of the Royal Sanitary Commission*
RSC2	*Second Report of the Royal Sanitary Commission*
SCPB	*Report of the Select Committee on Private Bills*
SLT1	*First Report of the Commissioners for inquiring into the State of Large Towns and Populous Districts*
SLT2	*Second Report of the Commissioners for inquiring into the State of Large Towns and Populous Districts*
Urquhart (1985)	R. M. Urquhart, 'The Burghs of Scotland and the Burgh Police (Scotland) Act 1833 (3 & 4 Will. IV c. 46)'

Urquhart (1987)	R. M. Urquhart, 'The Burghs of Scotland and the Police of Towns (Scotland) Act 1850 (13 & 14 Vict. c. 33)'
VICM	Ventnor Improvement Commissioners Minutes

I

Parliament and the Localities

1. INTRODUCTION: CENTRAL AND LOCAL GOVERNMENT

In the eighteenth and nineteenth centuries the relations between central and local government were worked out in parliament. Peers, of course, attended parliament in their own right, while Members of the lower House, whose constituencies varied so greatly in size, represented, contemporaries reassured themselves, not numbers, but interests. There was much truth in this, but Members of Parliament also stood for localities. Peers took local titles. Members of the House of Commons were returned by counties or boroughs, and were referred to in debate by the names of the places they represented. These localities had needs of their own, and in the British parliamentary system of the eighteenth and early nineteenth centuries initiatives could pass in both directions, from the centre to the localities and from the localities to the centre. The traffic was reflected in two distinct forms of legislation, which, before the end of the eighteenth century, was divided into public general Acts and private Acts. Public general Acts applied to the whole of one or more of the three kingdoms, England and Wales, Scotland, and Ireland. Private Acts, which, somewhat confusingly, were divided in the statute-book into two categories of 'Local and Personal Acts' and 'Private Acts', were passed upon petition by a local body, the promoters of a joint-stock company, or even by an individual person.[1] The difference between public and private

---

[1] Until 1854 Private Bill legislation was divided into (1) Local and Personal Acts, and (2) Private Acts. Local and Personal Acts included company, gas, water, paving, improvement, lighting and watching, police, road, and railway Acts, while Private Acts included inclosures and estate Acts. In 1855 there was a change and Private Bill legislation was classified as either (1) Local Acts, or

was revealed in the different formulae expressing the royal assent, 'le roi le veult' and 'soit fait comme il est desiré'. Private Acts were not as glamorous as public ones, and they were usually summarised rather than printed in full in the statute-book, but they were an important part of parliamentary business, and between 1800 and 1884, they outnumbered public Acts by 18,497 to 9,556.[2]

In the case of public general Acts, the ministers who introduced and the parliaments which passed them were faced with the problem of agency. Upon whom were they to lay the responsibility for carrying them out? There were three ways of implementing public general legislation. The first was through the Lord-Lieutenants of the counties and the Justices of the Peace in counties, and the corporations and Justices, or Magistrates, in boroughs; the second was through the much more numerous parish meetings and vestries; and the third through specially created statutory bodies like the Commissioners of Sewers (whose task it was to conduct surplus rainwaters off the land, via the rivers, to the sea), the Land Tax Commissioners, and the Excise Commissioners. There was some overlapping in personnel between the three forms, but each of these agencies may be said to have approached its role in central–local government relations from a different point of view. The JPs stood in the middle—they accepted their position as executive (and judicial) agents for the central government in the localities, and also saw themselves as representatives, within the administrative system, of the localities to the Home Office.[3] On either side of them stood the vestries, whose loyalties were to their own localities, and the Commissioners who owed their existence to and normally rendered their allegiance to the central government.

For any government in the early nineteenth century the choice between these three posed a dilemma. Early nine-

(2) Private Acts. The confusion caused by there being two categories of Private Bills, one of which was also called Private, has to be encountered.

[2] F. Clifford, *A History of Private Bill Legislation*, 2 vols. (1885), i, p. vii.

[3] A. P. Donajgrodski, 'The Home Office, 1822–48', Oxford University D.Phil. thesis 1974, *passim*.

teenth-century reforms in the legal system involved the downgrading of many offences, and their transfer from the higher to the lower, summary, courts.[4] At a time when the Magistrates' judicial work-load was increasing, was it practicable to add to their administrative burdens as well? Just how far could any government trade upon the good-will of an unpaid Justice? Then, there was a further complication. In the counties the Justices were still in full control. But in the towns many of the municipal corporations with which the Justices were closely identified, had degenerated into closed and co-opted bodies. Popular opposition was growing, and the 'elective' principle was gaining ground at the expense of the 'prerogative' or 'privilege' principle.[5] If political prudence dictated inclining towards an elected agency, then the parish vestries, many of which were still popular bodies, covered too small areas, for many purposes, to be effective, and were too numerous to be supervised. In Whitehall and at Westminster the parish officers, the overseers of the poor, were a byword for ignorance and inadequacy. If efficiency was the desideratum, then how could government ministers escape the conclusion that administration ought to be placed in the hands, neither of amateur JPs, however conscientious, nor of oligarchic corporations, nor of semi-literate overseers, but in those of a professional executive commission, staffed by paid agents, issuing directives, and employing inspectors to supervise a corps of obedient functionaries. But having reached that conclusion, they came up against the fact that parliament itself was jealous of commissions, and that JPs and vestries might be expected to make common cause against anything that smacked of jobbing, 'London knows best', and the establishment of a 'French' system. Early nineteenth-century governments, then, for all their astonishing success, between 1793 and 1815, in financing and waging the wars against France, and in overthrowing a much more visibly

---

[4] L. Radzinowicz and R. Hood, *A History of English Criminal Law* (1986), v, pp. 618–24; L. Sweeney, 'The Extension and Practice of Summary Jurisdiction', Cambridge University Ph.D. thesis 1985.

[5] J. Redlich and F. W. Hirst, *The History of Local Government in England* (1903).

organised and structured regime than their own, were short of agency.

Were things any better when looked at from the other end, from the point of view of the localities? In the course of the eighteenth century it seems to have become accepted, in both English and Scottish law, that a corporation was not a person. A person was allowed to do anything which was not forbidden by law, but a corporation, or public body of any kind, including commercial enterprises like canal and water companies, was not allowed to undertake anything not specifically permitted by statute. Hence the necessity for every locality, except, perhaps, a royal borough, which wished to improve itself, to promote a private Bill.[6] Every county which wished to erect a new bridge, gaol, or asylum, and every town which sought to widen, pave, light, or watch its streets, or to bring in a supply of fresh water—every locality, in short, which wished to carry out works affecting the rights of property, requiring the compulsory purchase of lands, or the right to levy rates, tolls, fares, or other charges, and to make by-laws, had to go before parliament with a petition for a private Act. For the locality, the attraction of this arrangement was that it gained a title which could not be overthrown in the courts. For parliament, the advantage lay in the fact that all business, throughout the United Kingdom, passed under its observation and through its own hands. The sovereignty of parliament, although never spoken of in the same breath with that of the monarchs of the *ancien régime* on the Continent, was absolute.

A private Bill, like a public one, had to pass through both Houses of Parliament. In both Houses proof of compliance with standing orders had to be supplied before a Bill could be proceeded with. It was essential, therefore, to employ an experienced solicitor, or parliamentary agent, to draft one's Bill, and serve notice upon interested parties. In both Houses a private Bill which was opposed would be referred to a Select Committee, and counsel had to be briefed to argue cases. In the early nineteenth century both Houses

[6] A. N. Schofield, *The Councillor* (1950), p. 1; B. K. Lucas and P. G. Richards, *A History of Local Government in the Twentieth Century* (1978), pp. 28–9.

were operating an 'open' committee system, according to which any Member might attend and vote, or even come in at the last moment and vote without having heard the previous discussion. The standing orders and the committee procedures of the two Houses differed, and in addition to the services of a solicitor and a barrister, localities were well advised to secure the help of the officials of the two Houses, who had many opportunities to promote or frustrate private Bills and knew how to exploit them.[7]

It is no wonder, then, that private Bill legislation acquired an unenviable reputation for expense. A country solicitor would charge 5 guineas a day for attendance in London.[8] His travelling expenses, and the expenses of witnesses (all of whom had to be brought to Westminster) called to prove compliance with standing orders had to be met. An inclosure Act cost between £1,000 and £2,000,[9] and in the 1830s the average cost even of an unopposed town improvement Bill was £1,627.[10] Exceptional cases cost much more, and in 1846 an experienced parliamentary agent who was asked what was the greatest number of witnesses he had ever known to be called to prove compliance with standing orders upon a Bill, answered 'four hundred', and added that their expenses had amounted to £10,000.[11] Opposed Bills were always expensive. Manchester lost £6,000 on a water Bill which failed,[12] and in 1846, Liverpool was reputed to have spent over £100,000 upon private Bill legislation in ten years.[13]

These were large sums even by the standards of large towns, and faced with examples of this kind, it is difficult to keep a sense of proportion, and avoid caricaturing private Bill legislation. Parliamentary agents milked, but

---

[7] Clifford, *Private Bill Legislation*. F. H. Spencer, *Municipal Origins, an Account of English Private Bill Legislation relating to Local Government, 1740–1835* (1911), ch. 3; O. C. Williams, *The Historical Development of Private Bill Procedure and Standing Orders in the House of Commons*, 2 vols. (1948); D. L. Rydz, *The Parliamentary Agents, a History* (1979), ch. 4.

[8] *PP* 1846, XII, p. 139, *SCPB*, p. 131, Qns. 1267–8.

[9] *PD* LXXXII, 25, Trelawny.

[10] S. E. Finer, *Life and Times of Edwin Chadwick* (1952), p. 433.

[11] *PP* 1846, XII, p. 113, *SCPB*, p. 105, Qn. 954.

[12] Ibid. p. 22, *SCPB* p. 14, Qn. 160.

[13] Ibid. p. 14, *SCPB* p. 6, Qn. 47.

did not of course seek to kill the beast they fed on. The large towns, with rents and other incomes of their own, could, perhaps, afford to pay. Much more worrying was the predicament of a community like Rusholme. This village lay compactly both for a supply of water, and for drainage. The works themselves would cost between £1,000 and £1,200. But the expense of promoting a local Act would be £600 even if the Bill were unopposed, and would be twice or even three times as much if there were an opposition.[14] How could it ever be prudent for a small community to proceed when the risks were so great, and how many Rusholmes were there, unwilling to venture into the costly and hazardous world of private Bill legislation, and unable, therefore, to provide themselves with the elements of either town improvement or public health?[15]

In the early nineteenth century, then, parliament was faced with a situation in which instructions passed from the centre to the localities were likely to fail for want of reliable agents, and initiatives coming up from the localities to parliament were all too often frustrated by costly and cumbersome parliamentary procedures.

2. 1828–1833: MODEL CLAUSES ACTS AND PERMISSIVE LEGISLATION

Faced with a kind of sclerosis in central–local government relations, parliament turned to model clauses Acts, and permissive, or adoptive, Acts.

The best known of all model clauses Acts was the General Inclosure Act of 1801.[1] This was an Act 'for consolidating in one Act certain Provisions usually inserted in Acts of Inclosure'. The Act did not itself inclose anything. Nor did it save inclosers from the necessity of petitioning for a private Bill, for every inclosure which would have required statutory authority before the model clauses Act was passed, would still require its own Act. But it did provide a

---

[14] Ibid. p. 24, *SCPB* p. 16, Qn. 197.
[15] Ibid. p. 4, *SCPB* p. iv.
[1] 41 Geo. III c. 109.

piece of legislative meccano. Henceforth, inclosers could incorporate the clauses of the General Inclosure Act simply by citing them. Private inclosure Acts became that much easier to draft, and that much cheaper in consequence.

Inclosure reached a peak during the Napoleonic Wars,[2] when the rapidly increasing population must, after all, be fed, unless there were to be bread riots and threats to public order. But it was only one sector where private Bill legislation was commonly employed, and in the period after 1815, when there was plenty of cheap grain available for shipment from the Continent, the emphasis among private Bills began to shift towards matters of town improvement and public health. Problems associated with urbanisation and industrialisation were coming to a head, and when parliament addressed itself to these, it was, at first, by means of permissive, or adoptive legislation that it sought to proceed.

This was an approach to the problem, which, despite its importance in an age which set a high value upon local independence, and individual self-help, has scarcely received the attention it deserves. A permissive Act can be described as a model clauses Act, or a set of meccano pieces, with a motor in. It was a public general Act which the localities might adopt if they wanted to, and it offered a happy medium between central control and local initiative. Permissive legislation was not new. There had been permissive Acts passed in the eighteenth century, and the one which is, perhaps, most often referred to, is Gilbert's Act of 1782.[3] This Act enabled 'two third Parts, in Number and Value' of 'the Owners and Occupiers of Lands' within a parish, with the consent of two Justices of the Peace, to adopt the Act, and in conjunction with other parishes to form a union for the construction of a workhouse and the better relief of the poor. The Act was, in effect, a ratepayers' do-it-yourselves kit. Successive clauses set out the procedures which were to be followed, and the schedules

---

[2] There were 1,700 inclosure Acts passed before 1800 and a further 2,000 between 1800 and 1844, *PP* 1844, V, p. 25, *Report from the Select Committee on Commons' Inclosure*, p. 17, Qn. 185.

[3] 22 Geo. III c. 83.

contained the exact form of words which was to be used at every stage of the adoption process. Towards the end of George IV's reign, and at the beginning of William IV's, parliament began to extend this adoptive system into the closely connected fields of town improvement and public health. In the specialised world of central–local government relations three Acts were subsequently cited as models of what such legislation should be.[4] The first, an Act of 1828, made provision for the lighting, cleansing, and watching of towns in Ireland. The second, passed in 1830 (and repealed and replaced in 1833), dealt with the lighting and watching of parishes in England and Wales. The third, introduced in 1830, but not passed until 1833, was an Act to enable burghs in Scotland to establish what was called 'a general System of Police'—a police Bill in Scotland resembling, as a witness before a Select Committee put it, an improvement Bill in England.[5]

All three Acts could be put into operation in much the same way. In Ireland the initiative could be taken by twenty-one £20 householders. In England and Wales it could be taken by any three rated inhabitants. In Scotland it could be taken by twenty-one £10 householders in burghs of over 3,000 inhabitants, and by seven £10 householders in smaller burghs. In Ireland the application was to be sent to the Lord-Lieutenant, who was to decide whether a town meeting was to be called. In Great Britain the central executive was not allotted any role to play: the English and Welsh addressed themselves to the churchwardens, and the Scots to the Chief Magistrate of the burgh. In each case a meeting was then to be held. In Ireland the meeting was to be decisive: in Scotland (and in England and Wales after 1833) any five ratepayers could demand a poll. Rules were laid down for voting, and if the Act was to be adopted the proposal had to be carried by a simple majority in Ireland, by a three-quarters (reduced in 1833 to a two-thirds) majority in England and Wales, and by a three-quarters majority in Scotland. In each case, if the majority was achieved, the meeting must go on and decide how many Commissioners

---

[4] 9 Geo. IV c. 82, 11 Geo. IV c. 27, and 3 & 4 Will. IV c. 46.
[5] *PP* 1846 XII, p. 107, *SCPB*, p. 99, Qn. 905.

(in Ireland and Scotland) or Inspectors (in England and Wales) were going to be needed to carry out the Act, which was then deemed to have been adopted and to have come into force.

These three Acts appear to have been grounded in the belief that all over the United Kingdom good and active men existed, whose desire to take a lead in the improvement of their localities was being frustrated by a sinister interest of lawyers intent on maximising their fees from private Bill legislation. The localities liked permissive legislation because it was voluntary, simple, and cheap. Members of Parliament benefited from a reduction in the number of time-consuming private Bills, and the departments of state were satisfied because the Acts embodied the 'best practice'. Localities which adopted a public general Act could not be acting contrary to the accepted principles of English, Scottish, or Irish law. Further, if time revealed deficiencies and a need for amendment, this, too, could be carried out by parliament, at a stroke, and without expense to the localities. Finally, the adoption of these Acts in the localities was not likely to prejudice the creation, ultimately, if that was what parliament wished, of a compulsory and uniform scheme of town improvement or public health.

It was the Duke of Wellington's short-lived administration of 1828–30 which passed the first two of these Acts, and initiated the legislative processes which led to the third by bringing in the first Bill to establish a general system of police in Scotland in 1830. The point appears, understandably enough, to have passed unnoticed by the Duke of Wellington's biographers. In comparison with the by-election in County Clare which took place during the 1828 session, with Catholic emancipation, and with the excitement of the general election in 1830, none of these Acts was newsworthy. Nor, except in one respect, do they appear to have provided matter for a struggle between political parties. The exception, however, is important, and is worth explaining in some detail. All three Acts established what might be called ratepayers' democracies. The principal features of the Irish Act were the select nature of the democracy, which was limited to the safe hands of £20 householders, and the fact that the initiative had to pass through the Lord-Lieutenant. The most striking aspect of the Scottish Bill introduced in 1830, and the English and Welsh Act of 1830, is that in both cases, after the initiative had been taken and a public meeting called, the ratepayers' democracy was to vote according to a graduated franchise. In Scotland there were to be two scales, one for towns with populations of fewer than 1,000, and another for towns with populations over 1,000.[6] In England and Wales householders assessed at up to £50 to the poor rate were to have one vote, and those assessed for more than £50 were to have one extra vote for every further £25 of assessment up to a limit of six votes. Although no reference was made to this in the statute, the scale was identical with that laid down in Sturges Bourne's Act of 1818.[7] Sturges Bourne's Act had been intended to enable the middle classes to seize control of parish meetings or *open* vestries from the hands of the unruly democracy and reduce poor rates, and in 1819 a second Act had been passed to permit ratepayers, voting according to the graduated scale, to establish select vestries, or committees of management where business could be conducted with dispatch.[8]

The fact that Wellington's government followed where Sturges Bourne had led suggests that the duke set great store by the proportional representation of property. This system of weighted voting was highly controversial. Following the change of government in 1830, the Whigs lacked the resolution to repeal Sturges Bourne's Act of 1818, which remained in force until 1894. But the strength of party feeling upon the matter can be gauged from the fact that in 1831 Hobhouse introduced a permissive Act to enable parishes in large towns to escape from the clutches

[6] The Scottish Bill *For Establishing a General System of Police in the Burghs of Scotland* is in *PP* 1830 III, p. 123. In the first category £5 householders were to have 1 vote, £15 householders 2, £30 householders 3, and £50 householders 4. In the second category £10 householders were to have 1 vote, £30 householders 2, £60 householders 3, and £100 householders 4.

[7] 58 Geo. III c. 69 and 11 Geo. IV c. 27, s. iii.

[8] 59 Geo. III c. 12.

of *closed* vestries and to elect representative select vestries on a one ratepayer, one vote system.[9] The change was condemned by the Duke of Wellington as having laid the foundation 'for leaving the property of every man at the disposition of the rabble of his parish, particularly in the towns'.[10] However that may have been,[11] graduated voting was retained by the Whig government in the draft of the Scottish Bill of 1833,[12] but disappeared, presumably under pressure from backbench Scottish MPs, from the Act. In the same session the Lighting and Watching Act of 1830 for England and Wales was repealed, and a new Act substituted for it.[13] The clause relating to plurality of votes was excised, provision was inserted for any five ratepayers to demand a poll,[14] and the wording of the new Act, requiring decisions to be taken by a two-thirds majority of the votes cast appears to have been copied from Hobhouse's Act which had established one ratepayer, one vote.[15] The intention of the legislature would appear to have been clear, but parish law was a confusing thing at the best of times, and the inhabitants of the parishes themselves may, in many cases, have supposed that in counting the hands raised at a meeting, or the votes cast at a poll held to determine whether to adopt the Lighting and Watching Act of 1833, they were still bound to weigh votes according to the scale laid down in the Act of 1818.[16]

---

[9] 1 & 2 Will. IV c. 60.

[10] E. Halévy, *The Triumph of Reform* (1927), p. 126 n. 2.

[11] The Act was apparently adopted in only 5 London parishes and 8 others outside the Metropolis: B. K. Lucas, *The English Local Government Franchise* (1952), pp. 33–4.

[12] *PP* 1833 III, p. 260, *A Bill to enable Burghs in Scotland to establish a General System of Police*, p. 4.

[13] 3 & 4 Will. IV c. 90.

[14] Ibid. s. ix.

[15] 1 & 2 Will. IV c. 60, s. v, and 3 & 4 Will. IV c. 90, s. xii.

[16] I have yet to find a case or a legal handbook which raises and answers the question specifically. But *In re the Rate-Payers of Eynsham* decided on 23 Apr. 1849 (*English Reports* 116, pp. 917–18) provides an indication: 37 ratepayers attended the adoption meeting, 20 voted in favour, and the other 17 did not vote or propose an amendment. The chairman's ruling that the Act had been duly adopted was overruled in the Court of Queen's Bench which held that it was not sufficient for there to be a two-thirds majority of those present and voting but that there must be a two-thirds majority of those present (only those qualified were allowed to attend). There was no mention of plurality of votes, and the

Having stressed this one important detailed point at issue between the parties, it is time to make four observations upon this first batch of permissive town-improvement Acts. The first is the obvious one that the Acts really were intended to enable localities to bypass the private Bill system. John Tidd Pratt, the Whig lawyer who drafted the new Lighting and Watching Act for England and Wales in 1833, said that the statute was passed 'to enable parishes . . . with the consent of the ratepayers, to make a rate for the purpose of lighting and watching, without the necessity of incurring the great expense necessarily attendant in obtaining a local Act'.[17] He made no acknowledgement to his predecessors, who had drafted the Act of 1830, and his handbook to the Act gives no indication why the Act of 1833 was substituted for the Act of 1830.

The second point is that, with or without the weighted representation of ratepayers, the permissive legislation of this period involved the creation of representative institutions. This appears to mark a decisive choice from the many options employed in private Bill legislation. The greatest variety prevailed among private Acts passed between 1700 and 1835, and ex-officio, co-optative, and elected bodies were all to be found. One hundred out of the 330 Acts studied by F. H. Spencer did contain an elective element, but the majority contained none, and Spencer was surprised to find that private Acts passed late in the period showed 'no greater democratic tendency than those of a comparatively early date'.[18] It is a striking fact, then, that when parliament (and it was the old, unreformed parliament) introduced this first batch of permissive town-improvement Acts, it insisted upon representative procedures.

The third point is that the parliaments which passed the

question turned upon a head count. How, then, did other parishes behave? Whatever Sturges Bourne's Act or the Lighting and Watching Act said, many parishes, one suspects, had their own ways of conducting business and kept to them. It must always have been easier, at a public meeting, to conduct a head count.

[17] *The Justice of the Peace*, 1839, p. 812.
[18] Spencer, *Municipal Origins*, p. 130.

adoptive Acts of 1828, 1830, and 1833, were not looking to established bodies for enterprise and managerial skills. The initiatives were to come from citizens, the decisions were to be taken at public meetings, and the Acts were to be carried out by *ad hoc* bodies. At this stage there was a real possibility, it seems, that, in many towns, the ancient corporations would continue to hold the honorary functions, while the Commissioners and Inspectors carried out the utilitarian ones.[19] Nowhere was this more apparent than in Scotland where it was not the existing authority that became a police burgh, 'it was the residents therein who initiated the new local authority (with much wider powers than the old), so that a system of dual administration could come into being—one town maintaining, at the inhabitants' choice, two separate burghs.'[20] In this way many localities would come to replicate the situation in parliament itself, where there was an obvious distinction between the more honorary position of the House of Lords and the more useful functions performed by the House of Commons. The fourth point is that the Irish and Scottish statutes were large Acts, reaching far into the field of town improvement. The Scots, for example, could secure a supply of fresh water, construct sewers, demolish ruinous buildings and remove obstructions from the streets, pave the roads and sidewalks, erect lamps, appoint police, regulate shambles, build weigh-houses, and license hackney-carriages. Time was to reveal that both the Irish and Scottish Acts were deficient in borrowing powers, but for the time being the Irish and Scottish towns enjoyed far greater opportunities for seeking a permissive solution to their problems than the English and Welsh ones did. The consequence was that England and Wales were the countries most in need of further legislation, and that the conflicts which developed in the 1830s, 1840s, and 1850s over the correct manner in which local improvements ought to be carried out, took place mainly upon the English and Welsh scene.

[19] Lucas, *English Local Government Franchise*, p. 38.
[20] G. S. Pryde, *Scotland from 1603 to the Present Day* (1962), p. 196.

3.   1834–1846: WHIGS AND PEELITES

In 1833 the Whig government reworked the permissive Lighting and Watching Act for England and Wales enacted by Wellington's administration, and passed the permissive General Police Act for Scotland. Seven years later a Select Committee of the House of Commons on the health of towns commended the Act 9 Geo. IV c. 82, 'which is restricted to Ireland', as a model which might be copied in England and Wales.[1] Ministers did not follow up this suggestion, and at no time does Grey's government or Melbourne's appear to have considered whether there might be a connection between a permissive approach to central–local government relations and liberal principles, or even whether, in a parliamentary system, permissive legislation might be tactically advisable. On the contrary, they appear more often than not to have looked at the problem from the other end, not how parliament could facilitate the wishes of the localities, but rather how the localities could be brought into line with the objectives and policies of the centre. This caused them to become pre-occupied with the difficulties they experienced in finding agents to carry out public general legislation.

After fifty years in the wilderness the Whigs were, perhaps, in the mood to take the part of a rational government in a brave nation and undertake a complete reorganisation of the relations between central and local government. The opportunity to do this arose when they reformed the poor law in 1834.[2] The poor law union was a new unit of local government, which cut across the ancient distinctions between counties and Hundreds and parishes. The whole of England and Wales, both rural and urban, was divided into unions, which were smaller than the counties, larger than the parishes, and few enough to be placed under the authority of a centralised commission.[3] Union boundaries

[1] *PP* 1840 XI, p. 295, *Report from the Select Committee on the Health of Towns*, p. xix.
[2] 4 & 5 Will. IV c. 76.
[3] There were 587 unions under the 1834 Act in 1843 (*PP* 1843 XLV, p. 95, *Poor Law Amendment Act, A Return of the Name of each Union &c.*), and 50 more

were drawn to take account of present rather than past circumstances, and Edwin Chadwick, the Secretary to the
Poor Law Commission, hoped to place additional responsibilities for education and the provision of public health
upon these units.[4] In 1836 the unions did, indeed, become
the registration districts for births, marriages, and deaths,
and in 1840–1 they were selected as the agents for vaccina-
tion.[5] But the resistance of Members of Parliament, and
their antipathy to Chadwick himself, meant that it
remained impracticable, for many years, to extend the
scope of the unions any further, and make them the principal organs of local government, analogous to the French
départements.

In setting up the New Poor Law the Whigs bowed to the
Duke of Wellington's preference for weighted voting.
Under the 1834 Act, both owners and ratepayers were
eligible to vote at the elections of the Guardians. Owners
were to be allowed up to six votes on the scale laid down
by Sturges Bourne in 1818. Ratepayers emerged from the
debates with one vote for those rated at up to £200, two
votes for those rated at between £200 and £400, and three
votes for those rated at over £400.[6] The bands were wide,
and in 1844, when Peel and his ministers renewed the Poor
Law, they assimilated the ratepayers to the owners and
substituted a revised scale. Peel's formula, which was to
be carried over into the Public Health Act of 1848 and the
Local Government Act of 1858, enfranchised both owners
and ratepayers upon an evenly graduated scale:

those owning or paying rates upon property below £50 in
rateable value, 1 vote
£50 or above £50 and below £100 rateable value, 2 votes
£100 or above £100 and below £150 in rateable value, 3 votes
£150 or above £150 and below £200 in rateable value, 4 votes

surviving unions or single parishes under Gilbert's Act or local Acts (*PP* 1842
XXXV, pp. 37–44, *Poor Law (Gilbert's Union &c.), Returns of Each Parish and
Township &c.*).

[4] Finer, *Edwin Chadwick*, p. 93.
[5] 6 & 7 Will. IV c. 86, 3 & 4 Vict. c. 29, and 4 & 5 Vict. c. 32.
[6] 4 & 5 Will. IV c. 76, s. xl; A. Brundage, *The Making of the New Poor Law: the
Politics of Inquiry, Enactment and Implementation, 1832–39* (1978), p. 72.

£200 or above £200 and below £250 in rateable value, 5 votes £250 in rateable value, and above, 6 votes.[7]

A person could qualify both as an owner and as a ratepayer, and guaranteed this degree of security, with a very wealthy property-owner who also paid rates being able to cast up to twelve votes, the Members of Parliament were willing to accept the non-traditional union as the 'price' which had to be paid for the imposition of a more rigorous discipline upon the poor. But there was no chance, in the mid-century, of the unions being allowed to expand beyond the carefully delimited and marginalised sphere of poor relief. Like the poor, they were to remain a thing apart.

There was, therefore, to be no grand revolution among the units of local government. That being so, parliament had to continue along the old round, and entrust the implementation of new legislation to the familiar units, counties, boroughs, parishes, and specially created executive commissions.

In the counties the Justices continued to act as the government's right hand. In 1834 they gained places as of right, ex officio, among the new poor law union officers, the guardians of the poor.[8] This aroused the ire of the Radical wing of the Whig party, and for a time it appeared that Joseph Hume's proposal to replace the arbitrarily appointed Justices by elected county boards, might become a serious political issue.[9] But Whig ministers already engaged in a desperate struggle with the House of Lords over the proposal to appropriate the surplus revenues of the Irish Church, had little appetite for another battle. In 1839 the Whigs passed a permissive County Constabulary Act, and entrusted the Justices with the power, subject to the consent of the Secretary of State, of adopting it.[10] The Justices continued to hold their place

---

[7] 7 & 8 Vict. c. 101, s. xiv.

[8] 4 & 5 Will. IV c. 76, s. xxxviii.

[9] He brought forward Bills in 1836, 1837, 1838, 1849, and 1850. The series was continued by others.

[10] 2 & 3 Vict. c. 93. The Act was amended by 3 & 4 Vict. c. 88, which gave three-quarters of the Justices, in an area where the Act had been adopted,

in the administrative system, beyond the middle of the
century, and in many respects right up to 1888, and as late
as 1860 it was still possible for an Anglican clergyman to
refer, at a public meeting, to 'the good old English
principle which had been established a thousand years of
vesting the power in the local magistracy'.[11]

The Whigs appear to have drawn a sharp distinction
between the counties, where they were willing to persevere
with the traditional system of administration by Justices,
and the Municipal Corporations, whose control over lands,
house properties, and charities provided many means of
influencing the outcome of parliamentary elections. Here
the Whigs sought to recover public property which had
fallen into private hands and restore it to its rightful owners.
They insisted upon replacing the self-appointed oligarchies
by popularly elected town councils, one-third of whose
members were to retire each year. Melbourne and Russell
selected a ratepayers' franchise, and returned, in this urban
environment, to the principle favoured by their supporters,
of one man, one vote. They were pressed to go further and
ensure that the Justices (or Magistrates) in the municipalities would, henceforth, be elected by the town councils.
But the Municipal Corporations Reform Bill could not be
passed without support from the opposition, and the
Whigs had to settle for some features they would probably
rather have done without. The House of Lords insisted
upon the appointment of aldermen to 'moderate' what
was misrepresented as a naked democracy, and even then,
the Town Councils, thus constituted, were not allowed to
appoint Magistrates, though they were invited to forward
names of suitable candidates to the Home Secretary.

One hundred and seventy-eight corporations were
named in the schedules to the Act.[12] The new Town Councils were required to take responsibility for their own
police, and in 109 towns where there were local police or
watching Acts already in force, these were to be terminated

power, with the consent of the Secretary of State, if they thought that the
constables were 'no longer needed in their County', to give it up again.

[11] Revd C. A. Hulbert, *HE*. 17 Mar. 1860, 3d.
[12] 5 & 6 Will. IV c. 76.

on the day the new watch committees, which were required
to appoint 'a sufficient Number of fit Men' as constables,
took over.[13] Powers adopted under the Lighting and
Watching Acts of 1830 and 1833 could be transferred to the
Councils, and because 'for Want of such Lighting the
Efficiency of the Constables may be much diminished, and
great Facilities afforded for the Commission of Crimes and
for the Escape of Offenders', it was arranged that the lighting, if it did not already do so, could be extended to cover
the whole district. If there was no lighting at all, then the
Council could assume the powers conferred by the Lighting
and Watching Act.[14] In addition trustees acting under the
authority of local Acts, in any of the following fields,
paving, cleansing, watching, regulating, supplying with
water, and improving, were empowered to use their own
discretion whether to transfer their jurisdiction to the new
Councils or not.[15] This meant that the new Town Councils
could, where the trustees were willing to surrender their
responsibilities, undertake as much as had been done
before, but little more. There was a clause allowing the
Councils to make by-laws to repress nuisances,[16] but the
Act as a whole belonged to the lighting and watching
period, not to the public health period of local government. It was concerned with police in the narrow, English
sense, rather than police in the broader, Scottish sense,
and was not drafted with a view to extending the powers
of the new Councils to undertake town improvements.[17]

It is astonishing how little confidence the ministers who
had created the new Councils appeared to place in them.
Between 1828 and 1833 parliament had insisted that localities adopting Acts which fell within the general field of
town improvement and public health must establish representative institutions. Now that ratepaying democracies
had been installed in the corporate towns, the Town
Councils could have been forgiven for supposing that the
government would pass a new, permissive, town-
improvement Act for England and Wales, modelled upon

[13] Ibid. ss. lxxvi, lxxxiv.   [14] Ibid. ss. lxxv, lxxxvii, lxxxviii.
[15] Ibid. s. lxxv.   [16] Ibid. s. xc.
[17] Lucas, *English Local Government*, p. 9.

the Scottish Act of 1833, and entrust them with the power of adopting it. In the years which followed, the municipalities, which had not been offered many opportunities of demonstrating enterprise, began, not surprisingly, to acquire a reputation for not being enterprising. Chadwick concluded that, when it came to matters of town improvement and public health, there was not much to choose between the old corporations and the new Town Councils.[18] Neither the Melbourne government nor Peel's seems to have been in a hurry to expand the scope of municipal activity, though Normanby nominated the Town Councils as the agents required to carry out the provisions of his compulsory 'Building Regulations in large towns' Bill of 1841. This Bill, which was to apply to England, Wales, Scotland, and Ireland, was a fine example of the Whigs' determination to turn four nations into a United Kingdom.[19] But it did not pass, and it was left to two backbench MPs, Ewart (Dumfries) and Ashley (Dorset), to confer upon Town Councils the modest power of adopting the Museums Act (parent of the Public Libraries Acts), in 1845, and the Bath-houses and Washhouses Act in 1846.[20]

In a situation in which the new poor law unions were hated, the parish still retained some attraction as a unit which, for all its deficiencies, did at least cover the whole country. Successive governments turned to the parishes for the implementation of the Highway Act of 1835,[21] the appointment of village constables in 1842,[22] and, beyond the period covered in this chapter, for the execution of the Nuisances Removal Acts and the Diseases Prevention Acts.[23] A somewhat reactionary and romantic cult of the parish as the traditional unit of local government grew up

[18] R. A. Lewis, *Edwin Chadwick and the Public Health Movement, 1832–1854* (1952), p. 100. See, too, Rydz, *Parliamentary Agents*, p. 101, and Finer, *Edwin Chadwick*, p. 241.

[19] *PP* 1841 I, pp. 93–124, *A Bill, intituled, An Act for regulating Buildings in Large Towns.*

[20] 8 & 9 Vict. c. 43 and 9 & 10 Vict. c. 74.

[21] 5 & 6 Will. IV c. 50.

[22] 5 & 6 Vict. c. 109.

[23] 11 & 12 Vict. c. 123 and 12 & 13 Vict. c. 111, consolidated in 18 & 19 Vict. c. 121.

among backbench MPs, an 'Association of Parochial Representatives' was formed,[24] and the movement found an engaging publicist in Joshua Toulmin Smith, whose books, *The People and the Parish*, and *The Parish: Its Obligations and Powers, its Officers and their Duties*, were published in 1853 and 1854 respectively.

In the eyes of permanent officials staffing the departments of state in Whitehall, legislation which relied upon the parishes for agency, was carried out badly or not at all. The governments of the 1830s and 1840s preferred to entrust as many functions as they could to bodies or officials answerable to themselves. Whig governments received most (from J. T. Smith all) of the blame for this, but Peel, too, clearly favoured the executive commission, and he and his ministers, especially Lord Lincoln and Gladstone, were at least as *étatiste* in outlook as their opponents. The Whigs were responsible for the invention of the Revising Barristers, for Factory, Education, and Prison Inspectorates, and for the Tithe Commission, but Peel himself placed responsibility for the reorganisation of the Church of England in the hands of an executive commission, Lincoln succeeded in establishing an Inclosure Commission, and Gladstone sought to secure increased powers over the construction of railways for the Board of Trade. In recent years most of the debates upon central–local government relations in the nineteenth century have focused upon these innovations, and historians have asked whether they constituted a 'revolution' in government, and whether the Inspectors, especially, were, or were not capable of carrying out the tasks laid upon them.[25]

[24] Finer, *Edwin Chadwick*, p. 403.
[25] Especially O. O. M. Macdonagh, 'The Nineteenth Century Revolution in Government: A Re-appraisal', *Historical Journal* 1958, and *A Pattern of Government Growth: The Passenger Acts and Their Enforcement* (1961); H. Parris, 'A Re-appraisal Re-examined', *Historical Journal*, 1960, and *Government and the Railways in Nineteenth Century Britain* (1965); W. C. Lubenow, *The Politics of Government Growth: Early Victorian Attitudes towards State Intervention, 1833–48* (1971); A. J. Taylor, *Laissez-faire and State Intervention in Nineteenth Century Britain* (1972); V. Cromwell, *Revolution or Evolution: British Government in the Nineteenth Century* (1977); P. W. J. Bartrip, 'British Government Inspection, 1832–75', *Historical Journal*, 1982, and 'State Intervention in Mid-nineteenth Century Britain; Fact or Fiction?', *Journal of British Studies*, 1983; A. E. Peacock, 'The Successful Prosecution of the Factory Acts, 1833–55', *Economic History Review*, 1984.

What has, perhaps, not received sufficient attention is the fact that in the course of these experiments, the line between resolving local problems in the legislative arena, and resolving them in an executive framework, was continually being redrawn. Parliament was jealous of its rights, and, even when overworked, viewed any attempt to take the conduct of business out of its own hands with suspicion. In 1835, when Peel transferred responsibility for the reorganisation of the Church to an executive commission, his object was not to save parliamentary time, but to spare the Established Religion from being savaged at the hands of the Dissenters, and the proposals made by the Ecclesiastical Commission still had to be embodied in Bills and brought before parliament, where the final decisions were taken at the end of a formal debate. In the mid 1840s the invention of the Provisional Order marked a further, slight, but significant step towards making a higher degree of executive involvement acceptable to parliament. It was estimated that there might still be another 4,000 Inclosure Bills submitted to parliament before the whole country was inclosed,[26] and in 1844 a backbench MP, Lord Worsley (Lincolnshire), proposed that a centralised body of Inclosure Commissioners should prepare draft orders, which would come into force unless there was a petition to parliament, in which case the Commissioners' proceedings would cease and the matter would revert to parliament's own hands.[27] A Select Committee was set up, and the conclusion to which it came was 'that it appears to be both practicable and expedient, under the provisions of a General Inclosure Act, to entrust the superintendence of all applications for the Inclosure of Land . . . to some central body . . . but that the sanction of Parliament, in regard to all Inclosures authorized by a Central Board of Commissioners, should be requisite before their decision should have legal effect.'[28]

On behalf of the government, Lord Lincoln then introduced a Bill the following year. He was called upon by the

---

[26] Trelawny, *PD* LXXXII, 25, 4 July 1845.
[27] *PD* LXXIII, 423–27, 29 Feb. 1844.
[28] *PP* 1844 V, p. 4, *Report from the Select Committee on Commons' Inclosure*, p. iv.

Speaker unexpectedly, when a debate upon another topic finished early. He had by him 'not a note, paper, or memorandum', and yet managed, somehow, to make a very informative speech. Taking it for granted 'that everyone admits the extreme difficulty which attends private legislation, and the frequent injustice which it occasions', he proposed to enable persons wishing to inclose land to proceed through a commission. He accepted that the objection to a commission was that it would 'withdraw the control of such measures from the hands of Parliament'. But he countered this by suggesting that the commission, which would conduct its inquiries on the spot, would be of benefit to the poor, who had never been able to afford the time (even if their expenses were paid) to come up to Westminster to attend the meetings of Select Committees on private Bills. In every case, after the inquiries were completed, the Commissioners' proposals would take the form of a Provisional Order. Under the government's plan, all inclosure schemes would be forwarded to the Secretary of State, who would then lay them before parliament in Provisional Order Confirmation Bills.[29] The expense of preparing POCBs would fall upon the Consolidated Fund, and, whatever the poor had gained, the entrepreneurial proprietor had thus been offered a cheap way of promoting an inclosure. In the short term, Peel's ministers had, it appeared, done something for the landed and agricultural interest. In the long term (though the point has scarcely been noticed by Peel's biographers) they had invented a means of enabling government departments to intervene in the affairs of the localities which was to endure and grow.

While these experiments, inspired by ministers, were taking place among the agencies employed to carry out public general legislation, parliament itself, motivated, in part at least, probably, by the desire to render interference by the central government unnecessary, was busy carrying out improvements to private Bill legislation. In the 1830s and 1840s both Houses adopted new and more streamlined procedures. Examiners of Petitions were appointed, to

[29] *PD* LXXX, 23–9, 1 May 1845.

relieve Select Committees of their preliminary task of making sure that the promoters of a petition for a private Bill had complied with standing orders. The standing orders of the two Houses were gradually brought into line, and in due course it was reported that the time taken to prove compliance with standing orders had been halved. Open committees were abolished, Bills were grouped, and by reducing the number of Members required to sit upon a committee, the Houses were enabled to cope with the huge increase in private Bills occasioned by the construction of railways.[30] The result was that, for the large towns, private Bill legislation remained a practicable procedure right up to the end of the century, and most of the towns described by Derek Fraser in *Power and Authority in the Victorian City* (1979), took this road, and did make the system work for them.

In 1838 a Select Committee of the House of Commons suggested that model clauses Bills covering all the major topics of private Bill legislation should be prepared.[31] At this period, between 1834 and 1844 the number of local Bills, while fluctuating considerably, averaged 115 per annum. This was a manageable number, and for the time being nothing was done about the Select Committee's proposal. But then, with the railway boom, and a significant increase in the number of applications for new waterworks, local Bills increased to 205 in 1845 and 402 in 1846.[32] The flood threatened to overwhelm the public business of parliament. Members had always been inclined to complain of the 'fatigue and annoyance' of attending to so many Bills.[33] Now they felt they were being robbed, 'of their time, their comfort, their health, and their convenience'.[34] Nor could they help noticing that while they were being overburdened in this way, barristers engaged to promote or oppose these Bills, were earning between six and twelve thousand pounds a year, according to Wakley,

[30] Ch. I.1, n. 7, above.
[31] Clifford, *Private Bill Legislation*, ii, p. 522.
[32] Ibid. Appendix A. These figures are for Local and Personal Acts, see Ch. I.1, n. 1, above.
[33] Thomas Greene, *PP* 1846 XII, p. 49, *SCPB*, p. 41, Qn. 356.
[34] Wakley, *PD* LXXVII, 179, 6 Feb. 1845.

and between ten and forty thousand a year, according to Brougham, in the committee rooms of the two Houses.[35]

It was not high policy, then, but pressure of business combined with a touch of envy that spurred Members on towards the passage of another series of model clauses Acts. This development was met by strong opposition from the parliamentary agents, who formed themselves into a trade association or trade union in the 1840s.[36] But Members persevered, and in 1845 Companies Clauses Consolidation Acts ('for consolidating in One Act certain Provisions usually inserted in Acts with respect to the Constitution of Companies incorporated for carrying on Undertakings of a public Nature'), Lands Clauses Consolidation Acts, and Railway Clauses Consolidation Acts (two of each, one for England and Wales, the other for Scotland) were passed.[37] Like their predecessor, the General Inclosure Act of 1801, these Acts did not dispense a company from the necessity of obtaining a private Act. But a railway Bill could now be built up of standardised clauses which did not have to be reprinted, but could be cited by reference to the parent Act. Railway Bills, which had hitherto been 100 pages long, shrank to one-tenth their former size.[38]

4.   1846–1848: MORPETH AND CHADWICK

The predominant impression left by a survey of the period 1834–46, is that both Whig and Peelite governments wanted to strengthen the hands of the central executive, encountered much difficulty in doing so, and never quite knew when to settle for an existing agency, second best as it appeared to them to be, or which one to choose. Nowhere were these frustrations more apparent than in the field of town improvement and public health. Once the problems

[35] Ibid. 177, and XCIII, 968, 28 June 1847.
[36] Rydz, *Parliamentary Agents,* p. 116.
[37] 8 & 9 Vict. cc. 16–20, 33. The Lands Clauses Acts provided for the compulsory purchase of land.
[38] Clifford, *Private Bill Legislation,* ii, pp. 529–30.

facing urban populations came to be seen in terms, not of
lighting and watching, but of public health, of the provision of water and sewerage, then the ideal administrative
unit was bound, as Chadwick said, to be a natural
drainage area, defined by topography. But ministers were
not living in an ideal world. The division of the country
into poor law unions had involved drawing new administrative boundaries across England and Wales, and the
reform of the Municipal Corporations had seen boundaries
redefined to take account of demographic changes. In
neither case had watersheds and the effects of gravity
upon fluids transported in egg-shaped pipes been the
determining factor. Granted that 'sanitary authorities . . .
must administer the whole drainage basin', where were
such authorities to come from? In 1842, when he published
his famous report on the Sanitary Condition of the Labouring Population, Chadwick 'ranged . . . over improvement
commissioners, municipal corporations, and Commissioners of Sewers', condemned them all, and concluded
that 'there must be new authorities nominated *by the
Crown'*.[1]

This was all very well, but ministers had to take account
of the feelings of Members of Parliament. Peel's government rightly decided that while Chadwick's report
showed that legislation was necessary, it did not itself
provide a basis for legislation. Peel appointed a Royal
Commission to inquire further into practical remedies for
the sanitary condition of the large towns. The reports of
this Commission were published in 1844 and 1845.[2] Late in
the session, in 1845, Lord Lincoln published a Public Health
(or Health of Towns) Bill.[3] This was what would nowadays
be called a consultative document, which was to be followed by a revised Bill in 1846. But in 1846 Peel and his
cabinet had other matters to attend to, and when the Whigs
came back into power at the end of June, they inherited the
whole burdensome and intractable problem of public
health.

[1] Finer, *Edwin Chadwick*, p. 225.
[2] *PP* 1844 XVII, 1845 XVIII.
[3] *PP* 1845 V, pp. 363–490, *Sewerage, Drainage, &c. of Towns Bill.*

There were, as earlier sections have shown, three ways of going about it. The first was to leave the local authorities to take the initiatives and to trust to private Acts. The second was to frame permissive legislation and to pass public general Acts which the local authorities might adopt if they wished to. The third was to pass a public general Act and require the existing authorities to carry it out, or to create new ones. Within a few days of the change of government the House of Commons was presented with the report of a Select Committee on Private Bills.[4] This committee was chaired by Joseph Hume, the Member for Montrose Burghs. Hume was a Radical who had entered the House in 1812. In the late 1820s he was much damaged by the scandals surrounding the expenditure of the money raised to advance loans to the Greek patriots,[5] and he never held ministerial office. But he had introduced the new Lighting and Watching Act to the House of Commons in 1833, and his constituency was among the first to adopt parts of the General Police Act for Scotland.[6] He possessed a remarkable insight into the business of the House, and as chairman he was knowledgeable enough to see that the whole range of policy options was laid before the Select Committee, and forceful enough, even had he not been prompted by Chadwick,[7] to give a clear lead.

The evidence taken before the committee provided classic illustrations of the problems inseparable from the system of private Bill legislation. These were not confined to high costs, the deterrent effect of these upon the smaller localities, and the fact that local Acts sometimes embodied principles contrary to statute or common law—the points which we have identified already. The supreme problem, as the committee saw it, was that in the case of the growing number of Bills promoted by businesses which hoped to sell services to the local authorities, the persons appearing before the Select Committees were all interested parties—

[4] *PP* 1846 XII, pp. 1–240, *SCPB*.
[5] C. M. Woodhouse, *The Philhellenes* (1969), pp. 91–2.
[6] *PP* 1847 LVII, p. 393, *Police (Scotland), Return from Each of the Burghs in Scotland; stating whether they have or have not adopted the Act 3 & 4 Will. 4 c. 46*.
[7] Lewis, *Edwin Chadwick*, pp. 134–7.

those proposing to undertake works, or those whose properties would be affected by them. There was nobody to represent the interests of the general public. In the case of town improvement and public health the public interest, Chadwick convinced the committee, lay in recognising that water and sewerage were natural monopolies. Competition between rival companies meant wasteful duplication, and administrative chaos. Competition within the field of service should cease, services should, so far as possible, be placed in the hands of a single authority, and competition between rival companies to buy the franchise or right to provide the service should then be encouraged.[8] But how was either a company or a local authority which contracted with a company, to be made cognisant of, and responsive to, the needs of the masses crowded into the yards, tenements, and cellars of the mushrooming towns? Capitalists could not, as a class, venture to be benevolent, and local authorities, which could, perhaps, have afforded to pursue enlightened policies, would invariably be taken over, in a system based on a weighted franchise, by the larger owners, who disdained to visit the cheaper quarters of the towns where fever was endemic, where public health was most needed, and where the availability of fresh water and the installation of drainage would yield the most beneficial results. Here, the only answer appeared to the committee to lie in subjecting the authorities to some form of supervision by a government department.

The committee recommended that in cases where private Bills were still necessary, or still preferred, there should be 'a previous local examination by competent and responsible public officers', in a mode analogous to that adopted by the Tithe and Inclosure Commissioners established in 1845. Private Bills should be sent first to the appropriate government department, which would appoint an Inspector to see that standing orders had been complied with, and to examine the merits of the case. If the Inspector found that private property would be 'seriously interfered

[8] Chadwick's evidence is in *PP* 1846 XII, at pp. 29–49, *SCPB*, pp. 21–41, Qns. 249–353. He was examined together with H. Hobhouse.

with', then the whole question should revert to parliament. In other cases the Inspector's report would provide the basis for the Select Committees on private Bills to hold informed discussions.[9] These recommendations were acted upon precipitately. Morpeth ordered a Preliminary Inquiries Bill to be drafted. It was introduced into the House of Commons on 12 August, and became law on 28 August 1846.[10] Under this Act, all petitions for private Acts relating to town improvements were to be sent first to the Commissioners of Woods and Forests, except those affecting ports and navigable rivers which were to be sent to the Admiralty. In each case the department would then appoint an Inspector, who would conduct an inquiry and make a report before the Bill came in front of the Houses of Parliament.

Addressing itself to the familiar problems of the localities which could not afford private Bill legislation, Hume's committee recommended that model clauses Acts (or clauses consolidation Acts) should be prepared for police and watching, waterworks and sewerage, lighting, improvement of towns, the regulation of buildings and streets, markets and fairs, cemeteries, bridges and ferries, harbours and docks, piers and quays, canals, rivers, and navigation. This would, in itself, of course, reduce costs. But the committee did not want to stop there. Taking the Irish Town Improvement Act of 1828, the Scottish General Police Act of 1833, and the Lighting and Watching Act for England and Wales of 1833, as their models, the committee recommended that these model clauses Acts should be upgraded into permissive Acts, which the localities might adopt if they wished to. This did not mean, however, that the committee supposed the localities ought to be allowed to proceed entirely without supervision. They, too, it was suggested, should be obliged to secure the sanction of the appropriate department, which would ensure that only one private Act was in force at any one time in any one place for any one object, that local entrepreneurs were not making excess profits out of the provision of public ser-

[9] The Committee's recommendations are at pp. 3–7, *Report*, pp. iii–vii.
[10] 9 & 10 Vict. c. 106.

vices, and that ratepaying democracies were not neglecting
the needs of working men and their families.[11] Hume did
not seek to force measures upon the localities—far from it.
In his opinion the localities were the best judges of their
own requirements, and parliament should facilitate initiatives taken by the localities subject only to their accepting
the state's right to insist upon a level of professional com-
petence.

That is where things stood when Morpeth began to consider what sort of public health legislation ought to be
introduced in 1847. Morpeth had no difficulty in agreeing
that there ought to be model clauses Acts, and clauses consolidation Acts relating to the regulation of bodies of
Commissioners, the provision of water and gas, the paving, draining, cleansing, lighting, and improving of towns,
for police, markets and fairs, cemeteries, and for harbours,
docks, and piers, were introduced and passed in 1847.[12]
The move helped to ensure that private Bill legislation
remained a viable, and somewhat less expensive, option.
But Morpeth did not attempt to put a motor into these
model clauses Acts and turn them into permissive Acts,
which even the smaller localities could adopt if they
wanted to, in the way Hume's committee had suggested.
The fear was that this might prove to be a recipe for in-
action—especially if the localities adopting the Acts were to
be required to place themselves under some form of
departmental supervision in the way Hume's committee
had suggested. Morpeth's mind was leaning towards a
general measure, involving a degree of compulsion, which
would place the localities in a more direct relationship with
the centre.

The Public Health (or Health of Towns) Bill of 1847 met
with a deal of vociferous opposition: it did not become law,
and for simplicity's sake it is probably better to pass straight
on to the Act of 1848. This Act established a General Board
of Health, with three members,[13] one of whom was to sit in
parliament (this was Morpeth himself), and one of whom,

[11] *PP* 1846 XII, p. 6, *Report*, p. vi.
[12] 10 & 11 Vict. cc. 14–17, 27, 34, 65, 89.
[13] 11 & 12 Vict., c. 63, s. iv.

only, was to be paid.[14] It was well understood that this was
to be Chadwick.

The next point to be settled was the means by which the
Act could be set in motion. Where was the initiative to
come from? Many formulae were discussed before Morpeth
settled for two. The first empowered the General Board to
intervene in towns where the death-rate, as revealed by
the Registrar-General's returns, compiled over the previous seven years, exceeded 23 per 1,000.[15] To place this
section of the Act in perspective, the average death-rate
over the whole country at this period was 21 per 1,000,[16]
and the figure selected meant that it was only in the worst
cases, where the members of the General Board might
hope to be able to keep public opinion with them, that
they were empowered to intervene.

The great legislative innovation came with the second
method of setting the Act in motion. In all other towns, the
power of initiating the public health process was placed in
the hands, not of the elected representatives, but, in
deference to Chadwick's view of the Town Councils as
narrow, grudging, and ignorant, in the hands of a minority of the inhabitants.[17] The original Bill made provision for
one-fiftieth of the *inhabitants* to petition the General Board.
By the time it became law the wording had been amended
to read one-tenth of the *ratepayers*. Chadwick was furious
about the change and complained, with exaggeration, that
it would make the Act unworkable.[18] In his rage he overlooked the magnitude of the novelty involved. In 1828–33,
the majority required to adopt a measure of town improvement had varied between a simple majority in Ireland, a
two-thirds majority in England and Wales, and a three-
quarters majority in Scotland. Now, a minority of the
ratepayers was being encouraged to go behind the backs
of their local council or their local commissioners (the *Leeds
Mercury* described it as a 'Bill for nullifying Municipal Corporations'),[19] and to appeal to the General Board. As one

[14] Ibid. s. vii.
[16] Finer, *Edwin Chadwick*, p. 325.
[18] Finer, *Edwin Chadwick*, p. 322.
[15] Ibid. s. viii.
[17] 11 & 12 Vict., c. 63, s. viii.
[19] *LM* 26 Feb. 1848, 4d.

scholar, by no means hostile to Chadwick and the aims of the General Board, has put it,

All the Act required was that a minority of ten per cent of the ratepayers should petition the Board on one single occasion; all subsequent developments rested entirely with the Board. . . . Nine-tenths of the local ratepayers might be opposed to the Act; nay, if the original petitioners should have changed their minds —*all* the ratepayers might be opposed to the Act; but, provided that, at one time or another a petition had been made in due form, the Board was at complete liberty to apply the Act.[20]

It is not difficult to see that this was a recipe for trouble.

In areas of excessive mortality, then, the General Board itself was to take the initiative: in other places a hitherto unheard of minority. How, next, was the General Board to proceed? The answer was by making extended use of the two most important procedural advances of the period, the Preliminary Inquiry which had become a part of private Bill legislation in 1846, and the Provisional Order, which had been introduced to facilitate Inclosure in 1845. When the General Board received a petition, it was to send an Inspector down to the locality to conduct a public inquiry into the sanitary condition of the place on the spot. The Inspector was then to report to the General Board, advise whether the Act should be enforced, and (with reference to 'the natural Drainage Areas') to say whether any boundary changes would be desirable.[21] This power, given to the General Board, to alter boundaries, was probably the most sweeping of all the provisions contained in the Act. The Inspectors' reports were to be published, and the procedures to be followed allowed for a second inquiry to be held in each case to consider the report, and to hear comments and objections.[22] The final decision whether to apply the Act then lay with the General Board, which promulgated an Order in Council (which could not be challenged in parliament) in towns where there was no private Act already in operation and where no boundary changes were proposed, and a Provisional Order in the remainder.[23]

[20] Finer, *Edwin Chadwick*, p. 433.   [21] 11 & 12 Vict., c. 63, s. viii.
[22] Ibid. s. ix.   [23] Ibid. s. x.

The expenses involved in conducting the public inquiries were to fall upon the localities, while the costs of preparing the Provisional Order Confirmation Bills were to fall upon the Consolidated Fund.[24] Localities which opposed the application of the Act, had, of course, to bear the costs of their own resistance.

The next decision to be made concerned the agents whom the General Board was to employ and supervise. As one of Chadwick's biographers says, among

the English municipal corporations only twenty-nine possessed Local Acts which conferred powers of drainage, cleansing and paving on the Mayor and Corporation. In sixty-six corporate towns such powers were exercised jointly with a body of *ad hoc* Commissioners; in thirty by commissioners independently of the Corporation. Sixty-two corporate towns possessed no local Act whatsoever . . . of the non-corporate towns in England, with more than 5,000 inhabitants, 175 had local Acts, but 296 were without.[25]

It was imperative to rationalise them. Chadwick would have liked to hand the new districts over to Local Boards of Health whose members would be nominated by the Crown.[26] Morpeth knew that this was not feasible. In ten years between 1832 and 1841 the Whigs had acquired a reputation for jobbery, and they could not now afford to pay attention to Chadwick's demands for public health authorities to be nominated in this manner. The Act, and the General Board it created, must turn, in the first instance, to existing authorities.

Morpeth had, then, to make use of the Town Councils and the existing bodies of Improvement Commissioners, most of whom had been established under private Acts. In boroughs where there was a Town Council, and the Town Council's jurisdiction covered the whole district, the Council was to become the Local Board of Health, and Commissioners acting under local Acts were to surrender their powers to it. In districts extending over areas covered

24 Ibid. s. xi.
25 Lewis, *Edwin Chadwick*, p. 173.
26 Finer, *Edwin Chadwick*, p. 226.

by two Town Councils, the Councils were to nominate a
Local Board between them. In cases where the Town
Council's jurisdiction took in a part, only, of the area
involved, Local Boards were to be composed of members
of the Town Council jointly with members elected by the
ratepayers living in the remaining areas.[27]

In other places, where there was a body of Improvement
Commissioners but no Town Council, the ratepayers were,
in effect, being given an open invitation by parliament to
substitute a Local Board of Health for the Commissioners
they had already. The General Board was empowered to
entrust Improvement Commissioners with the powers of a
Local Board of Health (and in Oxford and Cambridge it
was obliged to do so),[28] but it was also given power over
'the Repeal, Alteration, Extension, or future Execution' of
all local Acts,[29] and the assumption must have been that
the Board's remodelling would lead to a clear-out of the
surviving oligarchic and self-perpetuating Boards and their
replacement with ratepaying democracies. These measures
did, in fact, then, involve a considerable degree of rationalisation, but not, Morpeth must have hoped, one out of
keeping with the spirit of the times.

Finally, in those places where there was no local authority charged with public health functions (other than the
parish with its responsibility for carrying out the Nuisances
Removal Act and the Diseases Prevention Act) already in
existence the General Board was empowered to form one.
Here, the owners and ratepayers were to elect a Local
Board of Health, one-third of whose members, as in the
Town Councils, was to retire each year.[30] The property
qualification for members of these Local Boards was to be
fixed in each instance by the General Board, and would
vary from place to place.[31] In these localities, as in every
other where elections took place under the Act, voting was

---

[27] 11 & 12 Vict., c. 63, s. xii.
[28] Ibid. Oxford and Cambridge, s. xxxi.
[29] Ibid. s. x.
[30] Ibid. s. xiii.
[31] It was not to be set higher than ownership of property worth £1,000, or
rated upon an annual value exceeding £30, ibid. s. xvi.

to be according to the scale established in Peel's Poor Law Act of 1844.[32]

In all cases, the Local Board, once erected, would continue to be subject to guidance, interference, reprimand, and even direction from the General Board. The Board was given power to extend the boundaries of districts from time to time,[33] and all by-laws made by the Local Boards had to be submitted to it and approved before they came into force.[34]

Almost as if to underline the formidable nature of the innovations, the Act returned, at one point, to the easily acceptable device of permissive legislation. Although the Act was commonly referred to as a Health of Towns Act, any locality, however small, was entitled to petition the General Board to send an Inspector and set the machinery in motion. Few small places would need or want to do this, and in order to cater appropriately for their requirements, section 50 provided for any locality, even the smallest rural parish, to make a bid to cleanse itself. It was laid down that, if it should appear to a majority of three-fifths of the rated inhabitants of 'any parish or place containing less than two thousand inhabitants', in which the Act had not been applied, 'that it would contribute' to their health and convenience 'that any pond, pool, open ditch, sewer, drain, or place containing or used for the collection of any drainage, filth, water, matter, or thing of an offensive nature . . . should be drained, cleansed, covered, or filled up, or that a sewer should be made or improved, a well dug, or a pump provided for the use of the inhabitants', they might obtain estimates and call a second meeting to sanction the improvement.

This, then, was the legislative hybrid fashioned by Lord Morpeth in 1847, and passed after he had become the Earl of Carlisle in 1848. The Act slighted the existing authorities at the moment of the initiative, yet turned, where possible, to the Town Councils for its execution. It set up unitary authorities with responsibility for the construction and maintenance of sewers, for streets, and the provision of

[32] Ibid. s. xx.   [33] Ibid. s. cxli.   [34] Ibid. s. cxv.

water.[35] In an uneasy compromise between public and private enterprise, local authorities were empowered to construct waterworks if they needed to, but not in places where there was a company willing to supply water 'upon terms'.[36] In order that the Local Boards might be able to carry out the necessary permanent works, they were given power, with the consent of the General Board, to borrow money on a hitherto unheard of scale up to a limit of one year's assessable value, and to mortgage the rates for up to thirty years.[37] At the same time the Public Works Loan Commissioners were authorised to make loans to the Local Boards,[38] so that the bitter pill of interference from the centre was sweetened with a financial incentive. The Local Boards were required to appoint a clerk, a treasurer, a surveyor, and an Inspector of Nuisances, and were allowed, but not compelled to appoint a Medical Officer of Health.[39]

Why was parliament willing to sanction so great a degree of state intervention and interference? It is not an easy question to answer, and one might be tempted at first sight to suppose that the explanation lay in Scotland. In 1847, inquiry revealed that fourteen years after the General Police Act had reached the statute-book, only twelve burghs in Scotland had adopted the Act in whole, and nineteen more in part. Another 132 reported that they had not adopted the Act, and a further twenty made no reply.[40] (We know now that a correct return would have revealed that thirty-seven burghs had adopted the Act in whole or in part.)[41] The Scots had evidently tempered enthusiasm for the opportunities made available to them by the permissive legislation of the earlier period with caution. But

[35] Ibid. ss. xliii, lxviii, lxxv.
[36] Ibid. s. lxxv.
[37] Ibid. ss. cvii, cxiii, cxix.
[38] Ibid. s. cviii.
[39] Ibid. ss. xxxvii, xl.
[40] *PP* 1847 LVII, pp. 393–4, *Police (Scotland), Return from Each of the Burghs in Scotland: stating whether They have or have not adopted the Act 3 & 4 Will. IV. c. 46.* These were the figures available to MPs.
[41] Urquhart (1985), pp. 37–40 and Table 2, lists 37 burghs which had adopted the Act in whole or in part by 1847, and a further 4 which adopted it between 1847 and 1850.

parliament itself showed no alarm, and its response was to do for Scotland what might have been done in England, and to pass one Act in 1847 allowing the elected Burgh Councils to take the initiative in adopting the Act, and to pass a second in 1850 to remedy the deficiencies, especially with regard to borrowing, which time had revealed in the Act of 1833 (see below, Chapter IV.2).[42]

Part of the answer must lie in the impact made by Chadwick's 1842 report, and the propaganda of the Health of Towns Association founded in 1844. Part, too, must lie in the fear of typhoid, which was present year in and year out, and was mentioned in the course of the debates upon the Public Health Act.[43] Finally, there was cholera which was spreading across Europe even as the debates upon the Bill were in progress. At the time of the first scare about cholera in 1831 and the first outbreak of cholera in 1832, the government had established a Central Board of Health, and Local Boards with power to take what measures seemed appropriate. Upon that occasion complaints had been made that the actions of the Central Board had been too timid.[44] Now it seemed right to supply the deficiency. The government grasped the opportunity to create a General Board of Health, and exploited the alarm caused by cholera to increase support for its plan to tackle the endemic problems of public health. The new and more powerful General Board was successfully established, in the first instance, for five years and one additional session of parliament.[45]

5. 1848–1858: RADICALS, PALMERSTONIANS, AND PROTECTIONISTS

As far back as 1836 Lord John Russell had written to Chadwick that the Whig government was endeavouring

to improve our institutions. Hitherto they have been lax, careless, wasteful, injudicious in an extreme; but the country

---

[42] 10 & 11 Vict. c. 39 and 13 & 14 Vict. c. 33.
[43] R. J. Morris, *Cholera 1832* (1976), p. 205.
[44] Ibid. pp. 112–13.
[45] 11 & 12 Vict., c. 63, s. iv.

governed itself, and was blind to its own faults. We are busy introducing system, method, science, economy, regularity, discipline. But we must beware not to lose the co-operation of the country. They will not bear a Prussian Minister, to regulate their domestic affairs. So that some faults must be indulged for the sake of carrying improvements in the mass.[1]

From the government's point of view the 1848 Act was an attempt to discover an acceptable degree of central intervention, and to bring order out of the chaos of local authorities. Whether the formula which Russell's government arrived at in 1848 was exactly the best that could have been found, it is impossible to say. To twentieth-century eyes the degree of state interference involved appears small, and members of the General Board fairly claimed that in many respects they carried out their responsibilities tactfully. 'The power to act on the authority of a return from the Registrar-General' when the death-rate exceeded 23 per 1,000 was 'exercised with the greatest caution'. In five years the Board 'directed inquiries into only twenty-eight places from which they had not received a petition'.[2] Nor should the towns be supposed to have boycotted the Act. As Lewis put it, 'the critics in Parliament and the Press, who tried to make out that the Board's intervention was everywhere resented . . . were amply rebutted by the evidence.'[3] Already by 1850 the Board had received applications from 192 places with a total population of 1,969,915, ranging from Birmingham (182,922) to Little Bowden in Northants (439). By July 1853 petitions had come in from 255 places, and 164 of these had already been brought under the operation of the Act, 78 by Order in Council, and 86 by Provisional Order. Before the end of 1853, petitions had been received from 284 towns, 243 had been reported on, and 182, with a population of 2,100,000 had been placed under the Act.[4]

These achievements should not be lost sight of when one turns, instead, to the torrent of complaints. Joshua Toulmin Smith led the way with his declaration that the Court of Star Chamber, which had been abolished in 1641,

[1] Lewis, *Edwin Chadwick*, p. 321.   [2] Ibid. pp. 290–1.
[3] Ibid. pp. 291–2.   [4] Ibid. pp. 290, 339.

had been re-established, with greatly increased powers in 1848.[5] This colourful remark fell upon ears attuned to listening to histories of parliament's struggle against the Crown in the seventeenth century. But it is not enough, in itself, to account for the chequered history of the General Board, and to explain that we must look elsewhere. The Act did not apply to London, but throughout the life of the Board, Chadwick himself was engaged in a desperate and very personal struggle to overthrow the powers of the London vestries and the London water companies, to put the capital under a single authority, and to cleanse it.[6] Animosities raised by this crusade merged into complaints about the 1848 Act itself. Then, the additional responsibilities thrown upon the Board at the time of the cholera outbreak made it appear more invasive than it would have wished to be. Chadwick discounted the possibility that the infection was water-borne, ordered the London sewers to be flushed out into the Thames, and actually spread the disease.[7] Even though this was not fully understood at the time, accusations of incompetence began to be added to charges of interference. Although the Act laid down that one member of the General Board must have a seat in Parliament, Members continued to express fears that the General Board was, in some way, outside the law. MPs disliked Inspectors and Preliminary Inquiries. For the time being, at least, they could not reach the Inspectors appointed under the 1848 Act, so they turned against those appointed under the Preliminary Inquiries Act of 1846 instead. The Act had been intended to rescue parliament from some of the excessive amount of work demanded by private Bill legislation, but it did not answer well. Preliminary Inquiries conducted into local Bills under the auspices of the Admiralty carried some weight. But those conducted by Inspectors reporting to the Woods and Forests commanded little respect in parliament, and received short shrift. The opinion that local inquiries necessitated delegating 'to other tribunals much of the

[5] Ibid. p. 167.
[6] Finer, *Edwin Chadwick*, bk. 9, 'The Struggle for London'.
[7] Ibid. p. 347.

authority of Parliament' gained ground. Members complained that the Inspectors' findings were not being made available until too late a period in the session. When the Bills did eventually come before parliament, the Inspectors' advice was not accepted, new evidence was introduced, and in 1850 a Select Committee reported that 'however fully the whole case may have been inquired into and discussed by parties interested on the spot, the Parliamentary investigation has generally proceeded as if no such local inquiry had been held'. In short, there was double discussion. Parliament concluded that 'local inquiries have not been successful in obtaining the principal objects for which they were instituted',[8] and five years after its introduction, the Preliminary Inquiries Act had to be repealed, the Admiralty alone preserving some part of its jurisdiction in a successor Act.[9]

Throughout this struggle to determine the manner in which private Bill legislation should be conducted, one can detect the hostility of the parliamentary agents. Success in overthrowing the Preliminary Inquiries Act spurred them on to attack the 1848 Act itself. In the early 1850s it seemed certain that the Health of Towns Act would reduce the number of private Bills passing through the House, and the agents intimated that 'the course adopted by the Board was an interference with their professional emoluments which would render it necessary on their part to raise opposition against the continuance of the Board itself'.[10] There is no need to follow every step in the chequered history of the Board. In 1852 Chadwick lost his struggle to overthrow the London water companies. As Finer said, 'The Board's span of life was due to end in 1854. Was Parliament likely to renew it? The shadows had begun to close upon the Board after the ignominious defeats of 1852; in 1853 they lengthened perceptibly.'[11]

The decision to abolish the General Board was taken in

[8] *PP* 1850 XIII, *First Report from the Select Committee on Local Acts (Preliminary Inquiries)*, pp. 531–656; *Second Report*, pp. 657–90.
[9] 14 & 15 Vict. c. 49.
[10] Finer, *Edwin Chadwick*, p. 461.
[11] Ibid. p. 453.

1854. It had, after all, been appointed in an emergency and for a trial period, and on 12 August Chadwick's official career came to an end. His biographers have done a disservice, however, by giving the impression that, with his departure, the whole public health movement collapsed. The Act of 1848 was still in force, and since it required the existence of a General Board for its operation, a stop-gap General Board had to be kept in being until such time as parliament could make up its mind what was to replace it. In 1854 the Board was turned, as a temporary expedient, into a department of state.[12] Sir Benjamin Hall became President, and in one year, in 1855, he succeeded in passing both an Act for the better local management of the metropolis,[13] in which parliament sanctioned a one ratepayer, one vote system,[14] and a Metropolitan Buildings Act,[15] before leaving to take charge of the Metropolitan Board of Works. Finding solutions to the problems of London was no mean achievement, and the General Board might have survived from year to year, and ultimately have recovered some of its former power and prestige, had it not been for Sir George Grey's determination, in 1856, to seize the opportunity presented by the army's being absent in the Crimea, to bring in a compulsory, general system of police, subject to Home Office inspection, in both counties and boroughs.

In the boroughs the Town Councils had provided their own police since 1835. Among the counties, twenty-four had already adopted the permissive Act of 1839, together with parts of seven others, but twenty were still outside it.[16] The Kington division of Herefordshire, which had adopted the Act in 1840 had given it up again ten years later, and dismissed its constables.[17] The new proposals were equally offensive all round, to the boroughs and

[12] 17 & 18 Vict. c. 95.
[13] 18 & 19 Vict. c. 120.
[14] Ibid. s. xvii.
[15] 18 & 19 Vict. c. 122.
[16] Sir George Grey, *PD* CXL, 231, 5 Feb. 1856.
[17] *PP* 1851 XLVI, p. 362 and n. 4 on p. 363, *Police Constables, Return showing the Number of Police Constables in each County or Division of a County in England and Wales, under the Act 2 & 3 Vict. c. 93.*

counties which had police and wished to retain control of them, and to the counties which had made up their minds they did not want them. The result was to bring many Members for large boroughs and Members for counties— two groups which it had been easy enough to keep apart in the heady days of the corn law agitation—into contact. Borough Members representing places with Town Councils disliked the way in which the right to self-government was being taken away from them again only twenty-one years after they had received it, while county Members tended to suppose that the historical independence of the localities was a guarantee against a successful revolution on the French model. The result was that Members for Bath, Birmingham, Leicester, Oldham, Sheffield, Stockport, and Walsall joined forces with those for Berkshire, East Kent, South Nottinghamshire, and the West Riding in opposing the Bill. Barrow (S. Notts) said he would resist every such Bill 'whether Whig, Tory, Radical or Composite',[18] and J. B. Smith (Stockport) pointed out that had the Bill emanated from the other side of the House, it would have been made the occasion for many 'an eloquent denunciation of Tory tyranny'.[19]

Sir George Grey relied heavily for his argument upon his ability to sensationalise the Frimley murderers. Frimley lay in Hampshire, which was the first county to adopt the 1839 Act, and in 1850 the Revd G. E. Hollest had been mur-dered by burglars operating out of Surrey, where no adoption had taken place. Patchwork adoption meant that the responsible citizens of Hampshire were at the mercy of the negligent Magistrates of Surrey. The murder had taken place a long time ago, but Grey was a persuasive man, the government won, and compulsory policing, subject to inspection by the Home Office, was rendered acceptable by the provision of grants taken out of central funds to every force pronounced by the Inspectors to be efficient. But this further instalment of Whig centralisation appears to have made the defeated parties more than ever deter-mined to make sure that there should be no reprieve for

[18] *PD* CXL, 2184, 10 Mar. 1856.   [19] Ibid. 2180, 10 Mar. 1856.

the General Board of Health. The drafting of a Bill to amend the Public Health Act of 1848 in such a way as to make it possible to abolish the General Board was begun in 1857 by Palmerston's stepson, W. F. Cowper, who had succeeded Sir Benjamin Hall as President of the Board of Health,[20] and completed in 1858 by Spencer Walpole and C. B. Adderley, after a change of ministry. Their work seems to reflect a joint Palmerston–Derby approach rather than the much more *étatiste* joint Whig–Peelite one which had held sway since 1832.

The new Act,[21] which came into force on 1 September 1858,[22] was known as the Local Government Act, and it has been shamefully neglected by historians. The first point to grasp about it is that it did not repeal the Public Health Act of 1848, which was amended where necessary, and remained in force, and was to be construed with it.[23] Like its predecessor, it did not apply to London, for which, as we have seen, separate provision had already been made in 1855. The new Act was informatively titled, 'An Act to amend the Public Health Act, 1848, and to make further Provision for the Local Government of Towns and populous Districts'. That is to say, it was an Act to enable the localities to continue to take advantage of the powers contained in the Public Health Act of 1848 in the new circumstances which would exist when the General Board was finally abolished. The 1848 Act had set out two ways in which the statute could be put into operation. Both ran through the hands of the General Board, and both, must, therefore, now be attended to. The first had allowed the General Board to intervene in cases of excessive mortality, and the second had set out a procedure according to which localities could petition the General Board to apply the Act. The first was simply allowed to lapse. There was to be no further forcing public health upon a reluctant town, and existing Local Boards were given their independence ('Whenever the Sanction, Consent, Direction, or Approval of the General Board of Health is required by Law to the Exercise of the Powers of Local Boards of Health . . . such

[20] A Bill was introduced on 10 Dec. 1857 by Cowper, *PD* CXLVIII, 499.
[21] 21 & 22 Vict. c. 98.   [22] Ibid. s. v.   [23] Ibid. s. iv.

Powers may be exercised without such Sanction, Consent, Direction, or Approval, or any Sanction, Consent, Direction, or Approval in lieu thereof, except in so far as is provided by this Act').[24] For the second, however, an alternative had to be found. There could be no question of depriving the localities of the opportunity to set up Local Boards of Health if they wanted them, and it is in the way in which this was to be done that the interest of the 1858 Act lies.

Since there was to be no power of discretion vested in a General Board, the Act had to take account of all cases. These were divided into those where there was already an existing authority, and those where there was not. The first category, in turn, was subdivided into two, those where there was an elected Town Council, and those where there was still an elected, or partly elected Improvement Commission or some other body of Commissioners.[25] Here, the power to adopt the Local Government Act was vested in the representative body. In case the representative body appeared sluggish, the Act contained a provision for any twenty ratepayers to forward a requisition to the mayor or chairman asking the Council or the Commissioners to put the matter to a vote.[26] In case the representative body appeared hasty, any ratepayer who moved in time could demand a poll.[27] For a resolution, however it originated, to succeed, there must be a two-thirds majority of those present.[28] The second category, too, was divided into two, places with a defined boundary,[29] and places without.[30] In the former, all that was required was a two-thirds majority of the owners and ratepayers voting according to Peel's graduated scale of 1844. In the latter, a shadow of the 1848 procedure remained. The parties favouring the adoption of the Act must number one-tenth of the ratepayers. They were to start by petitioning the Secretary of State to send an Inspector to establish a boundary. Once that had been done they could proceed in the same way as localities which already possessed a boundary, by a

[24] Ibid. s. viii.   [25] Ibid. s. xii (1), xii (2).   [26] Ibid. s. xiii (1).
[27] Ibid. s. xiii (4).   [28] Ibid. s. xii.   [29] Ibid. s. xii (3).
[30] Ibid. s. xvi.

two-thirds majority obtained at a public meeting, or, if one was demanded, through a poll. In December 1857 Cowper had said that the new Bill ought to allow 'every town in England, great or small', to enjoy 'the opportunity of acquiring . . . a local representative government'.[31] The Act achieved this, though it is worth noticing that it was noticeably more friendly to Improvement Commissioners established under private Acts than the 1848 Act had been. Many of these were, as was admitted, only partly elected bodies, but their credentials, and those of the business interests which had promoted them, were accepted. It was, however, true, that no part of the country was compelled to take it up, and no part was left without the means of doing so.

The Act opened the door to the localities to adopt powers contained in the Public Health Act of 1848, together with several refinements introduced as a result of experience, like the power to execute works outside their own district (which was particularly useful when seeking fresh water or a sewer outfall).[32] But it went even further than that because it also allowed the localities to adopt many of the relevant parts of the model clauses Acts, or clauses consolidation Acts passed in 1845 and 1847, just as Joseph Hume had wanted them to be able to.[33] There was, after 1858, a gigantic à la carte menu for the local authorities to choose from, and in accordance with the libertarian spirit in which the Act was framed, the localities were permitted to adopt the whole Act, or parts of the Act, or to add to their powers in instalments by successive adoptions, just as they wished, at their discretion.[34] All this could be done at no more cost than was involved in putting up notices, and paying for the hire of a room in which to hold a meeting.

At all times, then, the localities were to remain the judges of their own needs. Or were they? The General

---

[31] *PD* CXLVIII, 499, 10 Dec. 1857.
[32] 21 & 22 Vict. c. 98, s. xxviii.
[33] Ibid. ss. xliv, xlv, l, lxxv.
[34] Ibid. s. xv. The power of successive adoption seems to have been taken for granted in 1858, and was not formally enacted until 26 & 27 Vict. c. 17, s. 7.

Board was abolished, but a Local Government Act Office, occupying the same premises and engaging the same staff, had to be set up to administer the 1858 Act.[35] Localities without boundaries were obliged to go to the Secretary of State to procure them[36] (it is hard to see what else could have been proposed), localities which had adopted the Act were required to inform the Secretary of State that they had done so,[37] and to submit an annual report of the works carried out.[38] By-laws must still be forwarded to the Secretary of State for his approval.[39] Places where the conduct of the adoption meeting was challenged, and there was an appeal, had to submit to the decision of an Inspector sent down from London to hear the case.[40] Authorities which fell out with one another were obliged to accept the good offices of the Local Government Act Office, and places wishing either to incorporate themselves with an existing district or to separate themselves from the district they were in, had to go through the Local Government Act Office.[41] Every change of boundary involved resort to the Provisional Order procedure, and localities which wanted to purchase land by means of the Lands Clauses Consolidation Act had to start by petitioning the Secretary of State.[42] So sensitive were the localities that it still remained to be found out whether they would continue to see in these residual ties, the malign hand of the state.

The Act eliminated most of the more vexatious innovations introduced in 1848. The General Board disappeared, and with it the wholesale provision for one-tenth of the ratepayers to petition the General Board to apply the Act. It was still open to one-tenth of the ratepayers in a locality without a defined boundary to petition the Secretary of

[35] R. J. Lambert, 'Central and Local Relations in Mid-Victorian England: the Local Government Act Office, 1858–71', *Victorian Studies*, 6 (1962), pp. 121–50.
[36] 21 & 22 Vict. c. 98, s. xvi.
[37] Ibid. s. xix.
[38] Ibid. s. lxxvi.
[39] 11 & 12 Vict. c. 63, s. cxv.
[40] 21 & 22 Vict. c. 98, ss. xvii, xviii.
[41] Ibid. s. lxxv.
[42] Ibid. s. lxxv.

State, but the moment a boundary was established the power of decision was returned to a two-thirds majority of the ratepayers in the locality itself. Tails were no longer going to be allowed to wag dogs in the 1860s. The Act marked a return to older principles. Parliament's willingness to trust the local authorities reminded one of the way things might have been expected to move after 1835—and did go with the Museums Act of 1845 and the Bath-houses and Wash-houses Act of 1846. The selection of the two-thirds majority of the owners and ratepayers rule recalled the procedures laid down in the first batch of town–improvement and public health Acts in 1828–33. For all except the very large towns, private Bill legislation would henceforth be unnecessary. Good practice had been codified, the codes were available for adoption, permissive legislation had won the day against compulsory and coercive legislation, and the localities had triumphed over the centre. In parliament, Walpole announced that 'the Boards which might be constituted under the Act' were to enjoy 'the amplest powers of self-administration', and no longer be 'subjected to the necessity of referring to a central board in London'.[43] In the localities the Act was hailed as a 'Great Charter'.[44]

How had the localities coped and fared during the thirty years that parliament was groping its way towards the permissive system, and what use did they make of the cornucopia of powers which became available to them on 1 September 1858? For many years, now, it has been fashionable to look at these questions from a centralist point of view. In order to carry the argument beyond the rim of the Whitehall office desk and find out what happened on the ground, I shall look first at events in the Isle of Wight, and then at Huddersfield and its hinterland. The inhabitants of the Isle of Wight were connected to the old England of land, agriculture, sea captains, and loyalism. In the middle of the nineteenth century they were beginning to exploit their greatest natural resource, an equable climate, and were turning the island into a resort for fashionable society,

---

[43] *PD* CXLIX, 1555, 22 Apr. 1858.
[44] Lambert, 'Central and Local Relations', p. 124.

invalids, holidaymakers, and tourists, most of whom came from the South of England and from the capital. The people living among the valleys round Huddersfield belonged to the other England of manufacturing. They owed nothing to London and sought little from it. They had already passed through generations of early industrialisation before 1800, and in the first half of the nineteenth century their lives were dominated by the structural reorganisation of the woollen industry. Among them, awe at the expansion of their towns and pride in the quality of their products mingled with fear of their exposure to the fluctuations of trade. In the mills and among the cottages of the handloom weavers the novel experience of class war was as vivid as the rivalry of French and English was to the service captains on half-pay lodging in the boarding-houses of the Isle of Wight.

II
The Isle of Wight

1. INTRODUCTION: LAND AND THE RESORTS

The Isle of Wight lies in a strategic position off the south coast of England, and for centuries it was commanded by a Governor with quarters in Carisbrooke Castle. In the eighteenth century, when the chief function of British governments was waging transoceanic war, the island was useful to Britain as a marshalling ground. Armies were not easily recruited, and military units which it had taken months to enlist and train, were stationed in the island, where it was virtually impossible for the soldiers to desert before they were dispatched overseas. Warships, too, which were being brought into commission to form a fleet, lay at anchor in the lee of the island, at the Motherbank, where they did not interfere with the passage of vessels into and out of the arsenal at Portsmouth. The expedition which was sent in 1787 to found a new colony in Australia, stood in the roads off Ryde for months on end, while the component elements of seamen, convicts, and marines were assembled. The islanders, with an agricultural economy leavened by shipbuilding and chandlery at Cowes, supplied provisions to the army and navy authorities, while the more enterprising among them found additional outlets for their produce across the water in Portsmouth itself.

In 1782 Henry Jones dedicated a poem on the Isle of Wight 'to those Gentlemen and Ladies, who occasionally visit the Island, for health or pleasure, and express their admiration of its beauties . . .'[1] In the eye of the poet the Isle of Wight was the epitome of England, the island's isle,

---

[1] Henry Jones, *The Isle of Wight, a Poem in Three Cantos* (1782).

a garden within a garden. But it was not until the very end of the eighteenth and the beginning of the nineteenth century that one could speak of the island being transformed, with the discovery that it possessed, in its scenery and climate, natural advantages which could be bought, and marketed and sold. Turner came, for the first time, to sketch in 1795, Keats, to compose poetry, in 1817. In the meantime, while much of Europe lay under French occupation, wealthy aristocrats like the Duke of Buckingham and Earl Spencer, who might have made their way to wintering-grounds in the Mediterranean, took to the island instead. Naval captains on active service based at Portsmouth, lodged their families away from the thronging town, across the Solent, in the wholesome island. Retired admirals took up residence along the strand at Cowes or Seaview, where they could watch the ships come and go, and still cling by a picturesque thread of memory to the life of the Service. There, in the summer, they were joined by the wives and children of city merchants grateful to escape the heat and the humid stench of London. The island was mild in winter and fresh in summer: the mildness attracted residents with pensions (whose value increased by one-third or more with the deflation that took place after the war), and the freshness visitors—two groups which were to transform first Ryde, and then the eastern end of the island.

In the eighteenth century Ryde formed part of the parish of Newchurch, and consisted of one cluster of cottages down by the shore, and another on top of the hill.[2] The Player family owned both the manor of Ryde, and the estate upon which the town grew up, and in 1781 they laid out Union Street in order to join upper and lower Ryde together. When William Player drew up his will (he died in 1792), his main concern was evidently still to ensure that his widow kept the property intact. Accordingly, he insisted upon her granting only annual leases. Even under this restriction, many tenants, we are told, did accept Jane

[2] For Ryde see especially, J. M. Hocking, 'The Development of Ryde (Isle of Wight) as a Resort Town and Passenger Port, 1780–1914', thesis presented to Southampton University 1980.

Player's word that their leases would be renewed from year to year, and built houses or seaside villas upon their plots.[3] Already, by 1795, there were said to have been about 500 inhabitants. But a point was reached where further expansion of the town, and in the income of the Player estates, could only take place if tenants were granted long leases. In 1810, Jane Player, who was by that time well over seventy, obtained a private Act of parliament, enabling her to set aside the terms of her husband's will, and to grant leases for three lives or 99 years.[4]

Before Ryde could reap the benefits of this piece of entrepreneurial legal opportunism, there was one more facility that had still to be provided. To a passenger travelling from London, the route via Portsmouth, along an exceptionally well-constructed strategic highway, offered a short crossing protected from the open sea and from storms running up the English Channel. Landing, however, was a difficulty. Ryde possessed a quay, constructed in the 1750s, which could be used at high water, but no harbour, and visitors crossing at low tide were dumped, inhospitably, upon the sands, where their carriages sank, axle deep, into the mud. Recognising that Ryde was becoming 'a Place of great public Resort' for 'the Masters and Mariners of Ships and Vessels lying at *Spithead* and *The Motherbank*', for 'Persons passing and re-passing to and from the *Isle of Wight*', and for 'Persons frequenting the same as a Watering Place', a group of local capitalists, including the major landowners, Sir William Oglander, Sir Leonard Thomas Worsley Holmes, Barrington Pope Blachford, and George Player, formed a company and obtained a local Act of parliament enabling them to construct a pier and charge tolls for its use.[5]

In the half-century that followed, Ryde grew as fast as any showpiece industrial revolution town. The population increased from 1,601 in 1811, to 3,396 in 1831, and 7,147 in

[3] This is stated in the Act.

[4] 50 Geo. III c. 177, *An Act for enabling Jane Player, Widow, and Others, to grant Leases of certain Estates at or near Ryde . . . devised by the Will of the late William Player . . .*

[5] 52 Geo. III c. 196, *An Act for making a Pier and Landing Place at Ryde . . .* CRO/FAR/DD/85/1.

1851. Every year, while Ryde itself continued to grow, groups of 'overers' or 'overners' arriving in search of homes, winter residences, and summer lodgings, passed through the town and headed towards the south coast. Some were content to stop at Brading, where, at the beginning of the century, Legh Richmond had composed his evangelically inspired best-seller, the *Annals of the Poor*.[6] Others threaded their way through the gap in the hills to Sandown, where the bay was likened to that at Naples, and to Shanklin, whence they explored the Undercliff and the whole of the romantic coast from Luccombe to Blackgang. Further impetus was given to these developments when the physician, Sir James Clark, published a book called *The Influence of Climate in the Prevention and Cure of Chronic Diseases* in 1829, and pronounced the Undercliff particularly well-suited to the needs of 'invalids threatened with pulmonary disease'. In this respect, he added, Ventnor 'is probably superior to any place in this line of coast'. The principal objections to it, as a place of residence for invalids, he went on, were 'the scantiness of accommodations, and its distance from medical advice'.[7] These were deficiencies which could be remedied, and within a few years a small collection of fishermen's huts and an inn grew into a town which, already by 1851, recorded a population of 2,569.

The island had become fashionable, and a seal was set upon this development when, in 1845, Queen Victoria bought the Osborne estate from Lady Pope Blachford, and converted it into a family retreat, where she and Prince Albert could forgo the formalities of a court, and relax with their children. For their part the royal family, like other

[6] G. Brannon, *Sketches in the Isle of Wight designed to illustrate the Local Descriptions contained in the 'Annals of the Poor'* (1832), makes it clear that the cottages and graves of 'The Dairyman's Daughter' (Elizabeth Wallbridge) at Arreton and 'The Young Cottager' (Jane Squibbs) at Brading, and the beach at Whitecliff Bay where Richmond encountered 'The Negro Servant' (William), attracted large numbers of visitors.

[7] Sir James Clark, *The Influence of Climate in the Prevention and Cure of Chronic Diseases*, pp. 28–30. See, too, J. L. Whitehead, MD, *The Climate of the Undercliff, Isle of Wight, as deduced from Forty Years Consecutive Meteorological Observations* (1881), and Dr W. Thornton Parker, 'Ventnor as a Place of Health Resort', *New York Medical Journal*, May 1881.

owners of second homes, had to tread tactfully along the line between taking a lead in local affairs and failing to contribute to enterprises undertaken by the islanders themselves. Their response was to take no formal part—that, after all was the responsibility of the Governor—but to allow their name to be used freely in good causes like the construction of the new Royal Isle of Wight Hospital, the support of the Royal Isle of Wight Horticultural Society, the Royal Yacht Squadron at Cowes, the Royal Victoria Yacht Squadron at Ryde, the Ryde Royal Town Regatta, and in due course the Royal National Hospital for Diseases of the Chest at Ventnor. Commerce, too, made use of the royal name, and in the 1850s Ryde possessed a Royal Kent Hotel, a Royal York Hotel, a Royal Eagle Hotel, and a Royal Pier Hotel.[8] Perhaps the most attractive of all the many aspects of island life touched by the royal presence was the custom of celebrating the Queen's coronation day, 28 June, every year, as a public holiday, with picnics, outings, treats, sports, and other festivities all over the island.

The discovery of the Isle of Wight did much more than just set off a building boom: it changed the whole aspect of affairs. Like agriculture, the trade in visitors reached a seasonal peak in the summer, but to a greater extent than it is today, the business was well balanced. Every winter, while Cheltenham and Leamington endured cold fogs, the island boasted of its fine, clear, bracing weather 'which instead of repelling, actually invites, out of door exercise'.[9] In 1863 the *Isle of Wight Observer* spoke of 'the invalid, the convalescent, the man of business seeking relaxation, the tired soldier, the jaded lawyer, the pleasure seeker, the young gentleman in search of a wife with £300 a year, and the mother with her incomparable daughters' as all going to make up the community of a watering-place, and estimated that between 500 and 600 people in these categories would pass the winter at Ventnor.[10] Looking after winter residents sustained some of the momentum achieved by catering for the summer holidaymakers, and helped to convert what might otherwise have remained a part-time

[8] See 'The Fashionable List' published every week in *IWO*.
[9] *IWO* 13 Nov. 1858, 2e3a.   [10] Ibid. 14 Nov. 1863, 4a.

occupation into the sole, profitable, source of livelihood of many of the inhabitants. Catering for recreation and retirement became a major industry, with needs of its own. Newly arrived residents formed a fashionable society, demanded lending libraries, and founded Literary and Philosophical Institutes. They, and the businessmen who looked after them, formed a new 'interest', which began to challenge the dominance of land. At the same time the resorts at the east and south ends of the island became restless under the regime of the capital, Newport.

Newport lay at the head of the Medina estuary, close to the centre of the island. It could be reached, directly, by boat, from the mainland, and the borough lay claim to jurisdiction over the whole of the river estuary, as far as tide had ever reached and therefore over the waters of the harbour at Cowes.[11] For centuries Newport had been the meeting-place both for island society, which, in the seventeenth century, used to gather there from the outlying manor-houses for the winter,[12] and for the administration of the island's affairs. In the eighteenth century Newport was one of four Municipal Corporations in the island, the others being Brading in the east, and Newtown and Yarmouth in the north-west.[13] Three of these, Newport itself, Newtown, and Yarmouth were also parliamentary boroughs, each returning two Members to parliament. The island was not a county in its own right, being regarded, for shire purposes, as part of Hampshire. Freeholders could, if they wished, vote at elections for the county, but they must travel to Winchester in order to do so, and, as one commentator put it, for all the interest they had in the locality, they might just as well be voting in Yorkshire.[14]

[11] *Victoria County History, Hampshire and the Isle of Wight* (1912), v, p. 253. There is a map in *PP* 1837 XXVII, 352. Newport's jurisdiction extended a further 2 miles out into the Solent.
[12] P. D. D. Russell (ed.), *The Hearth Tax Returns for the Isle of Wight 1664–1674,* Isle of Wight Records series (1981), i, p. xxxi.
[13] *PP* 1835 XXIV, Brading, pp. 17–22, Newport, pp. 111–29, Newtown, pp. 131–6, Yarmouth, pp. 253–8, *Municipal Corporations, (England and Wales), Appendix to the first Report of the Commissioners, part II, South-Eastern and Southern Circuits,* pp. 677–82, 771–89, 791–6, 913–18.
[14] T. H. B. Oldfield, *The Representative History of Great Britain and Ireland . . . ,* 6 vols. (1816), iii, p. 555.

Those engaged in the administration of the island's affairs felt a strong sense of common identity. The island was the first place in England to form a union of parishes for poor law purposes, in 1771.[15] This meant that labourers and their families who had moved from one part of the island to another in order to secure employment, and had then fallen upon hard times and applied for relief, were not automatically returned to the villages they came from. The parishes contributed to the erection and operation of a common workhouse, but there was no attempt to equalise the rates, which continued to vary from parish to parish, Newchurch especially being proud of its low costs. In 1813 this strong sense of island identity enabled the Justices to obtain another Act of parliament which brought all the highways, with the exception of those within the borough of Newport, and after 1816 those within West Cowes, into a single system which was held out, in 1840, by a Royal Commission, as a model for the rest of the country.[16] The administration of justice, and of these, in some ways very enlightened, island-wide bodies of poor law guardians and highway commissioners all took place in Newport. The 'county', families and the larger tenant farmers were in control, and in the course of the eighteenth century the parliamentary boroughs had all lost their independence. Newport was treated as the property of the Holmes family, and Yarmouth fell into the same hands. Newtown was 'a decayed borough, consisting of only a few cottages, and paying no more than three shillings and eightpence to the land-tax', yet it sent 'as many members to Parliament as the county of Middlesex' which paid 'a sixth part of the land-tax of the whole kingdom, or the county of York'

[15] 11 Geo. III c. 43, *An Act to establish a House or Houses of Industry in the Isle of Wight for the Reception, Maintenance, and Employment of the Poor belonging to the several Parishes and Places within the said Island;* 16 Geo. III c. 53, *An Act to continue the Corporation of the Guardians of the Poor within the Isle of Wight,* repealed the previous Act.

[16] 53 Geo. III c. 92, *An Act for amending Roads and Highways on the Isle of Wight;* PP 1840 XXVII, p. 10, *Report of the Commissioners for inquiring into the State of the Roads in England and Wales,* p. 10. The roads were maintained by rates rather than by statute labour (as in an ordinary parish) or by tolls (as with a normal turnpike), see W. Jacques, *The Isle of Wight System of Roads* (1845), pp. 1–3.

which contained 'a population of near a million persons' and 20,000 freeholders.[17]

The Reform Act of 1832 dealt a shock to the Isle of Wight, which lost four MPs and gained one. Newtown and Yarmouth ceased to return Members. Newport continued to return two, and in addition the island was separated from Hampshire, and given a county seat of its own. In the county, polling took place at Ryde and West Cowes, as well as at Newport itself, but the announcement that there was to be an election and the declaration of the poll both took place at Newport, which thus remained at the hub of island politics, a situation epitomised by the fact that for many years a single solicitor, J. H. Hearn, held both the key posts, that of Town Clerk to Newport borough council, and that of Clerk to the Justices of the Peace in the county.[18]

Politically, the Reform Act restored life to the island. As in many other parts of the country, the annual registration of electors was fiercely contested. In 1832 the details of both borough and county registration contests were recorded almost verbatim by W. M. Manning, and published in a book which deserves to be reprinted by a Historical Records Society.[19] Contests were the norm, and although elections were said to be characterised by 'the intimidation practised during a canvass, and by the violence during a poll',[20] none of the three seats could be regarded as safe. The Liberals held all three seats between 1832 and 1837, and again for two years between 1857 and 1859, but the Conservatives held all three between 1841 and 1847. In 1852 the parties exchanged territories, the Conservatives winning the county from the Liberals, and the Liberals seizing the two borough seats from the Conservatives. If we accept the party labels used by McCalmont,[21] and

[17] Oldfield, *Representative History*, iii, pp. 562, 563, 570.

[18] In both the county and borough he kept the manuscript registers of persons entitled to vote, NBR vols. 210, 211.

[19] W. M. Manning, *Proceedings in Courts of Revision in the Isle of Wight before James Manning Esq., Revising Barrister . . .* (1836).

[20] *IWO* 23 Oct. 1852, 2b.

[21] F. H. McCalmont, *The Parliamentary Poll Book of all Elections from . . . 1832 to . . . 1879* (1880).

count the thirty-six years between 1833 and 1868, then in
the borough, with its two Members, the Liberal and Conservative Members tied with a score of 33½ each, while the
remaining five went to a Member described as a Liberal-
Conservative. In the county the Conservatives did establish
a winning margin, holding the seat for 20½ years against
the Liberals' 15½.

In the middle of the nineteenth century, then, the
borough of Newport had ceased to be the political fief of a
single family,[22] and even in the county the hold of the
landed interest was no longer unshakeable. The decline in
the fortunes of the landowners gathered pace during the
battle over the county highways. The struggle began in
Ryde, where the inhabitants, unlike those in Newport and
West Cowes, were subject to the highway rate. By the late
1830s Ryde found itself paying no less than one-fifth of the
total sum raised in the entire island, and receiving but a
fraction of its contributions back in the form of repairs to
its own roads.[23] The Highway Commissioners were landowners and tenant farmers, who were then perceived, 'as
a class', to have 'an interest distinct from that of the great
body of rate-payers, the householders of the island'.[24] In
1839 a committee was formed in Ryde to resist the Commissioners' demands. The first problem the protesters
faced was to procure a copy of the local Act, which none of
them 'had ever seen'.[25] When, at last, one was found, the
committee was advised by John Tidd Pratt (of Lighting and
Watching Act fame), that the power to levy rates had been
granted for twenty-one years only, and that it had therefore expired in 1835.[26] This was enough to encourage leading
citizens in Ryde to refuse to pay the rate. The Commissioners took the defaulters to court, and the Justices, all of
whom were commissioners themselves,[27] found against

[22] Description used in *PP* 1835 XXIV, p. 122, s. 47, *Municipal Corporations,
(England and Wales), Appendix to the first Report of the Commissioners, part II, South-
Eastern and Southern Circuits*, p. 778.
[23] Jacques, *Isle of Wight System of Roads*, p. 56.
[24] Ibid. p. 4.   [25] Ibid. p. 5.   [26] Ibid. p. 11.
[27] It was left to the Justices themselves to decide whether they would serve as
Highway Commissioners: 'The fact, however, is that all the leading magistrates
in the island have qualified; they have not only qualified, but act; they not only
act, but exercise a paramount ascendancy at the Board' (ibid., p. 8).

them. In 1841 twelve distress warrants were executed in Ryde in a single day,[28] and feeling in the town ran high. For their part the Justices accused Ryde of wanting 'to put the island into confusion',[29] and in 1845 the Commissioners obtained a decision in their favour from the Court of Common Pleas.[30] But by this time things had gone too far for the conflict to stop there. The tenant farmers themselves began to ask questions about the operation of the Act. The landlords replied by trying to turn the tenants off the Commission.[31] The tenants took their case to the assizes and won, and the Agricultural Society, over which the Earl of Yarborough and Sir Richard Simeon had presided, collapsed.[32]

The old order was beginning to crack even before the first railway surveyors appeared in the island in 1845. Upon this occasion the Earl of Yarborough, the Oglander family, the Simeons, and the Hambroughs, all opposed a development which would involve the compulsory purchase of land, the invasion of privacy, and the spoliation of natural beauty.[33] The project, like many others in a year of bubbles, came to nothing, and in 1852, when it was revived, the landowners leaned upon the borough of Newport to try and forestall the demand for a railway by promoting a Bill to enable the Town Council to deepen the channel of the Medina, and to levy dues upon coals landed at the town wharf.[34]

This second railway scheme was surveyed by Mr Fulton, and promoted jointly by the London and South Western Railway and the London, Brighton and South Coast Railway. The proposal was for two lines, starting at West Cowes and Ryde, to meet at Newport, and proceed across country, past Godshill, to Niton in the south of the

[28] Ibid. p. 26. [29] Ibid. p. 24.
[30] Ibid. p. 45. [31] Ibid. pp. 17, 34–6.
[32] Ibid. p. 38. [33] Summarised in *IWO*, 23 Oct. 1852, 2cd.
[34] 15 & 16 Vict. c. 21, *An Act to enable the Mayor, Aldermen, and Burgesses of the Borough of Newport in the Isle of Wight to raise Monies for the Improvement of the Navigation of the River Medina, within the Borough, and to alter and amend certain Ancient Tolls and Duties payable to the said Mayor, Aldermen, and Burgesses.* The Act was said, on one occasion, to have cost £2,000, *IWO* 11 Dec. 1852, 3ab, and on another £800, *IWO* 28 Nov. 1863, 3f4a.

island.[35] When the Bill came before the House of Commons in 1853, it was allowed a second reading before the land-owners showed their hand. The two (Liberal) Members for the borough prudently (and timidly) decided that it would not be advisable to speak against the wishes of their con-stituents, and absented themselves from the debate. The Member for the county, Colonel Harcourt, then spoke against the Bill. Vansittart (Berkshire) alleged the Bill was 'wholly promoted by strangers', Compton (Hampshire, South) claimed there was not 'the slightest necessity' for the Bill, because 'there was water carriage to all the towns which it proposed to benefit', and Inglis (Oxford Univer-sity) delicately suggested that it ought to be thrown out on the spot in order to save its opponents the expense of having to fight it in committee. Everyone agreed with Compton that 'all the landed proprietors in the island were opposed to this railway', doubt was thrown upon the claim that it had obtained 'the concurrence of a large number of the respectable tradesmen' in the towns,[36] and at the end of the day a majority of what the *Hampshire Independent* called 'forty-one of the rankest Tories in the kingdom . . . led on by Messieurs Vansittart! Inglis! Compton! Spooner! Newdegate!', threw the Bill out by 133 votes to 92. The defeat may not have been inflicted, as the newspaper suggested, by 'a Jesuitical system of organ-ised opposition', but the Bill's opponents were, notoriously, the dear-bread men of 1846. The fact that they 'could have no possible conception of the wants and wishes of the community', and that they were willing to veto 'any portion of Her Majesty's subjects being allowed the option of preferring the accommodation of a railway carriage to a stage waggon', was bitterly denounced in the Liberal press (which was embarrassed by the conduct of the Liberal Members for the borough).[37] In the autumn of 1853, it was reported that the promoters now planned to leave Newport out, and come before parliament again, 'the late Bill having been thrown out mainly through the

[35] Summarised in *IWO* 3 Sept. 1859, 2e.
[36] *PD* CXXV, 197–8.
[37] *IND* 19 Mar. 1853, 5d.

instrumentality of the borough solicitors and the promoters of the [Medina river] mud scheme'.[38] Nothing came of this, however, and for the time being there was little for the Liberal press to do but keep Colonel Harcourt's behaviour in parliament under scrutiny,[39] and endeavour to make sure that at the next election he would lose his seat.

In the meantime, in 1855, the balance of forces began to change, when the Earl of Yarborough sold Appuldurcombe House, which passed, by subsequent lease, into the hands of a joint-stock company for use as an hotel.[40] Even with one key strong-point converted from landowning to tourism, however, the third railway project, surveyed by Mr Birkinshaw, and promoted in 1858, failed like its predecessors. The breakthrough came the following year, when two separate projects, one for a line linking West Cowes to Newport, surveyed by Mr Ward, and another for an Eastern Section railway from Ryde to Ventnor, surveyed by Messrs Livesay and Saunders, were brought before parliament.[41] The first passed, and the line was established with a capital of £30,000 and power to borrow £10,000, and the second, which was defeated in the House of Lords, was reintroduced, and passed the following year, with a capital of £125,000 and a power to borrow £41,600.[42] The Cowes to Newport line which was only four miles long, was opened on 16 June 1862, the Ryde to Sandown and Shanklin line, eight miles, on 23 August 1864, and the extension, running under St Boniface down, to Ventnor, twelve miles from Ryde, on 10 September 1866. Links between the two systems, joining Newport to Ryde and Sandown, authorised by Act of parliament in 1863,[43] were not completed until 1875.

---

[38] Ibid. 6 Aug. 1853, 8f.
[39] Ibid. 8 July 1854, 5d, 'in seventy-four of the most important divisions' Col. Harcourt had voted upon 33 occasions 'contrary to the Members for the Borough', and 'on thirty-four of these same important divisions he was absent from his post'.
[40] L. O. J. Boynton, *Appuldurcombe House*, Official Guidebook (1967), p. 26.
[41] Summarised in *IWO* 3 Sept. 1859, 2e.
[42] 22 & 23 Vict. c. 94 and 23 & 24 Vict. c. 162.
[43] 26 & 27 Vict. c. 232.

The principal demand for a railway came, throughout, from Ventnor. The town stood single-mindedly behind a cause championed by its medical practitioners. It was probably an exaggeration to say that coaches took five hours to make the journey over the top of the downs from Ryde[44]—four must have been more normal. But there was an 'immense passenger traffic' between Ryde and Ventnor.[45] In 1858 it was said that 500 people a day passed through Brading in the season,[46] and on Good Friday 1859 visitors poured into Ventnor 'on the regular coaches, in buggy, gig, dog-cart, and tandem, and on foot by the scores'.[47] By 1863 the traffic between Ryde and Ventnor was reckoned to be worth £14,000 a year.[48] The delays in parliament caused a great deal of frustration in Ventnor. Visitors were deterred, and the expansion of the town was held back. Ventnorians grumbled about 'the great difficulty experienced by the merchant, the man of business, and the professional man in getting to and fro to visit their sick relations', and in 1858 at 'one of the most numerous attended meetings' ever held in the town, 'many persons of wealth and influence, neither lodging house keepers or exclusively doctors . . . pledged themselves to take shares' in a new railway, if one were promoted.[49] In 1862, frustrated by the uncertainty which still surrounded the Eastern Section's plans to extend its line from Shanklin to Ventnor, the citizens of Ventnor grasped at a scheme to construct a harbour of their own. Breakwaters were built, and the promoters looked forward, in a visionary way, to steamers plying direct to Ventnor from Stokes Bay or Littlehampton, and reducing the journey time from London to four hours.[50] But the breakwaters were carried away by storms, and the inhabitants were left with their 'insecure anchorage, a raging surf, a dangerous and rocky shore, and a precipitous cliff'.[51] The truth was they had been over-optimistic in more ways than one. Britannia did

[44] *TEL* 12 Sept. 1866, 3c.
[45] *IND* 6 Aug. 1853, 8f.
[46] *IWO* 2 Oct. 1858, 2e3a.
[47] Ibid. 30 Apr. 1859, 3e.
[48] *IND* 4 Feb. 1863, 2e.
[49] *IWO* 2 Oct. 1858, 4a.
[50] E. D. G. Payne, 'The Harbour and Piers of Ventnor, 1843–1914', Ventnor and District Local History Society.
[51] *IND* 1 Jan. 1853, 8bc.

not 'rule the waves smooth enough round Bembridge ledge and Dunnose point, for that route ever to become available for the transit of passengers, especially invalids'.[52] A further expansion in the fortunes of Ventnor would take place with a railway, but otherwise not at all.

Once it had become clear that the landowners were in retreat, and that a railway would eventually be built, the crucial question for Ventnor, as for the other towns on the island, was what railway was there to be? At this point the island had become caught up in the fortunes of the two railway companies, the London and South Western and the London, Brighton and South Coast, and the plans they put forward for making the connection from London and the Solent coast. Their rivalry accentuated the conflicts between different parts of the island. There were two ways of approaching the island from London, one via Southampton and the other via Portsmouth. Southampton was a small but an expanding town, Portsmouth a large town, but, since the end of the wars, a somewhat idle one, growing at a pace well below the national average.[53] The LSWR reached Southampton in 1840. It threw out a branch from Eastleigh to Gosport in 1845, and invited passengers for Portsmouth harbour to complete the journey on foot across a floating bridge. In 1848 it opened a line via Fareham, where it was joined by the LBSCR, and Cosham to Portsmouth. Both companies offered somewhat round-about routes from London to Portsmouth, and there was still a chance of Southampton becoming the main port of embarkation for the Isle of Wight, until the direct line of railway, built by a company which literally drove a track, via Guildford and Petersfield, down the middle between the other two, and then leased its line to the highest bidder (the LSWR),[54] was opened in January 1859. There was not much the island could do to affect the outcome of the competition between Southampton and Portsmouth, even though the result would have repercussions upon the

[52] *IWO* 26 Oct. 1861, 3f.
[53] The population of Southampton increased from under 8,000 in 1801 to over 19,000 in 1831, while that of Portsmouth grew from 41,000 to 50,000.
[54] *The Times*, 15 Apr. 1859, 11d.

fortunes of Cowes, Newport, and Ryde. If passengers could make the journey from London and Southampton to Cowes faster than they could make that from London to Portsmouth and Ryde, then Cowes and Newport would grow at the expense of Ryde, and Ventnor would be tempted to throw in its lot with any plans which the Cowes and Newport Railway might bring forward for extending their line across the middle of the island. In 1859 the Ryde newspaper, the *Isle of Wight Observer* had 'no hesitation in asserting that if Ryde people allow the stream of traffic to and from the Undercliff to be diverted from its present channel to that of Cowes, the sun of their prosperity will be set for ever', and in 1860 a rumour of new and faster ferries being ordered for the Southampton—Cowes run by an 'Improved Steamboat company', caused alarm in Ryde.[55]

Ryde had much to lose, and Newport to gain. In 1837, the Commissioner appointed to arrange the revised boundaries of the Municipal Corporation had commented upon the 'very slow' growth of population at Newport.[56] In 1831 the population within the limits of the parliamentary borough was 6,620: to this, the new and more extensive municipal boundaries added about 800 more.[57] But in 1851 the total was still only 8,047, and ten years later it had actually fallen to 7,934. In the ten years between 1851 and 1861 Ryde grew from 7,147 to 9,269, and left Newport behind. By 1866 the rateable value of Ryde was nearing £50,000, while that of Newport was a mere £20,000.[58] Hence Newport's desperate attempt to improve the Medina in 1852, and its opposition to any railway originating at Ryde.

It was fortunate for Ryde that the direct railway to Portsmouth came into service in 1859. Ventnor stood staunchly behind the Eastern Section railway, and it was

[55] *IWO* 13 Aug. 1859, 3a, and 3 Mar. 1860, 3d.
[56] *PP* 1837 XXVII, p. 354, *Municipal Corporations Boundaries, Report of Commissioners upon the Boundaries and Wards of certain Boroughs and Corporate Towns: part II (Folkestone to Nottingham)*, p. 354.
[57] Idem.
[58] *PP* 1867–8 LVIII, p. 808, *Local Boards (Areas), Return showing the Number and Names of the several Local Boards in England and Wales operating under the Authority of the Public Health Act or the Local Government Act.*

fitting that when the line from Ryde was finally opened on 10 September 1866, the directors of the railway were entertained to a dinner at the Marine Hotel, where 'most of the gentry and landowners in the neighbourhood were present, as were also a considerable number of the tradesmen of the town'.[59] Meetings of the Railway Company were held in the town. The extension from Shanklin to Ventnor brought a massive increase in receipts, from £2,989 for the sixteen weeks mid-September to mid-December 1865, to £5,092 for the corresponding period in 1866, and the Eastern Section railway promised 'when the traffic is fully developed, to be one of the most remunerative in the kingdom'.[60] The population of Ventnor increased from 3,208 in 1861 to 4,841 in 1871.

The opening of the Eastern Section railway meant that the island had two railways, one from Cowes to Newport, and another from Ryde to Sandown, Shanklin, and Ventnor. The two railways, and the axes upon which they were built, corresponded exactly to the state of the island. There was an old island and a new island, and for the moment the two had gone their separate ways. Ventnor and Ryde, the two new towns, had challenged the primacy of, and perhaps got the better of, the two older ones. But there was still, curiously enough, one thing that remained to be settled, and that was Ryde's ambivalent attitude towards Ventnor and the Eastern Section railway. The two Acts of parliament of 1810 and 1812, which set Ryde on its path of dizzy growth, had themselves contained a contradiction. Was Ryde to be a resort or a point of entry to the island? The pier and the approaches to the pier spoilt the foreshore, and in summer, especially, the crowds of travellers seeking to pass through the town, impeded those who wanted to rest and stay there. Ryde, of course, sought to have it both ways, to preserve its position as the point of arrival, and to detain those who were passing through for just long enough to make something out of them, while simultaneously keeping them out of sight lest they spoil the character of the place for the residents. The

[59] *IWO* 15 Sept. 1866, 4a.   [60] Ibid. 2 Mar. 1867, 4a.

result was that in 1860 the Eastern Section railway was forbidden by Act of parliament to come further north into the town than Melville Road. The terminus was built at St John's Road, and between the railway station and the pierhead, therefore, there still lay a distance of over a mile, for the people of Ryde to make what they could out of conveying travellers to Sandown, Shanklin, and Ventnor across the gap. The editor of the *Isle of Wight Observer* spoke out bravely against the short-sighted and beggar-my-neighbour attitudes of his fellow citizens, saying that he hoped to see the railway extended to the pierhead and 'a train run over the Esplanade every five minutes in the day'.[61] Despite this creditable lead, a majority of the people of Ryde appear to have taken a different view: 'Why box people up at the end of the pier and whisk them away to Ventnor. Could any "change" be got out of that?'[62] In 1864 a compromise was reached, and travellers were allowed to negotiate the pier itself by means of a lightweight tram, which came into service on 27 August 1864. This still left a gap between the Pier Gates and St John's Road. The railway company tried to exert its muscle, and promoted a Bill to enable them to extend their line from St John's Road and along a new pier to low-water mark. This had the desired effect of bringing the existing Pier Company and the town to terms, and the tram was extended from Pier Gates to St John's Road.[63] Finally, opinion in parliament appears to have turned against Ryde, and in 1879 the railway company obtained an Act to enable it to tunnel under the sea-front highway so important to Ryde as a resort, and to construct a double-track standard-gauge railway on a new pier, running alongside the existing one. The line was opened on 5 April 1880, and in due course a non-stop train, *The Invalid Express* ran from Ryde Pier Head to Ventnor in twenty-one minutes, which was what the town of Ventnor had waited more than a generation to achieve.[64]

Even then there was still the coal problem to settle. Mild

[61] Ibid. 10 Jan. 1863, 3c.
[62] Ibid. 21 Feb. 1863, 3b.
[63] Ibid. 8 Sept. 1866, 3d.
[64] V. Mitchell and K. Smith, *South Coast Railways, Ryde to Ventnor* (1985).

as the climate was, residents needed coals. Already, by 1863, 3,000 tons of coal were consumed in Sandown every winter,[65] and one of the objects of the Ventnor harbour scheme had been to land 6,000 tons of coal a year.[66] In the mid-century the price of coals in the resorts was 32*s*.–35*s*. a ton, and in March 1860 the price in Ventnor reached 45*s*.[67] The early railway projectors had hoped to reduce the price to 22*s*.–25*s*.,[68] and when standard-gauge trains were at last able to run direct from Ryde pierhead, it seemed inevitable that coal would become an important constituent of railway traffic. Ryde's hotel trade felt threatened by the dirt and noise associated with the handling and transportation of coal, and the supply to the east end of the island was increasingly diverted to Brading harbour, which was developed through Local Acts of 1874 and 1881.

2. OUTLINE

Small as it is the Isle of Wight offers examples of the various methods employed by the localities and by the centre to tackle the problems of town improvement and public health.

Four towns—Newport, West Cowes, Ryde, and Ventnor —possessed local Acts. In two places, Whippingham and West Cowes, ratepayers took advantage of the Health of Towns Act of 1848 and petitioned the General Board to establish a Local Board of Health, and West Cowes secured one. When the Local Government Act of 1858 was passed, the elected Commissioners at Ryde lost little time in adopting the whole Act, and in three places without any form of representative government—East Cowes, Sandown, and Shanklin—the Act was adopted by meetings of ratepayers. Finally, the elected Commissioners at Ventnor and the elected Town Council at Newport adopted the Act hesitantly in stages.

---

[65] *IWO* 28 Nov. 1863, 3f4a.
[66] Payne, 'Harbour and Piers of Ventnor'.
[67] *IWO* 24 Mar. 1860, 3e.
[68] Ibid. 23 Oct. 1852, 2d.

3. PRIVATE BILL LEGISLATION:
NEWPORT, WEST COWES, RYDE

Nobody seems to know where a copy of the Ventnor Act of 1844 can be found, and this examination is confined to the three Acts for Newport (1786), West Cowes (1816), and Ryde (1829) where the county Highway Commissioners maintained the roads but not the pavements, and the Town Commissioners exercised jurisdiction over behaviour in the streets.[1] We do not know what the Newport Act cost, but that for West Cowes was said to have cost £1,600, and that for Ryde £1,700.[2]

The thrust, and in many clauses the wording, of these three Acts is very much the same. They had, as might have been expected, a great deal to do with the growth of gentility in the late eighteenth and early nineteenth centuries, and little to do with the urgent necessity to make war against mortality of the mid-nineteenth century. The Acts were intended to repress hooliganism, the breaking of windows, and the discharge of fireworks, and popular sports, like bull-baiting, 'throwing' at cocks, and even bowling hoops and football. But they were also drafted in such a way as to regulate the conduct of almost every trade in the town. These early Acts were often referred to as paving Acts, and reading them one would be inclined to imagine that every man with wares to sell, and every man with beasts to dispose of stood with them in the streets, crying their points. Every self-employed workman in town, it might seem, carried out his calling upon the pavements—builders mixed mortar, masons dressed stone, sawyers cut timber, coopers tended casks, wrights repaired wheels, farriers shoed horses, and, most offensive of all, butchers slaughtered animals and scalded and dismembered carcasses in the open.

The Acts were intended to remove artisans and labourers into workshops and yards where they would be out of

[1] 26 Geo. III c. 119, 56 Geo. III c. 25, and 10 Geo. IV c. 39.
[2] *IWO* 11 May 1861, 3d; 23 Nov. 1861, 4b; 29 Nov. 1862, 3f4a. Captain Brigstocke said the Ryde Act cost only £800, *TEL* 18 Jan. 1851, 4e.

sight, and to drive street vendors of all kinds into formally organised markets, where they would cease to obstruct the highway and could be regulated and taxed. Newport already possessed a market, but West Cowes and Ryde gained markets from their Acts. In Ryde, butchers were to be charged 1s. a day for the right to set up a stall. For every basket of roots brought in for sale the tradesman had to pay 2d., for a dozen poultry 6d., for a horse or an ox or twenty sheep, 2s. 6d.[3] Thus far this new system of regulation might be interpreted as a conspiracy by the larger and more prosperous tradesmen to clear the free-lance competition, with its low overheads, off the streets. But the Acts also made war against substantial tradesmen with business premises, who had been guilty of encroachments upon the pavements. Catch-all clauses banned every category of 'projections',[4] ranging from the trade marks and emblems which denoted a person's 'Trade, Occupation or Calling', to show boards, flap windows, cellar-traps, and shopkeeper's awnings. Large and small householders alike had to adjust to a new regime under which their steps, scrapers, spouts, porches, and flowerpots might be held to obstruct passers-by, and might be condemned and removed. With the pavements thus cleared, tradesmen and householders alike were forbidden to 'lay, or cause to be . . . laid, any Coals, Coal Ashes, Wood Ashes, Cinders, Soot, Rubbish, Dirt, Dung, Blood, Offal, Soil, Filth, or any other Nuisance or Annoyance whatsoever'[5] in the streets, and were required to sweep the pavements outside their premises every day. Persons in charge of conveyances, together with people riding or driving animals, were forbidden to drive or ride furiously, or to park longer than was necessary for the setting down and taking up of passengers and goods.

It would be unwise to gauge the scale of the nuisances from the phraseology of the Acts. Laywers had their formulae, and the civilised norms which were, in future, to be enforced, were, no doubt, in very many cases, already

---

[3] The tolls are listed in an Appendix to the Act.
[4] West Cowes Act, p. 23.
[5] Newport Act, p. 21.

observed. Nevertheless, these local Acts do seem to reflect an extraordinary increase in the middle classes' sensitivity to smells, shouting, jests, high spirits, and horseplay, a rising tendency to think of all handwork as something dirty, a thing apart, to be separated from the sale and consumption of goods, and a growing willingness to invoke the law to create a sanitised environment. As an illustration of what people of means would have liked to accomplish, the Acts are instructive. Just what was achieved by them is another matter. At Newport thirty-one persons were named as Commissioners, and charged with responsibility for carrying the Act into effect. There were four esquires and one clergyman, four gentlemen, four brewers, one wine-merchant and one distiller, three bankers, three grocers, two surgeons, two merchants, one mercer, one tanner, one ironmonger, one carpenter, one stonemason, and one brazier. They were given power to co-opt additional Commissioners up to a total of forty-one, and vacancies were to be filled, not by election, but by co-option, the qualification being residence and the receipt of 'Rents and Profits' derived from property within the borough of £10 p.a. At West Cowes there were thirty-four Commissioners. Their occupations are not given, but they were headed, ex officio, by the Governor of the Isle of Wight, the Captain of Cowes Castle, the Minister of Cowes (Church of England) Chapel, and the Lord of the Manor of Debourne, followed by Sir Thomas Tancred and Sir John Coxe Hippesley. The whole body, composed of persons qualifying by residence and being in possession of rents or lands worth £20 p.a. or of a personal estate of £500, seems to have taken its tone from the top. Here, too, the Commissioners filled vacancies by co-option. At Ryde the Commissioners were to be headed by the Governor and Captain General of the Isle of Wight, and to include 'every male person in his own right or in right of his wife possessed of real or personal estate of £1,000'.[6] In this case, as in the others, elections were ruled out, and it is worth noticing that the qualification was set higher in 1816

[6] Ryde Act, p. 2.

than it had been in 1786, and was set higher still in 1829 than it had been in 1816.[7]

All these Acts vested sewers in the Commissioners, but there was no power to compel householders or businesses to join their premises to a public system. Nor, judged by later standards, could any very extensive new works be carried out. In Newport the Commissioners were allowed to levy a rate of up to 1s. in the pound p.a., and their borrowing powers were limited to £400. It would have been impossible for them to have undertaken any major works upon these terms, and in 1853 they appear to have carried out an important street improvement by public subscription.[8] The later Acts took a somewhat more realistic view of the magnitude of the problems involved in town improvement and public health, and in West Cowes and Ryde the Commissioners were allowed to levy a 2s. 6d. rate, and borrow up to £5,000.[9] Even these more extensive powers, however, were to prove inadequate when put to the test.

4. THE PUBLIC HEALTH ACT OF 1848: WHIPPINGHAM, WEST COWES

The first place in the island, and one of the first in England, at which the ratepayers resolved to petition the General Board to send an inspector and draw up plans to implement the Health of Towns Act, was the parish of Whippingham, which included East Cowes and Barton's Village (a suburb of Newport). East Cowes had been the original home of the Royal Yacht Squadron, which met at the Medina Hotel. But the Yacht Squadron had long since moved to West Cowes,[1] with its more upper-class tone, and Whippingham society consisted of two elements, resident gentry with farms and labourers, and mechanics

[7] Illustrating a general point made by Spencer, *Municipal Origins*, p. 130.
[8] *IND* 15 Oct. 1853, 5d.
[9] Both West Cowes and Ryde were required, if they borrowed money, to repay a minimum of one-twentieth every year.
[1] *Victoria County History, Hampshire and the Isle of Wight*, v (1912), pp. 197–8.

and wrights, who found occasional employment servicing the ships and boats using the Medina estuary.[2] It was an unlikely place to head the march of progress, and one cannot help wondering whether the decision to petition the General Board, which was reached on 21 January 1850,[3] was taken to please Prince Albert at Osborne. The prime mover appears to have been Roscow Shedden, Esq.[4]

On 5 March the Inspector, Mr Ranger, opened the preliminary inquiry, which was held at the Medina Hotel. He announced that 'for the accommodation of the working classes', who could not leave their employment during the day, he would hold a special session each evening at seven o'clock, 'to hear anything they might have to say by way of complaint or otherwise'. Upon the first evening, the room was crowded, and the proceedings were watched by 'Seyd Effendi, Yanko Effendi, and Ibrahmi Effendi, three gentlemen from Turkey', who were visiting Cowes, one imagines, in order to buy ships, and who were said to have been 'much pleased with the proceedings'.[5] Whatever the Turks really thought, it is clear where the Inspector's own interest lay. Whippingham was a rural parish of 4,390 acres with a population, in 1841, of 2,518. Persons engaged in retail trade and handicrafts outnumbered those employed in agriculture, but there were apparently twenty-two tenant farmers, fifteen of whom employed 169 agricultural labourers between them.[6] The inquiry presented Ranger with a wonderful opportunity for a display of virtuosity demonstrating that the Act of 1848 was not just a 'Health of Towns Act' as it was commonly called, but a Public Health Act which could be applied anywhere. For Ranger, this was rural England stripped of romance. The mortality, at 1.6 per cent p.a. was low, and compared with a rate of 1.9 per cent for the island. But low as the death-rate was, the deaths due to epidemic diseases, which Ranger regarded

[2] *IWO* 15 Oct. 1859, 3de.

[3] *Report to the General Board of Health on a Preliminary Inquiry into . . . Whippingham, by William Ranger* (1850), p. 3.

[4] *TEL* 9 Mar. 1850, 4f. Shedden later became a member of the East Cowes Local Board of Health, *IWO* 13 Dec. 1862, 4a.

[5] *TEL* 9 Mar. 1850, 4f.

[6] *Report . . . Whippingham, by William Ranger*, pp. 9–10.

as preventable, accounted for 19.8 per cent of the whole—a
figure which, he pointed out, exceeded that in Bristol,
which was the third most unhealthy town in England. One
in eight children did not survive the first year. Those that
did, suffered, the three medical practitioners assured him,
from 'want of good health'.[7] Everywhere, Ranger found
evidence of 'a perpetual struggle for cleanliness . . . in the
midst of foul gutters, [and] stagnant pools.' In East Cowes
there were houses 'standing literally over cess pools', and
privies so repulsive that they could not be frequented.[8]
Throughout the parish liquid refuse went into open pits
and soaked into the earth, while the solids were heaped
into middens which accumulated 'in close connexion with
the walls of the houses'.[9] In East Cowes Ranger found a
single public well which was liable to flood with seawater
at high tide:[10] in summer the level dropped, and 'it was
stated by the industrial classes that, in order to secure a
supply, they are obliged to attend as early as three o'clock
in the morning'.[11] There was little doubt that East Cowes
needed both a better supply of water and an improved
system of drainage. But doubts were expressed whether
'the costs incurred may be more than a needy and often
unemployed population can well afford to pay',[12] and in
particular whether a humble parish could afford to employ
the regular staff of officers required by the 1848 Act.[13]

Ranger, however, behaved as though he had a point to
prove. He took the view that 'the state of the habitations'
was not due to 'any inherent habits of the people themselves',[14] but to want of legal means which meant that it
was 'utterly beyond the power of the poor creatures themselves' to alter anything.[15] East Cowes could be furnished
with a constant supply of filtered water at high pressure

[7] Ibid. pp. 10–12.
[8] Ibid. pp. 14–15.
[9] Ibid. pp. 16 (Captain Chapman), 28.
[10] Ibid. p. 17, Mr Wheeler.
[11] Ibid. p. 15.
[12] *TEL* 9 Mar. 1850, 4f.
[13] *Report . . . Whippingham, by William Ranger*, p. 4.
[14] Ibid. p. 24.
[15] Ibid. p. 14.

from a catchment area of 130 acres lying in the park above the town and tapped by 'deep drainage by means of tubular pipe and catch-water drains'.[16] Barton's Village could be supplied from Newport (which itself drew its supplies from Carisbrooke). Ranger recommended that the Public Health Act should be applied to Whippingham, and that a Local Board of Health should be established with nine members, one-third of whom would retire each year. Each of the nine members would be elected out of the whole parish (i.e. there was to be no division into wards).[17] The General Board hesitated to act on his recommendation. There had always been a feeling, as Mr J. H. Hearn put it, that 'the petition for inquiry had not emanated from the whole parish, but merely from East Cowes'.[18] This was made the ground for an opposition, and it was alleged that 'the occupiers at Whippingham' had been 'reluctantly dragged' towards 'a participation of the exceeding benefits of the bill'.[19] A second inquiry was held. The printed report is missing from the British Library,[20] but we do know that the upshot was that it was decided not to apply the Act.

Interest in the Public Health Act was not confined to one side of the Medina. West Cowes had its local Act, and its Commissioners had not been idle. Extracts taken from their minute-books show that in the 1840s they had attempted to abate nuisances, and that they had addressed themselves to the problem of sewerage.[21] In eleven years before 1850 they spent £8,476 5s. 2d. upon their attempts to improve the town.[22] But the 1816 Act contained 'many glaring imperfections', and there was no provision 'for . . . apportioning the sum expended over properties deriving the benefit'.[23] Everything had to be paid for out of the

[16] Ibid. p. 25.
[17] Ibid. p. 39.
[18] Ibid. p. 22.
[19] *TEL* 8 Mar. 1851, 5ab.
[20] CT 160 (14).
[21] *Report to the General Board of Health on a Preliminary Inquiry into . . . West Cowes, by William Ranger* (1850), pp. 14–16, 17–25.
[22] Ibid. pp. 58–60.
[23] Ibid. p. 17.

general rate, and not surprisingly there was jealousy, and a ratepayers' opposition to the oligarchic Commissioners.

Much the most telling charge made against the Commissioners was that they were acting corruptly, in breach of the clause in their own Act which forbade interested parties to act.[24]

On the 26th October, 1845, a meeting of the Commissioners was held, at which twelve Commissioners were present, of whom nine were shareholders in the gas-works. At this meeting a resolution was passed for entering into a contract for lighting the town for the ensuing year. And at a subsequent meeting, held on the 9th November in the same year, fifteen Commissioners were present, nine of whom were shareholders in the gas-works, when a resolution was passed to light the town for a year at £3 10s. per lamp.[25]

Then again, after the formation of the West Cowes Waterworks in 1847, the Commissioners, many of whom were shareholders, voted in favour of allowing the Water Company to break up the streets in order to lay their pipes. The Commissioners were exploiting the authority conveyed to them for public purposes by Act of parliament to increase their own private profits, and upon this occasion a minority protest was entered in the minutes.[26] Further, Mr John White alleged that it had been 'perfectly understood that there were to be four public conduits to be given to the town for the benefit of the poor'. He complained that this had not been done, and withdrew, for a time, from the meetings of the Commissioners.[27]

The 1848 Act opened up new opportunities for the 'active' ratepayers, led by Mr C. Stokes,[28] a solicitor, who wanted to put an end to the dominance of the Ward family, who owned Northwood Court, and of the £500 men, and start a new round of improvements in the town. Early in March 1850, while Mr Ranger was in East Cowes, a party of ratepayers from West Cowes waited

[24] 56 Geo. III c. 25, s. 5.
[25] *Report . . . West Cowes, by William Ranger*, p. 8.
[26] Ibid. p. 32.
[27] Ibid. p. 31.
[28] *IWO* 23 July 1853, 3d.

upon him, and 'were pleased with the explanations given'.[29] Recognising the strength of feeling in the town, the Commissioners themselves then hurriedly seized the initiative, and called a public meeting which was held on 12 March 1850.[30] At that meeting Mr John White, stated that 'he had formerly been opposed to any application' to the General Board, but said that 'a more minute examination of the Bill had convinced him, in common with others, of the excellence of its provisions, if honestly carried out'.[31] He was supported by an estate agent, Mr Moore, who said later that 'the town was so tired of the present Act, that if they could not get the Health of Towns Act they would apply to parliament for another Act for themselves'.[32]

These threats, if threats they were, were sufficient to persuade the meeting to decide unanimously to petition the General Board to apply the Public Health Act to the town,[33] and the statutory inquiry, conducted by Mr Ranger, began at the town hall on 17 April. In Whippingham, Mr Ranger had been confronted by a rural parish which was entirely without provision for public health. Here he was faced with the limitations which the passage of time had revealed in a previous attempt to solve urban problems. Maps were laid before him which showed the routes taken by the existing water-pipes and sewers.[34] The basic necessities were already in place. And yet, there had been cases of cholera, 185 houses, only, out of a total of 879 which were listed in the rate-book were connected to the water supply, and Mr Prangnell, a fishmonger, complained that the water was so dirty he could not wash his fish in it— 'it would stain a turbot so that it could not be removed'.[35] The installation of water-closets was being held back by the high charge, 10s. a year, levied upon each one by the Water Company, and there was no public bath-house provided for the lower classes.[36] The sewage collected in

[29] *TEL* 16 Mar. 1850, 4ef.
[30] *Report . . . West Cowes, by William Ranger*, p. 1.
[31] *TEL* 16 Mar. 1850, 4ef.
[32] *Report . . . West Cowes, by William Ranger*, p. 23.
[33] Ibid. p. 1.   [34] Ibid. maps 1 and 3.
[35] Ibid. p. 31.   [36] Ibid. pp. 31, 61.

the drains was discharged at low tide on to the mud of the
Medina, where it offended the population of East Cowes
when the wind was in the west, and the inhabitants of
West Cowes themselves when it blew from the east.[37]
Then, there was the Point, a low-lying area 400 ft. long by
250 ft. wide, where a thousand people lived crowded
together among piggeries, dung-heaps, and pits for the
reception of offal from slaughterhouses. In due course one
of the maps accompanying Ranger's report showed the
area 'All built over & occupied by People and Pigs'.[38] As
Mr Ranger said, it was impossible not to conclude 'That
the provisions of the local Act have failed in its machinery
practically, as evidenced by the prevalence of the evils they
were intended to prevent.'[39]

The solution to all the town's problems, the Inspector
decided, was to apply the Public Health Act, set up a Local
Board of Health consisting of fifteen members, one-third
of whom were to retire each year, and to place the responsibility for the water supply and the sewerage in the same
hands.[40] The General Board accepted his advice, the Provisional Order constituting the Local Board of Health and
defining the area it was to cover (part of Northwood and
part of West Cowes township) was issued on 8 March
1851, and the first elections took place on 15 September
1851.[41]

The elections divided the town. The correspondent of
the *Hampshire Telegraph* reported that the popular party
attacked the self-elected nature of the old regime, and that
Mr Charles Taylor 'spoke in dispraise of the old commissioners, of their robbing the fatherless and widows, of
their numerous blunders, and their short-comings and
misdoings'.[42] But the newspaper acknowledged that there
was another party whose supporters held that the old
Commissioners had been men 'who were actuated by a
sincere desire to advance the prosperity of the town'. The
great majority of the old Commissioners were requested

[37] Ibid. p. 25.
[39] Ibid. p. 69.
[41] *TEL* 20 Sept. 1851, 4f.

[38] Ibid. pp. 13–14, and map 2.
[40] Ibid. p. 63.
[42] Ibid. 30 Aug. 1851, 4e.

'to stand for office under the new regime',[43] and the result was that the old guard never really lost control. They had played their hand very skilfully. They had joined the rate-payers in petitioning the General Board to apply the Public Health Act to the town. They had, in effect, emerged from the preliminary inquiry with a remodelled local Act obtained at no cost, and fifty-two sections of their original Act of 1816 remained in force.[44] Mr Ranger had been tender to existing interests. The rich men of Cowes sacrificed the self-perpetuating nature of the old Commission, made a bow in the direction of representative institutions, and secured an almost unchanged property qualification for the new body of £500 property or £15 rating.[45] No sooner were they back in power than they began to lay plans for the Board to purchase the local Water Company. They were able to cite Mr Ranger's report in support of this move, and there would not, of course, have been anything wrong with it were it not for the fact that a majority of the Board held shares in the undertaking, and stood to profit from its disposal. The clerk to the Board was the solicitor to the company, and the Inspector of Nuisances appointed by the Board was the company secretary. As the correspond-ent to the *Hampshire Telegraph* drily put it, 'it is to be hoped that the interests of the said Water Company will not be overlooked by those in authority'.[46] The ratepayers' party complained that the valuation agreed for the sale, £3,975, was too high,[47] and the purchase was apparently blocked by the General Board. When the General Board was abol-ished, the Local Board returned to the issue, and finally, in 1860, when 'the chief proprietors' of the company were still 'the leaders of the Local Board',[48] the purchase was completed. The West Cowes water works, with its 'cracked reservoir and rusty pipes',[49] became the property of the town. The purchase had been effected 'at an im-

[43] Ibid. 12 Sept. 1851, 4f.
[44] *Report . . . West Cowes, by William Ranger*, p. 70.
[45] Ibid. p. 71.
[46] *TEL* 8 Nov. 1851, 4e.
[47] Ibid. 17 Jan. 1852, 4e.
[48] *IWO* 3 Mar. 1860, 3d.
[49] Ibid. 17 Oct. 1863, 4b.

mense cost, far beyond its actual value as an engineering production, though probably not more than the original outlay for the same, including the ignorance and errors of the promoters'.[50] In this way did the private shareholders escape from any possible losses resulting from the incompetence of their servants and their own folly.

There was always something unattractive about the Local Board at West Cowes. Members of the Board claimed that, while the population increased from 4,786 in 1851 to 5,730 in 1871, they carried out the improvements they thought necessary for 'any locality of medical and fashionable resort'.[51] But they were no sooner back in power, with all the additional legitimacy they derived from having been elected, than they began to flaunt their independence of the General Board, to strike attitudes against the centralising tendencies of the Public Health Act of 1848, and to pose, despite their still very unrepresentative nature, as the champions of 'the great principle of self-government'.[52] They insisted upon appointing a person known to themselves to carry out the necessary survey of the town, even though the Public Health Act laid it down that this task was to be reserved for the Ordnance Survey.[53] At all times the odour of propertied men's and businessmen's connections and favours hung about the Commissioners' modest sense of their duty to the population at large. Nowhere was this more apparent than in the vital question of the town's landing-stage. In 1816, when the town obtained its local Act, care had been taken to provide for the construction of a public landing-place.[54] But 'subserviency to a dominant interest' prevented that scheme from coming to fruition, and in 1857, when Sir Charles Fellowes tried to persuade the Local Board to construct a public stage, and to break the monopoly of the Fountain Quay from which Mr George Ward secured an annual income of £525, the Commissioners, we are told, showed lack of spirit.[55] The Board did do something to improve the sewers, but instead of borrowing money from the Public Works Loan

[50] Ibid. 3 Mar. 1860, 3d.
[52] Idem.
[54] 56 Geo. III c. 25, p. 11.

[51] Ibid. 23 July 1853, 3d.
[53] Ibid. 30 Sept. 1854, 2d.
[55] *IWO* 6 July 1861, 3a.

Commissioners, or even from the Royal Exchange, which was willing to advance it, they borrowed £1,500 from the father of the Chairman of the Board, Dr Hoffmeister, which was not illegal, but was neither scrupulous nor prudent.[56] In the 1860s, alone among the towns in the island, the West Cowes Local Board disdained to answer reasonable queries from the Local Government Act Office about the dates when works were begun and completed, the gross estimated rental, and the rateable value of the town.[57] It is hard not to agree with Mr Stokes, who claimed that he had 'introduced the Public Health Act into the island', that 'socially and politically' the Act had been 'a great failure' in West Cowes, because 'those who have been called upon to carry out its provisions', did not really seek to carry out the Act in the way the legislature had intended.[58]

5. THE PUBLIC HEALTH ACT OF 1848 AND THE LOCAL GOVERNMENT ACT OF 1858: RYDE

Under the local Act obtained in 1829 anyone with property worth £1,000 could become a Commissioner. Residence was not required, and in the early days the influence of the heirs of the Player family and the lords of the soil, Captain Brigstocke and Dr Lind was 'quite irresistible'. 'The real management and business of the whole Commission' was handed over 'to five gentlemen, who were owners of property in the town', and within three years they had set a pattern of ambitious expenditure which was to remain characteristic of Ryde, whoever was in power, for half a century. Taking advantage of the clause in the Act which allowed them to borrow £5,000 against the security of the

[56] Ibid. 30 Sept. 1854, 2d.

[57] West Cowes is omitted from (because it had not answered) or entered with details left blank in *PP* 1866 LX, pp. 419–62, *Sanitary Works, Return of all Districts under the 'Public Health Act 1848', and 'Local Government Act 1858'*, pp. 5, 7, 1867 LIX, pp. 141–66, *Public Health and Local Government Acts, Returns . . . of Districts where 'The Public Health Act, 1848', or 'The Local Government Act, 1858', or both of them, are in Force*, p. 22, and 1867–8 LVIII, 789–822, *Local Boards (Areas), Return showing the Number and Names of the several Local Boards in England and Wales acting under the Authority of the Public Health Act or the Local Government Act*, p. 21.

[58] *IWO* 23 July 1853, 3d.

rates, they bought property to that amount, and then 'borrowed £4,000 more on the mortgage of the ground so purchased'. With that they built a town hall and market-house. These were assets to the town, but their hasty purchases meant that they were, as Mr Jacques put it, 'involved in debt from the beginning'. They had exhausted their borrowing powers at a stroke, and found themselves 'from the very outset . . . in a false position'.[1] In pursuing a single prestige project, they had mortgaged a great part of the maximum 2s. 6d. rates which they were permitted to levy for the payment of interest upon the huge sums borrowed. There was little left to meet other and more utilitarian needs such as the provision of sewers. The realities of the town's situation were driven home when, as the Revd A. J. Wade recalled, the place had to resort to a voluntary subscription to remedy the unhealthy state of the poorer quarters of the town, and 'the projected improvement was laid aside for want of sufficient support on the part of the public, and the inability of the poor people themselves to contribute anything towards it.'[2]

The result was that in 1847, when parliament was at last coming to grips with the whole problem of town improvement and public health, the Ryde Commissioners were obliged to obtain a second Act,[3] which released them from the obligation to pay off one-twentieth of all the money they had borrowed every year. The new Act also allowed them to escape from the Highway Commissioners, and to take responsibility for their own roads. This was a saving, because they had been contributing £700 p.a. to the island's highways, and, upon their own estimate, receiving only £300 back in repairs to the roads in the town.[4] But the Act did nothing to change the composition of the Commissioners, of whom there were, by 1851, sixty-one, forty-four of whom were resident and seventeen of whom were non-resident (the average attendance at meetings was about a dozen).[5] There were still to be no elections, and in Ryde, as

[1] Report to the General Board of Health on . . . Ryde, by William Ranger (1852), p. 58, W. Jacques.
[2] Ibid. p. 51.
[3] 10 & 11 Vict. c. 29.
[4] Report . . . Ryde, by William Ranger, p. 59.
[5] Ibid. pp. 53, 59.

in West Cowes, there was a strong feeling that 'the non-representative system and irresponsible government' ought to be changed to allow the smaller ratepayers and occupiers a voice in the government of their town.[6] The passage of the Public Health Act of 1848 allowed this feeling an opening. In 1851 144 ratepayers, headed by the clergy, seven doctors, and, more surprisingly, the chief ground landlords, the Brigstockes and the Linds, petitioned the General Board.[7]

The preliminary inquiry was held before Mr Ranger and opened on 9 December 1851. The town had suffered from cholera, worse, Sir Claude Wade suggested, 'than in any other town similarly circumstanced',[8] and the overall death-rate was found to be running at over 25 per 1,000. Admittedly, the figures were swollen by the number of invalids who came to Ryde when their chances of recovery were hopeless. But even when every allowance had been made for this factor, it had to be remembered, as Mr Ranger expressed it, that 'this more than average rate of mortality exists in a place which is frequented for the means of health it affords, and whose chief prosperity depends on its being able to maintain that character.'[9]

Everything then focused upon the sewers and the supply of water. The sewering was deficient. Some streets were without sewers altogether:[10] in others which did have them the Commissioners had no power to compel house-holders to connect to the public system.[11] In Ryde, as at West Cowes, sewage was discharged at low tide upon the beach,[12] which itself lay beyond the Commissioners' jurisdiction.[13] The water supply, too, was hopelessly inadequate. The Ryde Pier Company had constructed a waterworks from which it supplied ships at a cost of 3s. 6d. per ton.[14]

---

[6] *IWO* 27 Aug. 1853, 3e.
[7] Hocking, 'Development of Ryde', p. 139.
[8] *Report . . . Ryde, by William Ranger*, p. 52.
[9] Ibid. p. 9.
[10] Ibid. p. 10.
[11] Ibid. p. 58.
[12] Ibid. pp. 31–2.
[13] Ibid. p. 59.
[14] Ibid. p. 12.

Surplus water was offered to the town as an afterthought, houses with two rooms being asked to pay 8s. p.a., those with four 10s., those with six 14s., and those with eight 18s. The charge for supplying a water closet was 10s. p.a.[15] In summer the taps ran dry, and the want of water affected the letting of houses.[16] In 1844 the Pier works had been leased for thirty years to Mr Jonathan Dashwood, who had sunk a new well on his own property adjoining the town boundary, and installed a steam-engine and pumps at a cost of between £700 and £800.[17] Even then the increased supply was still not sufficient to keep pace with the growth of the town, and the combination of inadequate sewers and an occasional supply of water meant that in Ryde almost as much as in the parish of Whippingham people still drew water from private wells which were contaminated by neighbouring cesspits. There was little need to look any further to account for the high death-rate, and the final irony was that by 1851, even ships anchored off the Motherbank were abandoning Ryde pier and sending parties to Portsmouth for their supplies.[18] Scarcely surprisingly Mr Ranger recommended that the Act should be applied to Ryde, that the boundaries of the town should be extended to include the foreshore, and that there should be a twenty-seven-man Local Board of Health. In Ryde Mr Ranger showed himself, once again, exceedingly tender to existing societal arrangements, and he suggested that the qualification for becoming a Commissioner should be set at £20 rating or the possession of property worth £700.[19]

This was really very little different from the status quo. True, there would be elections, but the ratepayers' votes would be counted upon the graduated scale laid down in the Act, so that the owners of the larger properties had little to fear. Nevertheless the existing Commissioners began to have second thoughts, and an opposition emerged. In March 1852, when a public meeting was called to consider whether the ratepayers wished to see the Act applied or not, they voted by 267 votes to 227 against it.[20] But the

[15] Ibid. p. 67.   [16] Ibid. p. 16.   [17] Ibid. pp. 12–13.
[18] Ibid. p. 19.   [19] Ibid. pp. 46–7.   [20] *TEL* 27 Mar. 1852, 4f.

issue would not go away. In August Mr Ranger returned to hold a second (ways and means) inquiry, which was dominated by the single question of how, and where, Ryde was to obtain water.[21]

On 4 September, George Butler, the leading printer on the island, whose works occupied The Colonnade in Lind Street (and whose wife ran an agency for supplying domestic servants),[22] published the first number of a new four-page newspaper the *Isle of Wight Observer* (now, in 1988, the *Isle of Wight County Press*), which was founded with the stated aim of promoting the grand causes of representative government and public health.[23] Butler brought an excited style to his reporting of the town's affairs. The Town Commissioners were used neither to sarcasm, 'this glorious company of town contractors . . . the Pier, Water and Gas Company', nor to being castigated as 'profiters from filth'.[24] They resolved to poll the town again. Six hundred and fifty papers were issued: in a simple majority count 355 ratepayers expressed a wish not to have the Act applied, 35 voted in favour, 2 said they were neutral, and 258, objecting to the haste with which the Town Commissioners were proceeding before the publication of Mr Ranger's second report, refused 'the call of the self-elected Board', and boycotted the referendum.[25]

In January 1853 Mr Ranger's second report was published, and the whole issue of democracy in Ryde became inseparable from that of water and the source from which it was to be obtained. The Town Commissioners supported a scheme put forward by Mr Dashwood, the lessee of the Pier Company's works, for a joint-stock company to extract water from the Bloodstone Spring under Ashey Down. The opposition, marshalled by a committee sitting at the York Hotel, and supported by George Butler, preferred the alternative put forward by Dr Lyon Playfair in 1850 and endorsed by the engineer, H. Austin, employed by the

[21] *IWO* 25 Dec. 1852, 3ab.
[22] Advertised on the front page of *IWO*.
[23] Hocking, 'Development of Ryde', p. 144.
[24] *IWO* 25 Dec. 1852, 3bc.
[25] *IND* 1 Jan. 1853, 8d.

General Board, to obtain it from the south side of the downs, at Alverstone.[26] The distance would be greater, but water, emerging from the greensand, would be soft, and any extra costs involved in pumping it over the hills would be offset by pecuniary advantages 'in the consumption of tea, of soap, [and] in the wear and tear of washing'.[27]

At this point, perhaps because the death-rate had been running at a level which, if it had continued, would have justified the General Board in invoking its compulsory powers, both sides still expected the General Board to impose its will upon the town. In January 1853, when the Commissioners balloted for their offices, they all joked about it because they expected to have to yield them up before the year was out.[28] Upon the other side, Mr Oldfield gave a banquet at the York Hotel to celebrate the 'early anticipated provisional order'.[29] He might have done better to wait. In March, one week before he destroyed the Isle of Wight railway scheme, the MP for the County, Colonel Harcourt, met a delegation from the Town Commissioners in London, and conducted them to the offices of the General Board in London, where they were said to have achieved all they wanted from their deputation. In vain did a second deputation from the public health party travel up to London, in haste, to try and undo the damage done by the first.[30] The town was polled a third time, and the commissioners won by 213 votes.[31] The clerks at the General Board continued to prepare a Provisional Order, the Revd W. S. Phillips, vicar, and Mr Geo. Randall of the Pier Hotel were asked to allow their names to stand in the instrument as chairman and vice-chairman for conducting the first elections necessary to establish a Local Board,[32] and the Provisional Order was sent away to be printed. But by this time it was too late for it to come before parliament in 1853, the General Board itself was under attack in the House of Commons, and the Board let it be known that

[26] Ibid. 22 Jan. 1853, 8e.
[28] *IND* 15 Jan. 1853, 8d.
[30] *IND* 19 Mar. 1853, 5ef.
[32] Ibid. 11 June 1853, 5e.

[27] *IWO* 25 Dec. 1852, 3ab.
[29] Ibid. 19 Feb. 1853, 8d.
[31] Ibid. 9 Apr. 1853, 5ef.

it would not allow the Act to be applied to Ryde until a majority of the ratepayers voted in its favour.

The public health party clung to the hope that the Home Secretary might yet be persuaded to include Ryde among the Provisional Orders for 1854. They forwarded a memorial to Palmerston, rehearsing the whole history of the case, drawing attention to the 'clumsy machinery' by which the 1848 Act was 'either rendered mischievous or brought to a dead lock', and urged him to turn the Act into a compulsory one, binding upon all localities in the land, in the coming session.[33] Palmerston, who could scarcely have done more, thanked them for their letter 'complaining of the conduct of the General Board, in bowing to the opinions of a majority contrary to, or without authority from, the Public Health Act', and declined to interfere, adding that the majority would have themselves to blame if there was an epidemic.[34] It was an argument whose force was evidently appreciated in the town. The Commissioners' objections were not so much to public health, with all its opportunities for selling more water to the ratepayers, as to anything that smacked of a client relationship to the General Board in London. They decided, once again, to encounter the costs of applying for another local Act. This was an extravagant thing to do—the two Acts of 1847 and 1854 were said later to have cost £3,000,[35] but there was no shaking their determination to handle matters in their own way, and what happened next was very unusual. The public health party came to terms with the Commissioners, the former accepting that the town was going to follow the old-fashioned road, and the latter that the local Act would incorporate all the important clauses of the Public Health Act of 1848, including the election of Commissioners. In December 1853 a joint committee of Commissioners and ratepayers was reported to 'sit almost daily', combing their way through the clauses consolidation Acts, sorting out what was needed for Ryde.[36] There was one last half-

[33] Ibid. 12 Nov. 1853, 8d.
[34] Ibid. 10 Dec. 1853, 5e.
[35] *IWO* 23 Nov. 1861, 4b.
[36] *IND* 10 Dec. 1853, 5e; 7 Jan. 1854, 5d; 14 Jan. 1854, 5d.

hearted attempt to persuade the government to include Ryde among the Provisional Orders for 1854, but a memorial to support this move was received with apathy in the town,[37] and the new local Bill made rapid progress through the two Houses of Parliament, and became law in July.

The Act[38] established a new body of twenty-seven Commissioners, as recommended by Mr Ranger, and the first elections took place in August 1854. At the time the *Hampshire Independent* reported that the representative system had 'completely revolutionised the old prosy order of things', and added that 'the pucker and consternation this throws on the old slow and sure party is extremely ludicrous and amusing'.[39] From a somewhat longer perspective, taken in 1861, the *Isle of Wight Observer* said that 'the first three Boards elected under the Act of 1854 unquestionably represented the large property and trading interests of the town, and not the tenement owners or occupiers'.[40] The *Observer* was probably nearer the mark. Much was achieved by the new body, and in three years, 5,844 yds. of sewers were laid, 3,428 yds. of road were made up, 5,929 yds. of pavements were laid, and 5,229 yds. of gutters and kerbs put in place.[41] But in 1859 when it was reported that 300 new houses had been built in the previous five years, it was acknowledged that 1,181, only, out of a total of 1,640 houses were supplied with piped water.[42]

Water was nearly the undoing of Ryde. Too much of the 'judgement and decision' spoken of by the *Independent* in 1854[43] went, in much the same way that it had at West Cowes, into the purchase, for £1,000, of the defective Strand waterworks, which was then leased back and operated by the former owner, while the Commissioners set about securing a new supply.[44] The Act of 1854 gave

[37] Ibid. 11 Feb. 1854, 8e.
[38] 17 & 18 Vict. c. 83.
[39] *IND* 30 Sept. 1854, 8d.
[40] *IWO* 23 Mar. 1861, 3a.
[41] *IWO* 3 Apr. 1858, 2e3ab.
[42] Ibid. 12 Feb. 1859, 3a.
[43] *IND* 30 Sept. 1854, 8d.
[44] Hocking, 'Development of Ryde', p. 149.

the Commissioners power to borrow up to £23,000 for this purpose. Water did, indeed, run from the Bloodstone, but the stream was slow, and in summer it was liable to diminish, just when it was most wanted. As the *Observer* put it, 'crowds of visitors and a short supply occur in the same months; grumbling, loud and deep, is heard on all sides, and we are inundated with letters to expose the shortcomings of the Commissioners'.[45] For their part, the Commissioners accepted the advice of their engineers, Easton and Amos, sank a well, and installed a pump. When the supply was still deficient, the Commissioners released the engineers from the guarantee they had given to provide 300,000 gallons a day,[46] dug a deeper well, and lost all the water out of the first one. Within four years the Commissioners were approaching the limit of their borrowing powers. Under 'The Great Retrograde Movement', as the *Observer* called it, and 'the combination of "zeal" and "practice"', the position was that 'with powers to borrow £23,000 for water works, and £15,000 for sanitary works, we find the money nearly all spent; a water famine just at hand; the sewage works a failure; and the shore spoiled'.[47] A year later they still had only 28,000 gallons a day where they needed 90,000.[48] By the time the Local Government Act was passed in 1858, the Commissioners found themselves boxed into a situation in which they must either adopt that Act, at a cost of a few pounds, or promote yet another local Act at a cost, probably, of another £800 in lawyers' fees.[49] There was a good deal of crowing from the *Observer*, but the Commissioners knew when they were beaten, and having stood out so proudly against the Public Health Act of 1848, they lost little time in adopting the Local Government Act in October 1859.[50] Their motive was not to secure self-government, for the town enjoyed that already, but to increase their powers of borrowing. The irony was that by the time they were ready to turn to the south side of the downs for their water, the supply at

[45] *IWO* 8 Oct. 1859, 2e.
[46] Ibid. 10 Apr. 1858, 2d.
[47] Ibid. 17 July 1858, 3a.
[48] Ibid. 12 Feb. 1859, 3a.
[49] Idem.
[50] *IWO* 22 Oct. 1859, 2e.

Alverstone had already been earmarked for Sandown and Shanklin, and they had to turn to Knighton instead, where they encountered extortion from landowners.[51] The result was that they had to promote yet another Ryde Waterworks Act in 1861,[52] and to lodge additional requests with the Local Government Act Office to increase their borrowing powers still further, in 1862–3, when they exhausted the £43,300 limit allowed them under the Local Government Act, and still needed another £3,600 to complete the works. In 1865 they required another £9,000 on top of the £47,280 they had already borrowed, and in 1868–9 they had to ask for a further £5,000 for sewerage works and £1,000 for street improvements.[53] The comfort was that the Provisional Order Acts, prepared by the Local Government Act Office, cost the town nothing. To have gone on petitioning for local Acts would have added a crippling last straw to the burden of debt which Ryde was rolling forward into the future.

6. THE LOCAL GOVERNMENT ACT OF 1858, ADOPTION BY RATEPAYERS: EAST COWES, SANDOWN, SHANKLIN

The plan to apply the Public Health Act to Whippingham was abandoned in 1851. Since then both John Samuel White and Company, engineers, and the firm of Saunders had set up works in East Cowes.[1] The town was expanding, and meritorious enterprise upon one side of the Medina now confronted meretricious employment upon the other—honest and independent artisans engaged in productive labour in East Cowes, in West Cowes anxious tradespeople dancing attendance upon the wishes of the rich. The houses in East Cowes were modest, and the

---

[51] Ibid. 4 Jan. 1862, 3a.

[52] 24 & 25 Vict. c. 58.

[53] *PP* 1862 II, pp. 509–10, *A Bill to confirm certain Provisional Orders under the Local Government Act (1858)*, pp. 11–12; 1863 II, pp. 463–4, *A Bill to confirm . . . ,* pp. 35–6; 1865 II, pp. 653–4, *A Bill to confirm . . . ,* pp. 37–8; 1868–9 III, pp. 339–40, *A Bill to confirm . . . ,* pp. 25–6.

[1] *Victoria County History, Hampshire and the Isle of Wight,* v (1912), pp. 197–8.

rateable value was not high,[2] but the town was the point of entry for the royal family and their many visitors, who made their way from the quay up the hill to Osborne. In 1853 the electric telegraph from the mainland reached Cowes, and was extended to the royal house.[3] Six years later gas-pipes were being laid 'to lighten the darkness' of the inhabitants, and the *Observer* expressed 'no doubt' that the installation would receive 'the patronage of the Sovereign, which will enable the new company to extend their main to Osborne'.[4]

The Local Government Act was adopted without fuss in October 1859. The district covered the whole of the parish of St James, an area of 498 acres, with a population, in 1861, of 1,950.[5] A body of Commissioners, twelve strong, was set up, with the Revd W. V. Hennah in the Chair. The members were 'chiefly practical men', and possessed 'a desire to see their little town regenerated under the powers entrusted to them by the Act', due regard being paid to the ratepayers 'who are necessarily small'.[6] The pace was steady. Plans were made to construct sewers and a reservoir 'to supply the place with water, which had been so long needed'.[7] Compared with its more famous sister town on the left bank of the Medina, East Cowes was not judged newsworthy by editors and local correspondents. Accordingly, in December 1862, when the works were well advanced, a '"respectful communication", as the Chinese would say, was made to the local reporters', who were invited to attend meetings of the Board 'in order that the public outside might be made acquainted with the doings within'. The *Observer*'s correspondent claimed to have lost his way among the heaps of spoil thrown up by the contractors, and a fellow reporter who found the meeting-place complained that he was shown to a corner.[8] These

[2] PP 1867 LIX, East Cowes p. 149, Sandown, Shanklin p. 158, *Public Health and Local Government Acts, Return . . . of Districts where 'The Public Health Act, 1848', or 'The Local Government Act, 1858', or both of them, are in force*, pp. 9, 18, and 1867–8 LVIII, p. 808, *Local Boards (Areas), Return showing the Number and Names of the several Local Boards in England and Wales acting under the Authority of the Public Health Act or the Local Government Act*, p. 20.

[3] *IND* 5 Nov. 1853, 8d.

[4] *IWO* 15 Oct. 1859, 3de.

[5] PP 1867–8 LVIII, p. 808.

[6] *IWO* 13 Dec. 1862, 4a.

[7] Idem.

[8] Idem.

irritations notwithstanding, the Board's actions appear to have been admirable: it got on with its work quietly and effectively. There is no hint of strife, and the meetings were not, apparently, without their lighter side, for when the Board needed somebody to collect the rates, and a Mr Babbage applied for the post, one member turned to another and asked '*sotto voce* whether he was Babbage the calculator; if so, he was just the man for them'.[9]

For much of the eighteenth century Sandown consisted of a fort, and the villa occupied, for a time, by John Wilkes, who was not noted for reverence, but would very likely have agreed that 'a Divine Hand had made that glorious bay, five or six miles in length'.[10] The place was a part of Brading parish, where, in 1851, there were 3,046 inhabitants. Ten years later there were 3,709, and most of the increase must have been accounted for by Sandown, which was 'a rapidly rising town'.[11] By the time the place was enumerated separately, in 1871, there were 2,320 inhabitants.

It is not easy to form an unbiased view of the proceedings in Sandown, because so much of our information comes from the columns of the *Isle of Wight Observer*, whose proprietor, George Butler, used Sandown as a stick with which to beat a dog (his own town of Ryde). It is a case of what the Butler saw. Nevertheless, the contrast between the history of the two towns is striking. Sandown had no local Act, and by the time the inhabitants were beginning to think about town improvements and public health, the Local Government Act was on the statute-book. In November 1859, Butler printed a letter (did he compose it himself, one wonders?) from 'an old inhabitant', who said he had been against applying for a local Act, and against the Act of 1848. Now he understood there was a new Act, 'but I, as well as others, am ignorant of the powers and the mode of application of the Act in question'. The Editor stated that he would be happy 'to go over to Sandown at any time, and lay the Government

[9] *IWO* 27 Feb. 1864, 4a. He was a tailor.
[10] *IWO* 28 Nov. 1863, 3f4a.
[11] Ibid. 8 Oct. 1859, 2e.

Instructions before a meeting convened for that purpose'.[12] Public health had its evangelists, the inhabitants agreed that they wished to adopt the Act, and since the town had no defined boundary, they petitioned the Secretary of State to send an Inspector to carry out a preliminary inquiry and determine the boundaries.

The Inspector, who was already familiar with the island, was William Ranger, and the inquiry was held in September 1859. 'The evidence adduced . . . clearly showed that for the purposes of constructing streets, sewers, and generally improving the place, some governing powers were required', and a new district covering 500 acres was recommended.[13] The *Observer* wrote enthusiastically of the way in which 'this delightful watering place . . . is throwing off the garb of the grub, and [is] about to create some sensation with its gorgeous wings, by fluttering in the sunshine of FASHION'.[14] Things did not proceed entirely smoothly. The first adoption meeting turned out to be invalid, and there was an appeal, which was dismissed, against the second. The Act was not formally adopted until 25 August 1860, when it was agreed to elect a Board of fifteen members. Some elections, at least, were contested, and in 1861 there were nine candidates for five places.[15]

The Local Government Act gave the board power to treat with a company for the supply of water, and simultaneously with plans to adopt the Act, a prospectus was brought forward for a new water company. The scheme was the brainchild of Mr Robinson, the lessee of the tolls of the Ryde ferry company,[16] and the plan was to take the pure water at Alverstone, which the General Board had recommended the people of Ryde to secure for themselves, and which the Ryde Commissioners had spurned, and to offer it to the whole of the east end of the island excluding Ryde itself. The Isle of Wight Waterworks Act of 1861 provided for a company with a capital of £20,000, and power to borrow up to £5,000.[17] With the water supply

12 Ibid. 13 Nov. 1858, 3e.   13 Ibid. 17 Sept. 1859, 4b.
14 Ibid. 29 Oct. 1859, 4a.   15 Ibid. 28 Sept. 1861, 4c.
16 Ibid. 29 Oct. 1859, 4a.   17 24 & 25 Vict. c. 55.

assured ('we are going to be supplied . . . from Alverstone, and we shall be sure to get enough'),[18] the Board got down to work. In November 1861 they were said to be 'setting the place in order . . . laying down sewers . . . laying down pavement gradually, and making crooked ways straight'. By the next season, Sandown promised to be a well-drained town, and 'as well supplied with pure water as almost any town in England'.[19]

The conclusion must be that the work was cheaply and efficiently done. The cost of adopting the Local Government Act was put at £50,[20] and in November 1862 it was announced that the Board had borrowed only £1,830 out of the £3,798 which it was empowered to do.[21] Not surprisingly, George Butler held Sandown out as a model to his readers in Ryde of

the advantages afforded by modern legislation, in substituting General Acts for Local Acts by which to govern towns. . . . The state of Ryde in 1829, as regards population, size, and requirements, was in all respects similar to that of Sandown in 1859. But in 1829 . . . there was no legal machinery applicable for the government and sanitary regulation of towns, so Ryde had to go to Parliament for a Private Improvement Act, which, as usual, turned out very defective, at a cost of £1,700, whereas, in 1859, there was the Local Government Act, which the people of Sandown wisely adopted.[22]

Basking in Butler's praise, and taking to heart his warning to heed every bad example set by Ryde,[23] the Sandown Board decided to promote the prosperity of the town by building a public rather than a private enterprise pier. Property in Sandown was 'increasing in value, but it was now on too limited a scale'.[24] The season was too short, and if the ratepayers could be persuaded to pay for a pier this would enable Sandown to rival Brighton, with its three miles of made-up paths along the seafront, where 'the height of their season was from September to

---

[18] *IWO* 23 Nov. 1861, 4b.
[19] Idem.
[20] Ibid. 29 Nov. 1862, 3f4a.
[21] Idem.
[22] Idem.
[23] Ibid. 23 Nov. 1861, 4b.
[24] Ibid. 28 Nov. 1863, 3f4a, Mr Hearn.

December'.[25] At this point, in the full first flush of local enterprise, we may leave them.

Sandown's example was rapidly followed by Shanklin, whose development followed closely upon that of its neighbour. In 1851 the population of the parish was 355, and ten years later the population of the 241 acres of what became the Local Board area was 597. The houses were large, and the rateable value per inhabitant appears to have been the highest in the island.[26] In March 1863, the *Hampshire Independent* recorded that 'this delightful little village', which had been 'sadly neglected in the matter of cleanliness', had made a move in the direction of sanitary reform. The ratepayers had resolved to adopt the Local Government Act.[27] As at Sandown, the boundaries would have to be defined. But this was soon done, and the Act was formally adopted on 23 April 1863. Water was readily obtainable from the new company operating out of Alverstone, and the Local Board borrowed £2,000, and then a further sum of £1,700 for water and main drainage.[28] There is no mention in the newspapers of parties or of disputes, and indeed very few references to Shanklin at all. The 2.035 people who lived there in 1871 may well have reflected upon the happiness of a locality which has no politics and no history.

7. THE LOCAL GOVERNMENT ACT OF 1858, ADOPTION IN STAGES: VENTNOR, NEWPORT

There is no copy of the Ventnor Act of 1844[1] in the County Record Office, and some of its details remain obscure. But we do know that the Act, which cost £3,050 to obtain,[2]

[25] Idem. Mr Withers.

[26] PP 1867–8 LVIII, p. 808, *Local Boards (Areas), Return showing the Number and Names of the several Local Boards in England and Wales acting under the Authority of the Public Health Act or the Local Government Act*, p. 20.

[27] *IND* 21 Mar. 1863, 7f.

[28] PP 1866 LX, pp. 450–1, *Sanitary Works, Return of all Districts under the 'Public Health Act 1848', and 'Local Government Act 1858'; the expenses incurred &c.*, pp. 32–3.

[1] 7 & 8 Vict. c. 105.   [2] *IWO* 24 Sept. 1859, 3e.

provided for eighteen Commissioners, each of whom must own £1,000 of property and be rated at £30 to qualify.[3] The Commissioners went out of office by rotation, and vacancies were filled by election, so that the Act, as the *Observer's* correspondent at Ventnor said, was 'certainly a great improvement upon that [of 1829] of Ryde'.[4] Even so, the qualification for office was high, and so, too, was the electoral franchise. In the whole course of the High Street, it was calculated in 1864, there were 143 ratepayers, 'out of which there were but 45 qualified' to vote under the local Act.[5] The votes cast for the six successful candidates at the annual elections in 1860, for example, were 60, 59, 54, 53, 52, and 51, and in a dull year when the contest was not a serious one, 39, 39, 39, 36, 36, and 30 votes were sufficient to secure election.[6] The large owners were able to keep affairs in their own hands, and for many years the meetings were chaired by Dr Leeson. The consequence was that a popular opposition arose among the lesser ratepayers, who were able to make capital out of the deficiencies of the 1844 Act, and ultimately to wear down the oligarchy of the old Commissioners.

The possibility of taking up the Local Government Act appears to have been raised for the first time in October 1859, when the Ryde Commissioners were on the point of adopting it. Opposition came 'from those principally who have large properties in the town',[7] and upon this occasion the Commissioners voted 12–5 against adoption.[8] But the issue would not go away. Ventnor catered for bad lungs and genteel sensibilities. During the summer there was trouble with the sea-bathing. Men and women, some of them naked, became mixed up, and rough and saucy boatmen pried upon their ablutions. The Commissioners had no power, under the local Act, to control the bathing, and in August 1860 150 ratepayers attended the annual general

[3] Ibid. 16 Apr. 1864, 3ef.
[4] Ibid. 25 Sept. 1852, 3b.
[5] Ibid. 16 Apr. 1864, 3ef.
[6] VICM, 2 July 1860, and 1 July 1861.
[7] *IWO* 22 Oct. 1859, 3c.
[8] Ibid. 24 Dec. 1859, 4b.

meeting of the Commissioners, and Mr Dodd recommended adopting the 1858 Act. He was interrupted by the
'Muckabites', and answered by Sir Raymond Jervis, a
former Commissioner.[9] In October the owners and ratepayers returned to the charge and presented a requisition,[10]
and in November a special meeting of the Commissioners
was held in order to consider the adoption of the Act, 'or
the incorporation of such part of the said Act with the
Ventnor Improvement Act as may appear expedient'.[11]

Sixteen Commissioners attended the meeting, and it is
worth spelling out in close detail what happened, in order
to show to what lengths local bodies would go in order to
select what they wanted from the Local Government Act
while still refusing to adopt the whole Act for fear of losing
their independence. The business had been carefully prepared, and the first thing the Commissioners did was to
vote to adopt the fifth portion of clause 44 of the 1858 Act,
which gave them powers to police public bathing. That, it
was agreed by everybody, they must do. They then went
on to consider whether they should secure powers in other
areas where their own Act was deficient. They voted
upon, but did not adopt, clauses enabling them to lease
land for the purposes of storing, disinfecting, and distrib-
uting sewage, and constructing a sewer outfall.[12] Next,
they adopted clause 32, giving power to cleanse the streets
or contract for cleansing, clause 34, giving power to regulate the construction of new streets and buildings, and to
close buildings unfit for habitation, and clause 36, giving
power (with the sanction of the Secretary of State) to
purchase premises for the purpose of making new streets.
Turning, under the fifteenth section of the Local Government Act, to the Public Health Act of 1848, they adopted
clauses 49, 51, 52, 54, 57–60, and 63, which brought them
powers to ensure that no new house was built without a
water-closet and drains, to require water-closets to be
placed in business premises, to provide public conveniences
or 'necessaries', to cover offensive ditches, regulate the

[9] Ibid. 11 Aug. 1860, 4bcd.
[10] VICM 15 Oct. 1860.
[11] Ibid. 20 Nov. 1860.
[12] 21 & 22 Vict. c. 98, ss. 29, 30.

keeping of swine, purify houses on the production of a certificate by two medical practitioners, and to enter premises used for the sale of butcher's meat.[13]

At this point the exhausted Commissioners adjourned. When they reassembled on 11 December, they began by adopting clause 64 of the Public Health Act, which gave them powers over the establishment of offensive trades within the town, and then turned to the question of water. They adopted clauses 75 and 76 of the 1848 Act, which gave them power to provide water and require houses to be supplied with it. Reverting to the Act of 1858 they adopted clauses 51–53 which would allow them to carry water-mains through the streets, and empowered a water company to sell its works to the Board. Finally, turning back, once again, to the Act of 1848, they adopted clauses 79, 93, and 94, which gave them powers to impose penalties upon persons injuring waterworks, and to levy a water rate and cut off the supply from persons failing to pay it.[14]

In this way, the Ventnor Commissioners picked and chose among the options made available to them under the Local Government Act, and it is difficult not to admire their stamina. Whether they laboured in a good cause, is not quite so clear. They possessed some powers to construct sewers under their own Act, but they had no power to compel a householder to join a public sewer,[15] and were, apparently, entirely without the power of borrowing money.[16] They seem to have regarded it as a point of principle that they ought not to lay burdens of debt upon future ratepayers,[17] and that presumably accounts for their refusing to take responsibility for the capital-intensive functions of holding, treating and discharging sewage. Time alone, then, as the *Observer*'s correspondent in Ventnor put it, would show 'how far this bit by bit legislature will go towards the objects desired . . . still being an important step in the right direction, we feel bound to give them the

[13] VICM 20 Nov. 1860.
[14] Ibid. 11 Dec. 1860.
[15] *IND* 24 Oct. 1863, 7cd.
[16] *IWO* 24 Sept. 1859, 3e, and 8 Oct. 1859, 2e.
[17] Implied in *IWO* 12 Nov. 1859, 3ab.

support due, but should have been far better satisfied had they adopted the whole of the Act, which they will ultimately have to do.'[18]

While the committee appointed by the Commissioners was still drawing up by-laws to regulate the bathing, by requiring men to use the east and women the west end of the beach, with a gap in the middle, and by prohibiting boats from coming within forty yards of the bathers,[19] the old body of Commissioners received a blow from which they never recovered. At the annual general meeting in August 1861, the clerk, Mr Charles Bull, apologised for not having finished preparing the accounts.[20] One month later he resigned, and absconded from the town. The 'bull's run'[21] left the Commissioners without a leg to stand on. The cash-book had not been entered up since 1855, and no vouchers could be found for the whole period 1852–7.[22] This was very wicked of Mr Bull, but the disclosure reflected much more severely upon the Commissioners who employed him and trusted him, for what use was it placing the government of a town in the hands of gentlemen of property and distinction if they allowed themselves, and the ratepayers, to be cheated by the likes of Mr Bull? Nor did the Commissioners handle the resultant publicity well. In January 1863 they attempted to select which newspaper correspondents they would admit to their meetings. As the *Hampshire Independent* put it, 'the high and mighty magnates who act as Improvement Commissioners for that beautiful little town are anxious to assume to themselves an authority which is not claimed by the sovereign of England, by the two Houses of Parliament, or by the Judges of the land. They will not, forsooth, allow their proceedings to be commented upon in the public press.'[23]

In February the ratepayers met to consider 'the best means of ensuring a free and public report' of the proceedings of their representatives.[24] One of the Commissioners, Mr Moor, who was the proprietor of the *Ventnor Times*,

[18] Ibid. 1 Dec. 1860, 3cd.
[20] Ibid. 5 Aug. 1861.
[22] VICM 8, 16 Sept. 1861.
[24] Ibid. 4 Feb. 1863, 2d.

[19] VICM 7 Oct. 1861.
[21] *IWO* 23 Nov. 1861, 4b.
[23] *IND* 10 Jan. 1863, 5c.

was accused of bringing his opponents upon the Board
into disrepute by putting speeches into their mouths,
filling them with 'incorrect orthography and grammatical
blunders', and publishing them in his paper.[25] The Commissioners gave ground, but they did it with a bad grace,
and passed a resolution 'that it shall be competent for a
majority of the Board to exclude any Reporter who may
use any language in any comment he may make upon their
proceedings which such majority shall deem offensive and
objectionable'.[26]

There was no keeping this issue out of the public eye,
and in the following autumn the Commissioners were
losing heart and ready to surrender. In September 1863
they agreed to consider a new proposal to adopt the remainder of the Local Government Act,[27] which would
enlarge the franchise, require proper auditing, and confer
powers of borrowing, which they had striven so long to
avoid. When the time came, on 19 October, Mr J. B. Martin
announced that he had changed his mind and was now
ready to propose the adoption of the Act: 'an attempt had
been made to improve the [local] Act, by the adoption of
certain clauses from the Local Government Act, but . . . it
was found that they had not adopted sufficient, so that the
clauses they had were inoperative.' Mr Moor, seconding,
admitted that he was now persuaded that their own Act
was 'of no practical service', Mr Burt said the old Act was
'a perfect nullity', and at the end of the debate the Commissioners voted by the necessary two-thirds majority, by
10–5, to adopt the Act.[28] The new district, which came into
being in 1864, had an area of 235 acres, and a rateable value
of £14,873.[29] Dr Leeson did not wish to carry on in the new
conditions, and resigned.[30] The new and slightly more
democratic body, where the successful candidates in 1864

[25] Ibid. 7 Feb. 1863, 8d.
[26] VICM 4 May 1863.
[27] Ibid. 7 Sept. 1863.
[28] *IND* 24 Oct. 1863, 7cd.
[29] *PP* 1867–8 LVIII, p. 809, *Local Boards (Areas), Return showing the Number and Names of the several Local Boards in England and Wales acting under the Authority of the Public Health Act or the Local Government Act*, p. 21.
[30] VICM 13 June 1864.

secured 172, 170, 166, 159, 155, and 141 votes,[31] came into existence in good time for the opening of the railway, and the resumption of rapid urban growth in 1866.

Newport's local Act was the oldest in the island, and at first sight it seems astonishing that it continued in force for so long. But it was to some extent remodelled in 1835, when the powers of the Paving Commissioners were handed over to the new Town Council, which was, of course, elected by the ratepayers, and exercised, henceforth, by a committee. The 'Proceedings of the Commissioners [i.e. the committee] for paving, lighting and sanitation 1844–66' are among the borough archives deposited in the County Record Office, but a much more important document, the Corporation Minute-Book for 1850–64 is missing, so that our knowledge of what went on is sketchy.

It is difficult not to feel sad when writing about Newport, which at this period was still living upon the accumulated capital of its past ascendancy. The town remained the capital of the island. But it was not a watering-place: it did not share in the prosperity brought to the resorts of the east and south coast by England's discovery of the intoxicating and addictive beauties of the island. Visitors, whose expectations of cleanliness lay behind the drive to improve Ryde, Sandown, Shanklin, and Ventnor, made few demands upon Newport, save that it cease to obstruct the construction of an Isle of Wight Eastern Section Railway. As for the authorities in Newport, their first response in any situation appears to have been to believe that the rest of the island owed them a living. The municipality claimed harbour dues from vessels anchored at Cowes,[32] and when the West Cowes to Newport railway was opened in 1862 the Town Council demanded compensation for loss of income from the tolls levied at the town wharf under their foolish Medina Navigation Act of 1852.[33] Throughout the period, their income was small, but the need to keep up

---

[31] Ibid. 4 July 1864.
[32] NBR bks. 237–41, Cowes Harbour Dues, and bk. 241a, Receipts.
[33] NBR bk. 191, Finance Com., 7 Jan. 1858 [sc. 1859], 4 Oct., 19 Nov. 1862.

appearances meant that the municipality's bills for legal advice and for stationery, for example, remained high.

The first we hear of a proposal to adopt the Local Government Act comes in February 1860, when the Paving Committee forwarded a recommendation for its adoption to the Town Council.[34] There was an opposition,[35] and no action was taken. Three years later, when faced with the problem of extending a sewer, the proposals accepted by the Town Council included 'borrowing, according to the power conferred by the Act of Parliament for the health of towns',[36] and it appears that, at this point, the town must have adopted parts of the Local Government Act.[37] But it was not until another three years had passed, in September 1866, that the Town Council began to take the Act seriously, and appointed a committee to examine it.[38] In January 1867 the committee reported unanimously 'in favor of the adoption thereof by the parish of Newport', and by 'such parts of other parishes within the Borough as are now subject to Paving, Lighting, or Highway Rates, with the exception of those portions of East and West Cowes now under the Local Government Act'.[39] The adoption would cost nothing, because the government would bear the expense of the necessary Provisional Order, and the Town Council resolved to proceed.[40] Five hundred copies of a circular giving the reasons for their decision were printed for distribution among the ratepayers.[41] The Council sought to reassure doubters that: 'By the adoption of the Act, the Council will not subject itself to any Government control, nor will the Council be compelled to carry out any of its Provisions not suited to the requirements of the Borough, the Act being permissive, not compulsory.'[42] Even so,

[34] NBR bk. 197, Proceedings of the Commissioners for paving, lighting and sanitation, 1844–66, 6 Feb. 1860.
[35] *IWO* 11 Feb. 1860, 3b, and 18 Feb. 1860, 3d.
[36] Ibid. 7 Feb. 1863, 4b.
[37] In a discussion among the Commissioners at Ventnor, Mr Wale said Newport had adopted parts of the Act, *IND* 24 Oct. 1863, 7cd.
[38] NBR bk. 81, Corporation Minute Book, 1864–73, 12 Sept. 1866.
[39] Ibid. 15 Jan. 1867.
[40] Idem. and *IWO* 19 Jan. 1867, 3f.
[41] NBR bk. 80, Corporation Minute Book, 'Original Minutes'.
[42] NBR bk. 81, printed handbill pasted into the minutes for 15 Jan. 1867.

there was some opposition, on the ground that 'the principal body of ratepayers were working men'[43] (though they were not, by that time, one hopes, carrying out the business of their trades on the pavements), and when the day came, on 25 February, for the Council to make the decision, a memorial with 238 signatures 'by Owners and ratepayers' against adoption was handed in. But the Council was undeterred. The mayor, six aldermen, and fifteen councillors were present, and only two votes were cast against the motion.[44]

The Council's motives are clear. In the course of the nineteenth century a new town had grown up, in Carisbrooke, outside the old. The Town Council acted to remove 'the distinction between the old and the new Borough', and to place 'the management of the whole of the Borough in the hands of the Council, thereby avoiding the difficulties which so frequently occur from the present divided management'.[45] The point was that some parts of the roads, sewers, and pavements were liable to be kept in repair by the Town Council, and others by the county Highway Commissioners set up under the Act of 1813. One after another, the expanding towns had become jealous of the Highway Commissioners, and resentful of the disproportion between what they contributed by way of rates and the sums that were returned to them in the form of road improvements. In 1847 Ryde escaped from the control of the Highway Commissioners, ceased to pay their rates, and took charge of its own roads. Ryde, in turn, was followed by the towns which adopted the Local Government Act, East Cowes, Sandown, Shanklin, and Ventnor. Finally, the message got through to Newport, whose Council then had to decide where its loyalties lay. Self-interest spoke louder than any vestigial sense of belonging to the county. The adoption of the Local Government Act would lead simultaneously to a reduced burden of rates and an increased volume of services. The Town Council went before the inhabitants upon the principle

[43] *IWO* 9 Feb. 1867, 4a.
[44] NBR bk. 81, minutes 25 Feb. 1867; *IWO* 2 Mar. 1867, 3e.
[45] See n. 42, above.

that 'the Rates raised within the Borough, should be expended for the improvement of the same'.[46] Motivated in that manner they made a belated, and perhaps rather spiritless attempt to catch up with the times.

[46] Idem.

III
Huddersfield and District

1. INTRODUCTION: CLOTHIERS AND MILLS

To the west of the Great North Road, out of sight of travellers between the South of England and Scotland, the waters of the Aire, the Calder, and the Calder's tributary, the Colne, descend for twenty or twenty-five miles from the summits of the Pennine hills to Leeds and Wakefield. The area, with its soft water, was the home of the Yorkshire woollen industry. The trade had two branches, worsteds and woollens. The production of worsteds took place in and around Bradford, which acted as the focus for the upper valley of the Aire. In the Calder valley Halifax, too, dealt mainly in worsteds. Further south, in the Colne valley Huddersfield enjoyed its share of the plain woollen trade and specialised in fancy woollens, the most skilful part of the entire trade. Joseph Milner, who gave evidence to the Select Committee on Handloom Weavers in 1835,[1] and John Beaumont, whose home is now the Tolson Memorial Museum, both made cloth for stylish waistcoats. The three towns in their turn looked to Leeds, which was the commercial capital for the trade, the inlet for raw wool grown in the Midlands and the South, and the outlet for finished cloths. Leeds provided warehousing, marketing, and the whole complex of financial, insurance, and transport services needed by a great industry.[2]

---

[1] PP 1835 XIII, p. 79, Report from the Select Committee on Handloom Weavers' Petitions, Minutes of Evidence, p. 57.

[2] H. Heaton, The Yorkshire Woollen and Worsted Industries, from the Earliest Times up to the Industrial Revolution (1922); W. B. Crump and G. Ghorbal, History of the Huddersfield Woollen Industry, Tolson Memorial Museum Handbook ix (1935); D. J. Jenkins and K. G. Ponting, The British Wool Textile Industry 1770–1914 (1982); P. Hudson, The Genesis of Industrial Capital, a Study of the West Riding Wool Textile Industry c.1750–1850 (1986).

Huddersfield itself grew up at the confluence of the Colne and the Holme, and the town served the trade of the whole district comprising the valley of the Colne, together with the land drained by its tributaries the Holme and the Fenay. Seven miles to the west-south-west of Huddersfield, three streams merge at Marsden to form the Colne, which is joined on its way down the rugged valley, past Slaithwaite, Linthwaite, and Milnsbridge, to Huddersfield, by Golcar Brook and Longwood Brook. Nearly ten miles to the south of Huddersfield, the Holme rises on Harden Moss, and flows through Holmfirth, before coursing along a wooded valley to Honley and Armitage Bridge, and picking up Hall Dike, from Meltham, on the way. To the south-east, the Fenay passes through hangers and softer pastures below Shelley, Shepley, Kirkburton, and Kirkheaton, to join the Colne downstream from Huddersfield.[3] In the eighteenth and nineteenth centuries the whole area, extending over the ancient parishes of Huddersfield, Almondbury, Kirkburton, and Kirkheaton, was engaged in the one trade, and was almost as clearly defined as it would have been if it had been an island.

In the valleys of the Colne, the Holme, and the Fenay, agriculture was a hard and unrewarding business, and already, by the beginning of the eighteenth century, farming took second place to manufacturing. The evidence for this was, and in many parts still is, written into the landscape. The valley bottoms of the Colne and the Holme were narrow. Above the steep-sided river-valleys, where the ground shelved, or sloped gently as it rose towards the open moors, at an altitude of between 400 and 800 ft., the land was covered with little hill farms made up of three or four enclosures of 2–7 acres each, separated by drystone walls, with homesteads built of millstone grit. Each household kept a cow or two for milk, brought in hay for winter feed, and grew oats for its chickens. The farms themselves could not provide the population with subsistence, but 'every house, wherever set, had the gift of running water'

[3] D. F. E. Sykes, *The History of Huddersfield and the Valleys of the Colne, the Holme, and the Dearne* (1910).

essential to the processes of making woollen cloth,[4] and alongside the laithe and mistal stood a workshop, where the independent clothiers and their families, assisted by hired hands from the terraced cottages built into the steeper slopes towards the bottoms of the valleys, spun the wool into yarn and wove it into cloth.

In his *Tour* published in 1724–7, Defoe recorded how, upon approaching Halifax, he found 'almost at every house there was a tenter, and almost on every tenter a piece of cloth' drying and being stretched in the sun.[5] It must have been much the same around Huddersfield. The people Defoe described were busy and prosperous, and fifty years later Watson wrote equally rosily of 'a constant supply of work, good wages, and plenty of most other necessaries of life, so that I know not any country where, upon the whole, they live better'.[6] Every week the clothiers, inured to wind, rain, and cold, carried their finished pieces down the valleys to the towns, took up their stands in the local Cloth Hall, made their bargains with the merchants, and returned with a new supply of raw material. Every clothier was an independent agent, who owned the tools with which he worked, and the 'respectable domestic manufacturers worth their £50, or £100, or £200, who were able to make their cloth at home and go to sell it in the market' were 'the strongest bulwarks of the state'.[7] The clothiers of the West Riding were, in a few words, among the sturdiest and the most independent people in Britain.

Between 1780 and 1850, while the population of Huddersfield grew from 7,268 in 1801 to 13,284 in 1821 and 30,880 in 1851, and that of the whole district increased from 47,079 to 71,021 and 123,860,[8] the familiar world of the Yorkshire clothier was undermined by changes in the capitalisation

[4] W. B. Crump, *The Little Hill Farm, Calder Valley* (rev. edn. 1951), p. 23.

[5] D. Defoe, *A Tour through the Whole Island of Great Britain* (1724–26), with introductions by G. D. H. Cole and D. C. Browning, Everyman edn. (1962), 2 vols, ii, p. 194.

[6] J. Watson, *The History and Antiquities of the Parish of Halifax* (1775), p. 8.

[7] C. Driver, *Tory Radical, the Life of Richard Oastler* (1946), p. 131.

[8] Figures in *PP* 1852–3 LXXXVI, *Population Tables, England and Wales*, division IX, Yorks., pp. 6–7.

of the trade, and overthrown by advances in technology which redrew the lines between classes.

Proto-industrialisation had been proceeding unremarked for two centuries before 'The tendency toward centralisation of capital was endorsed, particularly in the Huddersfield area, by two . . . developments of the late eighteenth century: the use of wool of finer quality and higher price . . . and the expansion and diversification of the fancy fashion branch of the industry.'[9] Both necessitated closer supervision, the first in order to prevent embezzlement, and the second to ensure quality control. There were, therefore, already pressures tending towards a transition to a workshop or factory system even before technological change began with the mechanisation of the cropping, or shearing, of the cloth. Cropping was a skilled craft, and the members of an élite group, threatened with extinction, tried to defend their livelihoods by machine-breaking. In 1812, at the height of the French wars, when the British blockade of the European continent

had, by offending America, cut off the principal market of the Yorkshire woollen trade, and brought it consequently to the verge of ruin . . . certain inventions in machinery were introduced into the staple manufactures of the north, which, greatly reducing the number of hands necessary to be employed, threw thousands out of work, and left them without legitimate means of sustaining life.[10]

The result, as Charlotte Brontë went on to say, was to turn machine-breaking, or Luddism, into a mass movement, and in February and March, when the Luddites claimed the allegiance of '2,782 sworn Heroes' in Huddersfield alone,[11] chilling threats were sent by letter to holders 'of those detestable Shearing Frames', who were warned to remove them, or see their buildings burned 'down to Ashes'.[12] In April, the Luddites made a night attack upon Rawfolds Mill. The owner, William Cartwright, and his

---

[9] Hudson, *Genesis of Industrial Capital*, p. 35.
[10] Charlotte Brontë, *Shirley*, ch. II.
[11] M. I. Thomis, *The Luddites; Machine-Breaking in Regency England* (1970), p. 86.
[12] E. P. Thompson, *The Making of the English Working Class* (1965), p. 558.

employees were garrisoning their workplace and were armed, two of the insurgents were killed, and the assault was beaten off. In desperation, the Luddites then turned to assassination. Cartwright himself was fired at, and escaped injury, but William Horsfall of Marsden, another prominent owner of shearing frames was killed. For six months the names of those who had organised the attack on Rawfolds Mill and murdered Horsfall remained a secret which was kept by hundreds of the operatives, even 'though the Government offered a reward of £2,000 for information'.[13] Then, Benjamin Walker turned informer. The leaders of Huddersfield Luddism, Mellor, Thorpe, and Smith, were arrested, tried for the assassination of William Horsfall, and hanged at York. Five more men were hanged for the attack on Rawfolds Mill.

There can be little doubt that the scaffold acted as a deterrent, and that, as Charlotte Brontë expressed it, 'the terrors of Law vindicated' paralysed 'the sinister valour of disaffection'.[14] Luddism lost its attraction, and in the first of the post-war depressions the operatives turned from direct action at the scene of work, to much more ambitious projects for the reconstitution of the body politic. Huddersfield witnessed two risings in 1817 and 1820. Upon the first occasion 300 men gathered at midnight at Folly Hall Bridge. The plan was to seize the banks, open the prisons, take the magistrates hostage, and proclaim a republic, but the crowd melted away into the darkness after the yeomanry appeared. Upon the second occasion the elaborate and well-trumpeted arrangements made to invade Huddersfield in four divisions from north, south, east, and west, allowed the owners of property time to organise an armed association which held the town. Two men, both of whom had fought at Waterloo, were tried for high treason. They were sentenced to death, but the punishment was not carried out, and they were transported for seven years.[15] While they were serving their time, the excite-

---

[13] Sykes, *History of Huddersfield*, pp. 299–300.
[14] *Shirley*, ch. XXX.
[15] Sykes, *History of Huddersfield*, pp. 320–4.

ments of revolutionary challenge appear to have given way to a sullen acceptance of the inevitable.

In the meantime mechanisation proceeded apace. The introduction of the spinning mule led to the transfer of work from the relatively healthy atmosphere of the home and the little hill farm, to the mills, which were situated in the crowded valley bottoms and operated by water-power. The change altered the tempo of the working week. But this further revolution in working practices took place against a background of rising, if fluctuating, demand, and the erection of spinning-mills did not, on the average, reduce family incomes. It was not actively opposed, and the shift in the balance of power within the trade from the independent clothier with his small farm to the millowner with capital and the command of resources became irreversible. As 'The Clothier's Delight, or, the rich men's joy, and the poor men's sorrow' expressed it, when putting words into the mouths of the masters,

> In former ages we us'd to give,
> So that our work-folks like farmers did live;
> But the times are altered, we will make them know
> All we can for to bring them all under our bow.[16]

In the 1820s weaving was not yet mechanised, and most of the yarn spun in the mills was still sent out to the farms and cottages up to ten miles away to be woven. For the time being, then, factory spinning generated more work for the domestic weavers, who enjoyed a golden evening of full employment. Their high wages, running at 25*s*. to 30*s*. a week, could not, however, disguise the fact that it was the millowners who were now dictating terms, deciding what was to be made, and saying whom they would employ to make it. Nor could there really be any doubt that weaving, too, would ultimately follow spinning into the mills—the question was when? Sunsets do not last long on the east side of the hills. In the 1820s power-weaving was experimental. In the 1830s it became the

[16] J. Burnley, *The History of Wool and Woolcombing* (1889), p. 161.

norm for plain woollens,[17] and in 1833 Henry Hughes told the Select Committee on Manufactures, Commerce and Shipping that there were more new mills building in the town of Huddersfield than in any other part of Yorkshire.[18] Within a few years it was only the very finest fancy goods that were still being woven upon the handloom.

The operatives' response to these developments was to embark upon a new campaign to limit the hours of labour in factories. This was not conducted along the lines taken by the Luddites. The object of the ten-hours men was not to destroy machinery, but to regulate the manner in which it was employed. It was a cause which appealed strongly to a certain kind of old-fashioned Tory paternalist, and brought the working men a champion in Richard Oastler, Thomas Thornhill's steward, or land agent, at Fixby Hall. Oastler seems never to have given a thought to the conditions of employment in factories before his famous meeting with John Wood in September 1830. Having once heard this enlightened manufacturer say that there were cruelties practised 'in our mills on little children' which exceeded those committed against the slaves in the West Indies,[19] Oastler never looked back. Within twenty-four hours he had written a letter on 'Yorkshire Slavery' to the editor of the *Leeds Mercury*,[20] and the factory movement was born.

Oastler himself was an evangelical churchman, opposed both to universal suffrage and to Nonconformity, and it was not at first apparent that his humane concern for women and children could be merged with the operatives' desire to limit the hours of work of adult males who formed 75 per cent of the factory work-force.[21] But Oastler's sympathies were enlarged by contact with the factory hands, and in June 1831 he promised the members of the Huddersfield short-time committee, including Joshua Hobson,

[17] J. H. Clapham, *An Economic History of Modern Britain: The Early Railway Age, 1820–50* (1950 edn.), p. 145.

[18] *PP* 1833 VI, p. 85, *Report from the Select Committee on Manufactures, Commerce, and Shipping*, p. 81, Qn. 1289.

[19] Driver, *Tory Radical*, p. 40.

[20] Ibid. pp. 42–4.

[21] Hudson, *Genesis of Industrial Capital*, p. 81.

whose family had resided on the Thornhill estate, to par-
ticipate in their campaign for a ten-hour working day.[22]
The employers replied by insisting upon a twelve-hour
one.[23]

In 1832, Sadler, the Member of Parliament for Leeds,
obtained the appointment of a Select Committee of Inquiry
into the conditions of labour in factories. A series of stirring
rallies in support of his campaign to regulate factory hours
culminated in April 1832, when the supporters of the entire
short-time movement, embracing Leeds, Bradford, and
Huddersfield, marched to York, the county town. On
Easter Monday 'Oastler's Own' assembled in the market
place at Huddersfield at five a.m., 'there to await the
coming of the other divisions from Holmfirth and Honley
and the surrounding hamlets'.[24] It had been 'in the strag-
gling villages around Huddersfield, some of them miles
from anywhere, that Luddism was most strongly established and most effective'.[25] The clothiers, as they had
formerly been, the handloom weavers, as they were now,
came pouring down like tributary streams from the hills to
join up with the torrent and march the forty-six miles to
the county town. Oastler strode with them every step of
the way, and the rally was held on Tuesday 24 April within
a few yards of the spot where Mellor, Thorpe, and Smith
had been hanged for the assassination of William Horsfall
nearly twenty years earlier.

In April 1832 York still lay at the centre of the largest and
the most populous county constituency in England—the
only one which returned four Members. In 1783 and 1807
the shire had elected William Wilberforce, and thus played
its part in the campaign for the abolition of the slave trade.
In 1830 it had supported Brougham, whose election contributed to the downfall of Wellington's government and to
Grey's decision to introduce a Reform Bill. Britain, it might
have been hoped, was accustomed to taking some notice

[22] Driver, *Tory Radical*, pp. 86–8; S. Chadwick, *'A Bold and Faithful Journalist'*:
Joshua Hobson 1810–76 (1976), pp. 8, 12.
[23] Driver, *Tory Radical*, p. 153.
[24] Ibid. p. 157.
[25] Thomis, *The Luddites*, p. 157.

of what was said and done in Yorkshire. And so, perhaps, it was. The trouble upon this occasion was that Yorkshire did not speak with one voice. The millowners accused the Select Committee of bias, and in December Sadler himself lost his seat at the elections for the first reformed parliament. The honour of promoting the ten-hours cause in parliament passed to Lord Ashley, and in 1833 the Whig government appointed a Royal Commission to go over the whole case for factory regulation again. When the members of the Commission reached Huddersfield, the short-time committees shadowed them wherever they went, and exposed how many meetings they held with the employers, and how little intercourse they had, by comparison, with the working people themselves.[26]

The ten-hours movement was, at least, partly successful. In 1833 the government brought in a Factory Bill, which restricted the hours of labour of children, young persons, and women, and appointed Inspectors to see that the law was carried out. The operatives wanted more, of course, and regarded the absence of a clause limiting the hours of adult males as a defeat. The campaign was continued, and led ultimately to the establishment of a ten-and-a-half-hour day in 1850, but in the meantime the single-mindedness of the short-time committees gradually gave way before other issues.

In 1834, at a moment when 'a very great number' of the weavers employed in their own homes worked sixteen hours a day, earned perhaps 5s. to 7s. a week, 'could not obtain sufficient food of the plainest or cheapest kind', were clothed in rags, possessed no furniture, and in some cases slept on straw,[27] the government introduced a new Poor Law. Parliament signalled its determination to compel parishes to form unions and build workhouses, and to take away the right to outdoor relief. Low wages were one thing, the fear of being separated from one's family, and being thrown into a distant workhouse and dying there was another. In January 1837, when the Poor

[26] Driver, *Tory Radical*, pp. 223–24, 230–1.
[27] John Fielden, quoted in Thompson, *Making of the English Working Class* pp. 288–9.

Law Commissioners' agent, Alfred Power, finally arrived to put the new system into effect, the dependent wage-earners of Huddersfield, supported by those in Todmorden and Bradford, were looking for ways of frustrating the law.

As Cecil Driver wrote 'it was the old Ten Hours organisation that provided the cadre for resistance'.[28] Committees were set up in every village, where 'hundreds and thousands' of formerly self-reliant men were 'living on a short allowance of water-porridge and potatoes'.[29] On the day Power was to meet the newly elected Board of Guardians, the operatives poured into town. The room was crowded out, and the Guardians were intimidated and refused to act. The next year, the Poor Law Commissioners and their supporters among the employers in manufactures resolved to overcome all opposition. When the Guardians refused to elect a clerk, the chairman appointed one: when the annual elections were held, and both sides claimed a majority, the chairman simply declared the supporters of the law elected. The working classes of Huddersfield were not to be so easily borne down. On 7 May the meeting of the Guardians was invaded by a crowd led by Feargus O'Connor and J. R. Stephens, the 'pros' were thrown out, and the 'antis', left in possession of the field, rescinded all the resolutions taken by their opponents, and dismissed the clerk. 1838 ended with no New Poor Law established in Huddersfield. But prosecutions followed the riot, there was a shift in sentiment among the ratepayers, and in 1839 the 'antis' were defeated at the annual elections.[30] The law finally came into force, but not before the daring of the people of Huddersfield, who had defied the centralized bureaucracy of the Poor Law Commission in London, had become a legend throughout the North of England, and the Commissioners themselves had tacitly conceded that outdoor relief would have to be condoned in manufacturing areas upon the occurrence of a depression.

In no part of the country, not even in Lancashire, were

[28] Driver, *Tory Radical*, p. 335.
[29] Ibid. p. 281.
[30] Driver, *Tory Radical*, chs. XXV–XXVII and ch. XXIX s. 6. See, too, N. C. Edsall, *The Anti-Poor Law Movement, 1834–44* (1971).

the changes associated with the Industrial Revolution more traumatic than they were in Huddersfield and the surrounding district. In no part of the country were the responses more articulate, or more heroic. But the termination of the Anti-Poor Law Movement seems to mark the end of an era. In 1842, towards the end of the long-drawn-out recession of 1837–42, when no fewer than 11,000 people in the Huddersfield Poor Law union were in receipt of outdoor relief, and families were surviving on 'seven pennyworth of oatmeal per week and two or three pints of blue milk per day', the district appears to have played, by its own standards, a somewhat passive role in the Plug Riots. On 12 August thousands of operatives from Lancashire and Cheshire streamed over Standedge Moor, heading for the mills in the Huddersfield district. When they crossed the border into Yorkshire, the well-disciplined columns divided. Some made for the Holme valley, where plugs were drawn from the boilers at Honley, Meltham, and Armitage Bridge: others for the Colne, where they stopped the mills at Marsden, Slaithwaite, Linthwaite, Golcar, and Longwood. On 13 August they reached Huddersfield itself, and 'from three to six o'clock they had complete possession of the town'. They were met with sympathy among the working class, but nobody joined them, and two days later they were dispersed by troops and the strike was over.[31] Did the Huddersfield hands, one wonders, like the Home Secretary, Sir James Graham, suspect that the turn-out had been organised by the Anti-Corn Law League to further middle-class ends (cheap bread and lower wages)?[32]

By the time public health and town improvement became the great issues of the day in the period following the repeal of the Corn Laws, the employers with their Liberal politics and *laissez-faire* values held the whole district in their grasp. Over a period spanning two generations they had been faced with machine-breaking, threats of general insurrection, and a political combination of workmen's radicalism with Tory paternalism. But, as Engels himself

[31] *LM* 23 July 1842, 7b, and 20 Aug., 6d and Supplement 1f.
[32] J. T. Ward, *Sir James Graham* (1967), pp. 190–2.

acknowledged, the amount of raw material worked up by the wool-textile industry had risen from 101 million lb. (7 millions of which were imported) in 1801, to 182 million lb. (of which 42 millions were imported) in 1835.[33] The wool trade was expanding, and the principal factor still holding it back remained the uncertainty of access to foreign markets. The masters blamed the protectionist policies of the British government for this state of affairs, and in 1845, when the Anti-Corn Law League was busy buying up property and dividing the ownership into freeholds which would support county votes, the test case in which the legality of their tactics was determined concerned property in Lockwood. Messrs Crosslands sold a terrace of cottages, next to their mill and occupied by their employees, to a consortium of thirty-five of their political supporters, each of whom emerged from the transaction with a 40s.-freehold and a vote in the West Riding. The terrace was called Cobden's Row, and the day the purchase was completed the cottages were leased back to Messrs Crosslands. The transaction was a blatant piece of electoral engineering, but it was held to be in order,[34] and the incident reveals how, even in matters of protest, or 'pressure from without', the initiative had now passed to the masters.

Seventy years exposure to technological change and the vicissitudes of international trade had ended in the establishment of a new order of society. The employers had come out on top, but the scars remained, and in the 1850s the Huddersfield district (the Choral Society, founded in 1836, apart) was not a nest of singing nightingales. Masters and men continued to watch each other warily. But neither had cause to look to government or to London for support. The former had espoused the self-help ethos, and the latter had been abandoned to it by a regime which disregarded all cries for help no matter how extreme the distress. Time and again, agents of the central government who came to visit Huddersfield, from the members of the Royal Commission on Factories to the Assistant Poor Law Commissioner, were given a boisterous reception—so much so that

[33] F. Engels, *The Condition of the Working Class in England* (1958 edn.), p. 17.
[34] J. Prest, *Politics in the Age of Cobden* (1977), pp. 92–3.

one wonders whether James Smith, who was dispatched
to make inquiries on behalf of the Health of Towns Commission, and described the town as lying 'on a bank of land
rising from the river Calder',[35] actually went there. A local
man, on the other hand, who defied the Westminster
system, like Joshua Hobson, and produced an unstamped
newspaper, the *Voice of the West Riding*, was fêted as a
hero. When he was prosecuted in August 1833, Hobson
chose to go to prison rather than pay a fine, and his journey
'to Wakefield was a triumphal procession accompanied by
bands'.[36] When he was released in January 1834, his
supporters waited until the factories were 'loosed', before
they assembled at Green Cross, Moldgreen, formed a
torchlight procession, and stage-managed a triumphal re-
entry into the town.[37] The people of this area might differ
bitterly from one another about the rights and wrongs of
labour, but they were, as Charlotte Brontë said, 'a North-
of-England–a Yorkshire–a West-Riding–a West-Riding-
clothing-district-of-Yorkshire' people,[38] and would rather
settle their differences, and all their affairs, for themselves,
than suffer any interference from outside.

2. HUDDERSFIELD TOWN

The town of Huddersfield lies in a favoured situation on a
gentle southward-facing slope above the river Colne, and
in 1845 the Health of Large Towns Commission reported
that the place was open to the prevailing winds, and that
the surface water ran off easily.[1] In the eighteenth and
nineteenth centuries the entire town, and a great deal of
land to the south of it, stretching away beyond Almondbury, belonged to the Ramsden family, who were the lords
of the manor and the ground landlords.[2] Nothing could be

[35] *PP* 1845 XVIII, p. 671, *Appendix—Part II to SLT2*, p. 311.
[36] R. Brook, *The Story of Huddersfield* (1968), p. 124.
[37] Chadwick, *Joshua Hobson*, p. 22.
[38] *Shirley*, ch. XIX.
[1] *PP* 1845 XVIII, p. 671, *Appendix—Part II to SLT2*, p. 311.
[2] Plan in Jane Springett, 'Landowners and Urban Development: The Ramsden Estate and Nineteenth-Century Huddersfield', *Journal of Historical Geography*, 1982.

done in Huddersfield without the agreement and support of the Ramsden family or the Ramsden estates, and it is essential, therefore, to start by giving an outline of the way in which the property was managed. The story falls into three periods associated with Sir John Ramsden, the trustees for his grandson Sir John William Ramsden, and Sir John William Ramsden himself.

Sir John Ramsden was only fourteen years old when he inherited the estates in 1769 as a tenant for life.[3] He lived till 1839 and in the entire course of his life, which lasted eighty-six years, he came to Huddersfield only twice, in 1800 and in 1822.[4] In the early nineteenth century the lands were managed for him by the steward of the family's property at Byram, John Bower, who visited Huddersfield twice a year and generally stayed for a fortnight taking the rents and auditing the accounts. When Bower grew old, he left the work to a local agent, Joseph Brook.[5] Throughout the crucial period of the demographic revolution and the Industrial Revolution, then, Sir John was an absentee. That does not necessarily mean that he was not a caring landowner. Contemporaries made free with the image of 'a wise, enterprising and honorable proprietor',[6] who facilitated 'the progress of improvement', and compelled 'the formation of wide streets, and the building of good straight houses'.[7] It was said that he employed Joseph Kaye, who at one period had 1,100 workmen on his books,[8] to plan and raise the town for him,[9] and in 1844 Engels declared that 'the charming situation and the modern style of building of Huddersfield have made it the most beautiful of all the factory towns in Yorkshire and Lancashire'.[10]

[3] This account draws heavily upon R. J. Springett, 'The Mechanics of Urban Land Development in Huddersfield 1770–1911', Leeds University D.Phil. thesis 1979.
[4] Ibid. p. 153.
[5] Ibid. p. 155.
[6] James Smith in *PP* 1845 XVIII, p. 671, *Appendix—Part II to SLT2*, p. 311.
[7] Joseph Kaye in *PP* 1844 XVII, pp. 705–6, *Appendix to SLT1*, pp. 177–8.
[8] Idem.
[9] John Betjeman said 'he did for Huddersfield what John Nash did for London', Brook, *Story of Huddersfield*, p. 114.
[10] Engels, *Condition of the Working Class*, p. 49.

Looked at in another way, a different picture emerges. Sir John's estates were tied up by two marriage settlements. The first, made when he married in 1787, created what came to be known as the settled estates, and the second, drawn up when his son married in 1814, created the devised estates. Like many other landowners who were tenants for life, Sir John had no power to alienate land, and leases, which would terminate with his life, were almost worthless. In these circumstances development took place, as it did at Ryde before 1810, upon the basis of tenancy at will, the parties 'relying upon the honor of the family of the superior'.[11] Bower and Brook 'did their best to promote this kind of development', little control was exercised over building, and Sir John's agents inculcated 'a feeling amongst the tenants that they were unlikely to be disturbed'.[12] Huddersfield did not grow up in a fit of absence of mind, but the management of the estate was indulgent, or even negligent, and most tenants, we are told, 'appear to have viewed tenancy at will as a cut-price perpetual lease for which there was no renewal fine to pay'.[13]

When Sir John died in 1839, the devised estates passed to his grandson, Sir John William Ramsden, who was only seven years old, and would not come of age until 1853. In the meantime both the settled and the devised estates were placed in the hands of three trustees, Earl Fitzwilliam, Lord Zetland, and George Fox. Earl Fitzwilliam, especially, was experienced in the management of a West Riding inheritance. While attempting to develop the property in the interests of the heir, the trustees took a realistic view of the need to accommodate the tenants at will, to conciliate the town, and to encourage building. Finding that many people had erected buildings upon the Ramsden lands without asking permission, and that their names had never yet been entered in a rent book, the trustees took a grip upon the management of the estate, and appointed George Loch as steward, who in turn selected Alexander Halthorn

[11] James Smith in *PP* 1845 XVIII, p. 671, *Appendix—Part II to SLT2*, p. 311.
[12] Springett, 'Urban Land Development in Huddersfield', p. 159.
[13] Idem.

as his local agent. They did not attempt to abolish tenancies at will, but did promote two private Acts of parliament, in 1844 and 1848, to enable them to grant sixty-year leases upon the devised estates and the settled estates.[14] It seems likely that the estate never was better managed than in this period between 1839 and 1853.

When Sir John William came of age in 1853, and the trustees bowed out, Loch resigned. For the next six years the affairs of the estate were placed in the hands of a London solicitor named Nelson, and the management took a decisive turn for the worse. With extreme insensitivity, the new regime decided to put a stop to the relaxed system under which Huddersfield had grown and prospered. There were to be no more tenancies at will, and henceforth tenants were to be charged economic rents. Then, in 1859, Sir John William dismissed Nelson, took control of the estates himself, obtained yet another private Act of parliament to enable him to grant 99-year leases upon his estates,[15] and followed this up by serving notice to quit upon any tenant at will who failed to apply for a 99-year lease. When this move was contested in the Courts, Sir John William had the satisfaction of winning the case— but not before it had been taken to the House of Lords, and not until several years had passed.[16] By 1866 the damage had been done. Developers had stopped looking to the Ramsden estate for land, other proprietors were willing to supply Sir John William's place, and the Thornhill estate, in particular, was offering leases just outside the town in Lindley upon very much better terms.[17] In order to keep up with the competition, Sir John William was compelled to go before parliament again with another private Bill, which was passed in 1867, enabling him to grant not just 99- but 999-year leases.[18] However much he then spent buying up new supplies of freehold land in order to retrieve his monopoly—and between 1844 and 1884 the trustees

---

[14] 7 & 8 Vict. c. 21; 11 & 12 Vict. c. 14.
[15] 22 & 23 Vict. c. 4.
[16] The judgement was reported in *HC* 12 May 1866.
[17] Springett, 'Urban Land Development in Huddersfield', p. 127.
[18] 30 & 31 Vict. c. 2.

and Sir John William between them bought no fewer than 942 acres[19]—the estate never recovered. By 1890 it was mortgaged for over one million pounds, and the interest charges swallowed £35,317 out of the rental income of £58,910.[20]

Because the Ramsdens owned the town, there were few freeholds, and the inhabitants of Huddersfield never took much part in the elections for the county. At the time of the election in 1807 there were only sixty-six county voters resident in Huddersfield, and two-thirds of these polled for freeholds lying outside the town.[21] The parliamentary life of the town began in 1832, when it was allotted a single borough Member, and 415 £10 householders cast votes at the first election in 1832. It was taken for granted, in the 1830s, that the Ramsdens' Whig interest was to prevail at the elections, and even Oastler, a local hero enjoying both Radical and Tory favour, whose supporters threatened to 'mark' the premises of shopkeepers who voted the wrong way,[22] failed when he attempted to challenge the lord of the soil in 1837 and 1838. In 1841, when Peel won a convincing victory at the general election, the Conservative party in Huddersfield was unable even to field a candidate. As late as 1859 a meeting called to support the formation of a volunteer rifle corps ended in uproar when the inhabitants denounced it as 'a Tory plot to divert the people from their social evils'.[23] When a parliamentary contest did take place, it was almost always between different shades of Whig and Liberal, between Stansfield (a Whig or moderate Liberal who lived at Esholt Hall and was supported by the Tories) and Cheetham (a Liberal) in 1847, Stansfield and Willans (the grandfather of H. H. Asquith) in 1852, and between Akroyd (a worsted manufacturer, a magistrate, the chairman of the Leeds, Bradford and Halifax railway, and the last of 'the sour and frigid Whigs') and Cobden in 1857. In 1859 the electors went some way towards expun-

[19] Springett, 'Landowners and Urban Development', p. 131.
[20] Idem.
[21] Sykes, *History of Huddersfield*, p. 408.
[22] Driver, *Tory Radical*, pp. 347–8.
[23] Brook, *Story of Huddersfield*, p. 152.

ging their sense of guilt at having rejected Cobden by replacing Akroyd with Leatham (a Liberal banker from Wakefield). Six years later it was Leatham's turn to be ousted by T. P. Crosland (a local manufacturer), but Leatham retrieved the seat in 1868 and held it throughout the period between the second and third Reform Acts.[24]

The progressives could afford the luxury of contesting the seat among themselves because Huddersfield was not divided by two great interests, in the way Ryde and Ventnor were divided from Newport in the Isle of Wight, for there was but one interest, the woollen trade. The tenant farmers in the area surrounding the town were not injured by the repeal of the Corn Laws, because they grew no wheat, and had already made the adjustments needed to enable them to serve a manufacturing population. They were now specialist dairymen, selling milk and butter to the industrial work-force in the towns and townships, and may even have benefited from cheaper animal foodstuffs.[25] In the absence of pressure from their tenants there was nothing to stop the landowners actively encouraging the growth of the woollen industry and the expansion of the urban rents from which they had, already, for several generations, derived the greater part of their incomes.

Sir John Ramsden built the famous Cloth Hall at Huddersfield in 1765–6, and brought the 'broad' canal (inevitably the Ramsden canal) into the town in 1780. Why should he not do so? Neither he, nor the other great proprietor, Thomas Thornhill, who owned land to the north and west of the town, at Fixby and Lindley cum Quarmby, resided in the area. The Ramsdens did not keep up a mansion in Huddersfield. They preferred their seat at Byram, near Knottingley, and lived for much of the time in London. For his part, Thomas Thornhill abandoned Fixby Hall for Riddlesworth in Norfolk. No romantic regret for the spoilt beauty of the countryside interfered with the development of distant estates, which became yet more valuable when the 'narrow' canal under Standedge Moor was opened in

---

[24] Sykes, *History of Huddersfield*, pp. 377–450, and Dod's *Parliamentary Companion*.
[25] Crump, *Calder Valley, passim*.

1811 and Huddersfield was linked by water, lock, and (except in the tunnel itself) towpath to Manchester. A generation later the railway line connecting Huddersfield to London followed the route favoured by the landowners, and when it was constructed the Ramsden trustees seized their chance to sell their canal interests to the railway company.[26] Trains began running to Huddersfield in 1847, and in 1848, when a second tunnel under Standedge Moor, driven parallel to that cut by the canal proprietors, was completed, the town lay half-way along the most direct line of railway connecting the two centres, Manchester and Leeds, of the two great textile industries of the North, cotton and wool. Once having reached the area, the London and Yorkshire Railway threw out branches to Holmfirth (1850) and Meltham (1868), while the London and North Western constructed a line to Kirkburton (1867). By that time there were over 300 trains a day using Huddersfield station.

3. PRIVATE BILL LEGISLATION: HUDDERSFIELD

In the first half of the nineteenth century there was only one locality in the Huddersfield district which made use of private Bill legislation for the purposes of town improvement, and that was Huddersfield itself.

In the early part of the century Sir John Ramsden kept a guiding hand upon the layout of the streets and the construction of buildings, but did not attempt to hold back development. In the same way he co-operated with the inhabitants in the changes they wished to make in the government of the town, while continuing, from a distance, to reserve his own rights as the lord of the soil. In the early nineteenth century such administration as there was took place in the vestry, where the vicar took the chair, and the Court Leet, presided over by the lord of the manor's steward.[1] The arrangements were old-fashioned,

---

[26] Springett, 'Urban Land Development in Huddersfield', p. 65.
[1] Sykes, *History of Huddersfield*, p. 451.

and in 1820 the leading citizens and the proprietor co-operated to promote a local Act to enable them to light, watch, and clean the town.[2]

The Act applied to the parish of Huddersfield within a radius of 1,200 yds. from the site of the old cross in the market-place. On the south, it reached, but did not extend beyond the river Colne. To the west, north, and east, it took in parts of the neighbouring townships of Marsh, Fartown, Deighton, and Bradley. The Act set up a body of fifty-nine Commissioners, including Sir John Ramsden and four other members of his family, whose names were placed first. Each of the other Commissioners was required to be a householder, leaseholder, or occupier in Huddersfield, and to own property worth £1,000. Vacancies were to be filled by co-option, and new members had to be approved by the lord of the Manor. The Commissioners were to meet every three weeks, and to hold an annual meeting open to the ratepayers on the last Friday in August. Their books and accounts were to be open to inspection by the ratepayers.[3]

In many respects the Act bore a close resemblance to those for Newport, West Cowes, and Ryde. There was the same concern to clear the streets of obstructions, and to force artisans of all kinds to labour out of sight. Workmen were forbidden to hew stone, saw wood, hoop casks, repair carriages, shoe horses, or slaughter animals in the street. Householders were warned not to obstruct the pavements by hanging out washing, and not to erect lines for this purpose. Nobody was to 'show or expose any Stallion or Stonehorse' for fear of pandemonium among the females and neuters of the species, and mastiffs, bulldogs, and other dangerous animals were not to be allowed to roam at large. Nobody was to discharge a gun or pistol, break windows, light a bonfire, let off fireworks, 'or play at Football, or any other Game or Games'. Dangerous driving and inconsiderate parking were to attract penalties.[4]

But the main thrust of the Act, not surprisingly in a period when machine-breakers and revolutionaries moved by night, was towards lighting and watching. The

[2] 1 Geo. IV c. 43.   [3] Ibid. pp. 1–6.   [4] Ibid. pp. 22–8.

Commissioners were empowered to provide lamps and to contract for gas to light them. They were to appoint watchmen to apprehend all malefactors and disorderly persons, and innkeepers were forbidden to 'harbour' watchmen. The Commissioners were given power to contract for the cleansing of the streets, and, following the Tuesday market, scavenging (i.e. refuse collection) was to be carried out 'on every Wednesday in every Week'.[5] For all these purposes rates were to be levied on all buildings, yards, and gardens, with the exception of the Cloth Hall, charitable buildings, churches, chapels, and 'all Cottages or Dwelling Houses under the yearly value of Six Pounds'.[6] The last was a large exception, which must have made the collection of rates relatively easy, and may have been intended to defuse complaints that the Act was a conspiracy to enable the rich to tax the poor. All householders, however, whether they paid rates or not, were required to sweep the pavement in front of their premises. This was to be done before 9 a.m. on Wednesdays.[7] In the middle of the week the town was to be returned to its best appearance.

No sooner was the Act passed than a group of capitalists, headed by Godfrey Berry,[8] who was a Commissioner under the local Act, formed a Gas Company. The company did not secure an Act of parliament, and one must assume that the promoters enjoyed the confidence of Sir John Ramsden, who allowed them to lay pipes under the streets. The proprietors remain a shadowy body, but they appear to have proceeded step by step. First they made sure of their customer. On 22 December 1820 the Town Commissioners resolved to enter into a contract for the purchase of gas.[9] Then, on 2 April 1821, they formed their company, with a nominal capital of £4,000, made up of 200 £20 shares, and a paid-up capital of £3,500.[10] The streets were lit for the first time on 30 September 1821:[11] twenty years later the Company was supplying 260 lamps owned

[5] Ibid. pp. 9–16.
[6] Ibid. pp. 17–18.
[7] Ibid. p. 16.
[8] MPPI Qn. 1063.
[9] Ibid. Qn. 1008.
[10] Preamble to 24 & 25 Vict., c. 56.
[11] K. O. M. Golisti, *The Gas Adventure and Industry in Huddersfield and Vicinity* (1986), p. 30.

by the Commissioners,[12] and these were apparently sup-
plemented 'by individual acts of generosity by members of
the public who undertook responsibility for specific
lamps'.[13] Gas was expensive, 46s. per lamp for seven
months of the year in 1828.[14] In the 1840s the practice was
for the streets to be lit by 'Sun Moon or Gas': the lamps
were lit from the first moon in August to the first moon in
May, and the townspeople had to forgo illumination for
two nights before full moon, the night of full moon, and
two nights after full moon.[15] The price did not come down,
and in 1843 the contract was for 47s. per lamp. In Leeds, at
the same period, the cost was 41s. for 365 nights in the
year:[16] not surprisingly, therefore, it was rumoured in
Huddersfield that the proprietors were making excessive
profits.[17] Throughout the 1830s and 1840s the link between
the Town Commissioners and the Gas Company was
close, and in 1843 when a new contract was signed by
eight persons, two on behalf of the Commissioners and six
on behalf of the Gas Company, three out of the six men
who signed for the Company also held office as Commissioners.[18] Their critics contended that this was illegal,
under the clause in the Act of 1820 which prohibited interested parties from acting.

Having attended to the watching and lighting, the next
requirement was to obtain a supply of fresh water, and this
was achieved by another local Act of parliament in 1827.[19]
The Act named Sir John Ramsden, other members of the
Ramsden family, and his agents, together with 111 other
citizens, all of whom had to own property worth £1,000, as
Commissioners. The word was significant. The supply of
water was being placed, not in the hands of a private, profit-
making company, but in those of a public non-profit-
making body. When the Act was drafted it was estimated

---

[12] MPPI Qn. 1018.
[13] Golisti, *The Gas Adventure*, p. 30.
[14] MPPI Qn. 1011.
[15] Ibid. Qn. 1004, and Golisti, *The Gas Adventure*, p. 32.
[16] *LM* 12 Feb. 1848, 8de.
[17] MPPI Qns. 1071–3.
[18] Ibid. Qns. 1032–41.
[19] 7 & 8 Geo. IV c. 84.

that 120,000 gallons a day would be sufficient to supply the needs of the town.[20] For sources the promoters pointed to springs in Longwood and Lindley cum Quarmby.[21] At this point, however, they came up against the fact that industrialisation had got under way before urban engineering. They were obliged to concede that New Mill, Clough Bottom Mill, Bank House Mill, and Longroyd Mill, were 'at present supplied from these sources' and might 'be injured by the Waterworks'. In order to protect the mills' interests the Commissioners had to agree to construct a separate reservoir at Leys, to hold 2,400,000 cu. ft. of water 'for the sole Purpose' of affording a regular supply to the mills.[22] The Commissioners were authorised to borrow up to £20,000 for their works,[23] and a maximum scale of water rents was laid down (those for a house under £10 in value were not to exceed 20s. a year).[24] As the borrowed moneys were repaid, water rents were to be reduced 'so that the Proceeds thereof . . . shall only cover the current Expenses attending the Execution of the Powers of this Act'.[25]

The water Act was an enlightened piece of legislation, but the population of the town continued to grow, from 19,035 in 1831 to 25,068 ten years later, and the demand for water increased even faster. There were, at that time, only 100 water-closets in the town.[26] But their use, as Joseph Kaye said, was expected to spread. 'In the areas for good houses we now put water-closets for the servants; they are becoming very common here. . . . The servants prize them very much. . . . Indeed the water-closets have been built for the servants, in consequence of the servants using those made for their masters, instead of going to their own privy in the yard.' Kaye made no doubt that, by this means, water-closets 'will become common for labouring men'.[27] In 1845 the Commissioners secured a new Act,[28] which followed closely upon that of 1827. One clause em-

---

[20] Ibid. s. xxii.
[21] Ibid. Preamble.
[22] Ibid. s. xxii.
[23] Ibid. s. lxvii.
[24] Ibid. s. lxxxi.
[25] Ibid. s. lxxiv.
[26] MPPI Qn. 1623, Mr James Brook.
[27] *PP* 1844 XVII, p. 706, *Appendix to SLT1*, p. 178.
[28] 8 & 9 Vict. c. 70.

powered the Commissioners to enlarge their reservoirs at Longwood,[29] and another compelled them to impound more water for the benefit of the mills in the Colne valley. The Leys reservoir was enlarged to 6,500,000 cu. ft.,[30] and the Ordnance Survey map of 1854 boldly marks the two reservoirs 'Supply' and 'Compensation'. The extraction of water from 'Supply' was to be regulated, to some extent, by an additional rent, which was not to exceed 10s. a year each, on water-closets and private baths.[31]

In the meantime the 1820 Act itself was beginning to look dated. Huddersfield aspired to become a Municipal Corporation, and in 1842 a deputation from the town 'had an interview with Lord Wharncliffe, Lord President of the Council . . . respecting a charter of incorporation'.[32] Since the promotors had secured the support of the Ramsden trustees,[33] it is not clear why they failed. But fail they did, and the initiative gradually passed into the hands of Mr T. W. Clough, a local solicitor, and Joshua Hobson, who wanted to promote a new local Act. Opinion formed slowly, and as a result the new Bill was not drafted until after parliament had passed the model clauses Acts in 1845 and 1847, and the Preliminary Inquiries Act in 1847. The Huddersfield Bill then became one of the first local Bills to be brought under the operation of the new procedures, and both the Inspectors appointed by the Department of Woods and Forests to conduct the Preliminary Inquiry, Henry Horn, barrister, and Ambrose Poynter, architect, and the solicitor, Mr Clough, presenting the reformers' case, appear to have been conscious, when the proceedings opened on 8 February 1848, that they were making history.

The inquiry lasted eleven days, and was completed on 21 February, after 2,805 questions had been asked and answered. Mr Clough praised the lighting of the town, and said that in this respect the Commissioners under the Act of 1820 enjoyed all the powers they needed. Watching was not so satisfactory, however. The Commissioners had

---

[29] Ibid. s. iii.
[30] Ibid. s. vi.
[31] Ibid. s. xxi.
[32] *LM* 12 Mar. 1842, 7d.
[33] *HC* 21 Dec. 1867, p. 7.

no power to employ watchmen during the day, and even at night they did, in fact, provide only twelve. Admittedly a further two parochial constables were appointed and paid by the vestry under Peel's Act of 1842, but the constables so chosen were subject to annual elections, and whenever they went 'into the lower parts of the Town amongst the Beerhouse keepers' they were told that they would be ousted 'at the next annual day'.[34]

Then there was the whole problem of sewerage. There was not 'a District perhaps anywhere possessing a better natural area for Drainage'. And yet there was not a single clause in the 1820 Act which would allow the Commissioners to construct a sewer, and the General Highways Act of 1835 authorised only surface drainage. Four or five miles of sewers had been constructed upon the authority of the lord of the manor,[35] but many streets were still without sewers when Irish immigrants came flooding into the town in 1847, and the cholera returned to Britain in 1848. Worse still, the courts and yards where a majority of the poorer inhabitants lived were regarded as being outside the jurisdiction of the authorities altogether. Only 800 out of 3,211 houses, Mr Clough said, were connected to the sewers. Fifty-four drained into cesspools, 1,111 had only 'a sort of drainage', and 1,246 had no drains at all.[36] Joshua Hobson told the inquiry how, when he held the office of Inspector of Nuisances, he had found, not a hundred yards from the room where Mr Horn and Mr Poynter were sitting, a group of dwellings with one privy, only, for 109 persons.[37] Clearly, despite Huddersfield's high reputation and many advantages, there was still much to be done. When the Department's Inspectors made their tour through the town, the sights they were shown, were, according to the *Leeds Mercury*, 'not to be outmatched in any town in the kingdom'.[38] Mr Clough found a sympathetic audience when he spoke of the need for the new

[34] MPPI opening speech of T. W. Clough, Tues. 8 Feb.
[35] Idem.
[36] Idem.
[37] Statement handed to the inquiry on Fri. 11 Feb. but not included in MPPI. Reported in *LM* 12 Feb. 8de.
[38] Thurs. 10 Feb., idem.

body of Commissioners to take over the control of the streets from the Ramsden trustees who laid them out, and the Board of Surveyors under the General Highway Act of 1835 who maintained them. The whole administration of the town ought to be placed under one management.

At the Preliminary Inquiry the two Inspectors, well briefed as to the significance of the changes that had been taking place in the procedures relating to local Acts, kept on coming back to the point that the new Bill was drafted to include clauses taken from the Lands Clauses Act of 1845, and the Commissioners Clauses Act, the Towns Improvement Clauses Act and the Police Clauses Act of 1847. Mr Horn stressed that those Acts were to be read 'if this Act be passed as if the clauses were expressly introduced into it', and added that they gave very extensive powers to the Commissioners.[39] The Bill, as he was saying, was really quite incomprehensible unless one followed up the citations and ascertained what it was that was contained in the Clauses Acts. To take one example. All the long phrases employed in the local Acts for Newport, West Cowes, Ryde, and Huddersfield itself banning workmen from carrying out their callings in the streets were reduced to a single reference to section 28 in the Town Police Clauses Act.[40]

In Huddersfield the Preliminary Inquiry went off smoothly, with no more than one point of real substance raised against the Bill by the trustees of the Wakefield and Austerlands Turnpike. Parliament itself seems to have accepted the Inspectors' findings, the Bill became law, and the *Leeds Mercury* pointed out that, 'If the same care as is evinced in this case had been taken with the private bills affecting large towns passed during the past half century, some most curious legislative blunders and strange anomalies would have been prevented.[41]

The Act, which was to be known as 'The Huddersfield Improvement Act, 1848',[42] repealed the Act of 1820, and

---

[39] MPPI opening remarks of Mr Henry Horn, Tues. 8 Feb., p. 2.
[40] 10 & 11 Vict. c. 89.
[41] Report of proceedings on Wed. 16 Feb., published 19 Feb., 7ef.
[42] 11 & 12 Vict. c. 140.

established a new and more wieldy body of twenty-one
Commissioners, of whom the lord of the manor was still to
be allowed to appoint three. In order to qualify, Commissioners must reside within five miles of the town, and own
£1,000 worth of property, or receive £50 a year in rents, or
be rated to the poor in respect of property 'of not less than
thirty pounds rateable yearly value'.[43] One still had to be a
wealthy man, then, if one was to become a Commissioner.
But the Commissioners were, at least, henceforth to be an
elected body. The local Act laid it down that 'every male
person rated under this Act to the general rates thereof
shall be entitled to vote in the election of Commissioners'.[44] The wording bore the appearance 'at first sight
of a very wide and liberal basis of franchise'.[45] But
Alexander Horn himself had determined that this clause
was to be carried out according to section 181 of the Towns
Improvement Clauses Act, which laid the responsibility
for paying the rates for all property under £10 in value
upon the owners.[46] Section 184, which permitted ratepayers under £10 to lodge a claim to be allowed to pay the
rates in person, was never acted upon, and the franchise
which had appeared so wide, was, in the event, narrow.[47]
Even then, of course, the votes cast by both owners and
occupiers were summed up, according to the weighted
scale established in 1844.

The Commissioners were given powers over the lighting, watching, paving, cleansing, sewering, draining,
watering, regulating and improving of 'all streets, courts,
passages, and other places'.[48] They were given power to
regulate offensive trades newly established (blood-boiling,
bone-boiling, fellmongering, soap-boiling, tallow-melting,
tripe-boiling were mentioned),[49] and under the Towns
Improvement Clauses Act they were authorised to lay

---

[43] Ibid. pp. 8–9.
[44] Ibid. p. 9.
[45] *HC* 21 Dec. 1867, 7a–f, 8a–c.
[46] MPPI at the commencement of proceedings on Fri. 11 Feb., pp. 1–2.
[47] *HC* 21 Dec. 1867, 7a–f, 8a–c.
[48] 11 & 12 Vict. c. 140, p. 11.
[49] Ibid. pp. 13–14.

down by-laws for the control of lodging-houses.[50] A special clause extended the house-drainage clauses in the Towns Improvement Clauses Act to include other buildings, and allowed the Commissioners to insist upon 'separate privies or water closets' being built and set apart 'for the separate use of males and females respectively in any mill or factory'.[51] This clause alone, it might be argued, justified the Commissioners' decision to persevere with private Bill legislation. The Commissioners were given power to borrow up to £50,000, one-thirtieth of which must be paid off every year.[52] They were to levy a general 'Improvement Rate', which would fall upon every householder rated to the relief of the poor, and in addition they were empowered, since some parts of the town possessed sewers already and others did not, to divide the area into districts and levy a separate sewer rate in each.[53]

Finally it is worth noticing that the Act compromised over the issue of the area to be covered by the new authority. The townships, as they were called, of Marsh, Fartown, Deighton, and Bradley, were in no hurry to be merged with the city. The Act was drafted, therefore, in such a way as to extend immediately to the same area, 1,200 yds. from the cross in the market place, as the Act of 1820, and prospectively to the four townships, if the Privy Council approved of an enlargement.[54] No action was taken under this clause. Even so, by 1861 the area controlled by the Commissioners contained 6,955 houses and 34,877 inhabitants.[55]

---

[50] Ibid. p. 14.
[51] Ibid. p. 15.
[52] Ibid. pp. 15–16.
[53] Ibid. pp. 17–18.
[54] Ibid. p. 7.
[55] *PP* 1862 L, p. 194, *Population (England and Scotland), Census of England and Wales: Population Tables; Numbers and Distribution of the People*, p. 160.

4. HUDDERSFIELD, THE IMPROVEMENT COMMISSIONERS,
THE GENERAL BOARD OF HEALTH, AND THE
LOCAL GOVERNMENT ACT

At the Preliminary Inquiry held in 1848 the reformers raised many complaints about the secretiveness and jobbing of the Commissioners acting under the 1820 Act, whom they stigmatised as 'an *unaccountable unaccounting body*'.[1] From the moment the new Commissioners took over, at the end of August, they were bound by the rules laid down in the Commissioners Clauses Act. They held regular monthly meetings. Every year they made up their accounts at the end of April, and presented them, together with an itemised list of all the contracts which they had entered into, to the statutory annual meeting at the beginning of June. In August, just before the annual elections, the attendance record of every Commissioner upon every committee was totted up and entered, formally, in the minute-books. No opportunity was missed to equate elective with responsible government in the eyes of the town, and to contrast the new with the old regime.

Open government, it was believed, would eliminate graft, and reduce costs. It may, indeed, have helped to do this, but that did not mean that the new regime was to prove a cheap one. The new Act itself had cost £3,586 11s. 7d.,[2] and Clough, who became a Commissioner, and Hobson, who became the clerk to the Board of Works, were filled with zeal to cleanse Huddersfield and make it a model town. To achieve this the Commissioners would have to spend heavily. There was no need, as was pointed out, for this to be 'present burdensome'.[3] The Act had given the Commissioners authority to borrow up to £50,000,[4] and they did not hesitate to use the powers they had obtained, and raise loans, mainly from the Atlas

[1] *LM* 12 Feb. 1848, 8de.
[2] Figure given in the new model accounts pasted into ICMB.
[3] *LM* 12 Feb. 1848, 8de, reporting Mr Clough's opening speech.
[4] 11 & 12 Vict. c. 140, p. 15.

Assurance Company.[5] Sewering, of course, is front-end loaded, for the capital expenditure comes first, and it was not until May 1854 that the Commissioners were able to charge for the service and levy their first sewer rate. A second followed in September 1860. In the meantime they were busy raising General Improvement Rates. The rates were not then, as they were later to be, levied once a year, and at the same time each year. The Commissioners raised a sum, and then, when it was nearly all spent, they raised another one. In their first ten years the new Commissioners set twelve Improvement Rates. The average time between rates was ten months, and in 1852 and 1857 they demanded two.[6] This was a facility which was not available to the ordinary businessman or householder, and it is not surprising that the successive calls made upon the ratepayers led to the new Commissioners in their turn being accused of profligacy.

The trouble began with the cemetery. In Huddersfield, as in most other towns, the population explosion of the late eighteenth and early nineteenth centuries brought about an interment problem. The rotting corpses in the burial-grounds attached to the various churches and chapels within the town offended the nostrils of the living, and were widely believed to be a cause of infection. Huddersfield desperately needed a new cemetery, the Improvement Commissioners began to look for one, and the Ramsden trustees, as ever, were considerate at a price, and offered to sell the town a site of twelve acres at Edgerton.[7] Since this was not an eventuality the town's Act provided for (Mr Clough appears to have slipped up here), the Commissioners approached the General Board of Health in November 1849, and sought its help in preparing the necessary orders under the Nuisances Removal and Diseases Prevention Acts of that year.[8]

[5] ICMB, the accounts for 1848–9 refer to a payment to the Atlas Assurance Company's solicitor for preparing a deed of security for a loan of £5,000: on 13 Aug. 1852 the Commissioners resolved to borrow a further £10,000 from the Atlas, at 4%.

[6] Detailed in the annual accounts.

[7] ICMB 4 Apr. 1851.

[8] ICMB 7 Feb. 1851 rehearses the case.

The General Board appointed an Inspector, William Lee, to visit the town and conduct a public inquiry, which was held on 9–10 January 1850. Joshua Hobson prepared the local evidence with care. The registers showed that, between June 1584 and January 1850, 38,298 people had been buried in the ground attached to the parish church, 4,334 of them within the previous nineteen years. The Inspector thanked Hobson, and contrasted the present case with that at Todmorden, where he had to elicit the facts and figures from the registers for himself.[9] The Improvement Commissioners naturally expected the inquiry to be followed by a report, and the report by the preparation of a Bill. But nothing happened. No report was presented, and in April they were informed by the General Board that the powers contained in the Nuisances Removal Act were insufficient for their case. The representations sent from Huddersfield would be used to try and persuade the legislature 'to extend the provisions of the Metropolitan Scheme for Extra Mural Sepulture to Provincial Towns'.[10]

The 1850 session came to an end with nothing accomplished, and the Improvement Commissioners turned to the Bishop of Ripon, who agreed that burials ought to cease, but lacked the authority to prohibit them.[11] In 1851 the Commissioners attempted, respectfully, to try and persuade the General Board to attend to their plight. The General Board prepared a Bill 'for providing a cemetery and for the regulation of interments in the Township of Huddersfield'.[12] Everything appeared to be going smoothly, and at the beginning of August the Commissioners thanked Clough and Hobson 'for the perseverance, judgment, and ability' which they had displayed.[13] But the congratulations turned out to be premature. Within a week the Commissioners were informed by the General Board that the President was obliged, under direction from the govern-

[9] Inquiry reported in *LM* 12 Jan. 1850, suppl., 10bcd.
[10] ICMB 7 Feb. 1851.
[11] Idem.
[12] ICMB 15 Aug. 1851.
[13] Ibid. 1 Aug. 1851.

ment, to abandon the scheme for the time being.[14] To be fair to the General Board, which had troubles enough of its own, this kind of upset towards the end of a long session would scarcely have come as a surprise to anyone familiar with the parliamentary scene. But, for their part, the Commissioners, not surprisingly, complained of the inattention, and the lack of expedition given to their case by the General Board.

The Huddersfield Burial Ground Act, which incorporated sections of the model Cemeteries Clauses Act of 1849, finally reached the statute-book at the end of June 1852.[15] The Improvement Commissioners immediately borrowed £10,000 to purchase the new cemetery,[16] and prepared to close the overcrowded burial grounds. Even then their troubles were not over. Half the new cemetery, the Act said, was to be reserved for the Church of England, and consecrated by the bishop of the diocese, while the other half was to be kept for the remaining denominations. It was agreed that there should be two chapels where the funeral services could be held. For aesthetic reasons the Commissioners wanted to connect them with a stone wall. This brought down upon them the wrath of the vicar of the parish church, who alleged that they were denying that there was any difference between the Established Church and the dissenting churches. Clergy, magistrates, and parishioners were all mobilised in support of a physical separation between the two.[17] The Methodist clergy and the dissenters took the other side. The hapless Commissioners discovered that the breezes of controversy may blow around the heads even of an active and public-spirited body of men.

The Commissioners possessed powers to control common lodging-houses,[18] but the difficulties they experienced in doing so, led them to consider whether they ought not, as Joshua Hobson suggested, to go further and adopt

[14] Ibid. 15 Aug. 1851.
[15] 15 & 16 Vict. c. 41.
[16] See n. 5, above.
[17] *HC* 8 Jan. 1853, 5c.
[18] 11 & 12 Vict. c. 140, p. 14.

Ashley's Labouring Classes Lodging Houses Act of 1851,[19] and build or buy a model lodging-house of their own. In August 1852 they expressed themselves 'deeply impressed with the manifold evils' arising from 'the present system', and declared that they believed the adoption of the Act of 1851 would go far to remedy them. The proposal raised an outcry from interested parties, and the Commissioners agreed to defer a decision for three months in order to allow 'private parties to provide a better class of Common Lodging Houses'.[20] In November they took the plunge and adopted the 1851 Act.[21] Six months later they borrowed £3,600 to complete the purchase of a warehouse and dwelling house in Chapel Hill,[22] which was converted to provide model accommodation in separate departments for males, females, and married couples, together with a mechanics home.[23]

In the twentieth century Huddersfield's historians have tended to esteem the model lodging-house as the jewel in the Commissioners' crown.[24] Among contemporaries the easy way in which the Commissioners spent the ratepayers money and infringed the sacred rights of private enterprise was not so warmly received. The proposal to adopt the Lodging Houses Act appears to have been the point at which the annual elections, which took place at the beginning of September, became the occasion for the ratepayers 'to make an effort to return . . . men who were . . . Mr. Hobson's most personal and public opponents'. Upon every occasion thereafter the reason assigned for the want of harmony amongst the Commissioners was 'the official presence of Mr. Hobson among them'.[25] The town, it was alleged, was spending recklessly, and slipping ever further and further into debt. In 1854 the disgruntled ratepayers and their representatives upon the Commission found what they were looking for. John Jarratt, the Inspector of

---

[19] 14 & 15 Vict. c. 34, introduced by Lord Ashley. This Act could be adopted in any Municipal Corporation, in any place under a Local Board of Health, and, with the approval of the Secretary of State, in any parish in England with a population of over 10,000.

[20] ICMB 25 Aug. 1852.
[21] Ibid. 24 Nov. 1852.
[22] Ibid. 4 Feb. and 6 May 1853.
[23] HC 21 Dec. 1867, 7a–f, 8a–c.
[24] Brook, *Story of Huddersfield*, p. 155.
[25] HC 8 Apr. 1854, 5bc.

Nuisances and Superintendent of Scavengers was accused of embezzlement.[26] The amounts involved in his 'defalcations' were small, £2 17s., £2 4s. 6d., and £1. But the Commissioners had no alternative but to prosecute Jarratt at the assizes in Pontefract, where he was sentenced to six weeks' hard labour.[27] To the joy of the low spenders, his fall involved Joshua Hobson, who was suspected of having warned him that he was under suspicion, and who was subsequently found to have had a greenhouse built on his own premises at the expense of the ratepayers.[28] Hobson's explanation, that he was using it to grow plants for the new municipal cemetery, was never disproved. He was allowed to resign without a stain on his character, and within a year he found occupation in a situation where he could, if he wanted to, get his own back, as the editor of the *Huddersfield Chronicle*.[29]

Never again were the Improvement Commissioners to dare to be quite so progressive a body as they had been between 1848 and 1854. The truth was that the 'practical' men had already begun to fight back against the 'men of science'. In October 1852 when an Inspector employed by the General Board, Mr Lee, wrote to the Commissioners to say that the latest statistics appeared to show that the death-rate in Huddersfield had risen to 26 per 1000, and that he had been instructed to carry out an inquiry into the sanitary condition of the town, the Commissioners replied by passing a formal motion condemning the egg-shaped sewers beloved of Edwin Chadwick, because they were not as strong as 'properly turned Culverts well constructed of Stone'.[30] The Commissioners challenged Mr Lee's statistics, no inquiry appears to have taken place, and the pace of improvement and the need to borrow money gradually levelled off. By 1859 the town had repaid £9,206 of its accumulated debt of £45,046. In the early 1860s its affairs were sufficiently under control for the Commissioners to be able to budget for a whole year at a time.[31] In August 1863, a month before Joshua Hobson himself was

---

[26] Ibid. 1 Apr. 1854, 7def.
[27] Ibid. 8 Apr. 1854, 5e.
[28] ICMB 3 Apr. 1854.
[29] Brook, *Story of Huddersfield*, p. 156.
[30] ICMB 5 Nov. 1852.
[31] Annual accounts.

elected a Commissioner, the Commissioners appointed a committee to consider 'whether it be desirable to adopt any and what portions of the Local Government Act'.[32] There had been many complaints about the state of the markets,[33] the Commissioners arranged to take them over, with a lease from Sir John William Ramsden,[34] and in February 1864 they adopted Clause 50 of the Local Government Act which in turn included the Markets and Fairs Clauses Consolidation Act.[35] Just over a year later, on 1 March 1865 the Commissioners adopted 'the Act for the closing of Public Houses and Refreshment Houses between 1 and 4 a.m.'. The Act 'answered well in Manchester', and in fact, 'wherever it was adopted, crime and drunkenness decreased'.[36] Neither of these adoptions involved great expense—indeed the markets with their 'Stallages, Rents and Tolls' brought in an income[37]—and by 1868 the Commissioners had paid off £26,412 out of a total debt of £57,308.[38]

In 1861 the population of Huddersfield was 34,877, and the limit of 1,200 yds. radius set upon the operation of the 1820 and 1848 Acts was beginning to appear somewhat artificial. The surrounding districts were filling up, and by the mid 1860s it looked as though everything needed to be reworked. The Gas Company, which had been registered under the Joint-Stock Companies Act of 1844, and incorporated under that of 1856 (by which time its share capital was £39,000),[39] obtained new powers by Act of parliament in 1861 which enabled it to increase capacity and supply much of the surrounding area. The Waterworks Commissioners in their turn came under increasing pressure to accept responsibility for the supply of water to the outlying suburbs. By the middle of the decade they had already exceeded their borrowing powers by £6,000,[40] and in 1866

[32] ICMB 5 Aug. 1863, followed by the election on 11 Sept. 1863.
[33] Ibid. 3 July 1861, 7 Oct. 1863.
[34] Ibid. 6 Jan. 1864.
[35] Ibid. 17 Feb. 1864, and *HE* 20 Feb. 1864, 6f.
[36] ICMB 1 Mar. 1865, and *HE* 4 Mar. 1865, 6c.
[37] ICMB 6 July 1864.
[38] Annual accounts.
[39] Preamble to 24 & 25 Vict. c. 56.
[40] *HC* 5 May 1866, 8e.

they promoted a Bill to enable them to construct a new reservoir at Blackmoor Foot, whence two mains were to be laid to Lockwood, and via Linthwaite to Lindley cum Quarmby. The Commissioners would then be in a position to supply Meltham, Lockwood, Newsome, and Moldgreen along one arm, and Linthwaite, Longwood, Lindley, Deighton, and Bradley along the other.[41] All this was coupled with a new scheme of government, providing for a mix of the old self-perpetuating Commissioners with representatives from the elected Local Boards.[42]

The scheme ran into almost every possible objection from the start. Communities living below the proposed reservoir on Blackmoor Foot were afraid that the structure would collapse and that they would become the victims of a disaster like that which took place at Holmfirth on 5 February 1852, when Bilberry reservoir burst, eighty-one people were drowned, and 7,000 more were put out of work for months.[43] It was calculated that, in the Meltham valley alone, there was £707,000 worth of property which would be swept away in the event of a flood. At Linthwaite there was another £241,000 worth.[44] Mill-owners expressed alarm about their streams, and resisted counsel's suggestion that 'it would be a positive blessing' if they were forced to convert to steam power.[45] When the Bill was introduced to the House of Commons, the mill-owners, the Ramsden estates, and the railway companies all succeeded in inserting clauses safeguarding their interests.[46] In May when the Bill came before the House of Lords, Mr Clough admitted, on behalf of the Huddersfield Improvement Commissioners, that 'public opinion . . . although in favour of an increase of water, is against the present Bill'. The upper chamber pronounced that 'public

---

[41] ICMB 7 Feb. 1866.

[42] Ibid. 4 Apr. 1866.

[43] Or like that which occurred at Sheffield on 12 Mar. 1864, when Bradfield reservoir collapsed and about 250 lives were lost, T. W. Woodhead, *History of the Huddersfield Water Supplies*, Tolson Memorial Museum Handbook X (1939), p. 58.

[44] HC 12 May 1866, 6de.

[45] Idem.

[46] ICMB 4 Apr. 1866.

necessity' should always be considered with reference to 'existing private rights', and the Bill was thrown out.[47]

The rejection concentrated minds upon the necessity for Huddersfield and the surrounding districts to get their act together and apply for incorporation. In 1867 the second Reform Bill was making its way through parliament, Huddersfield missed its chance to secure a second Member of Parliament, and the feeling grew that 'an unincorporated town . . . loses its due weight and influence in public and national affairs'.[48] The town was 'the butt of, and ridiculed by, all their neighbours round about.'[49] The Improvement Commissioners were aware that the local franchise contained in the 1848 Act was now 'strongly at variance with the declared policy of the legislature', which had extended the parliamentary franchise to all householders.[50] In May the Commissioners opened negotiations with the representatives of the surrounding districts, Marsh, Fartown, Deighton, and Bradley, which had lived for twenty years in the shadow of the extension clause in the Huddersfield Act of 1848, and Lockwood, Newsome, Moldgreen, and Almondbury where the population had also been increasing rapidly.[51] The project was forced forward, if we are to judge by the petitions that were received, even more by weight of rateable value, £106,782 to £16,606, than by numbers, 4,933 to 2,049.[52] When Huddersfield and the surrounding districts were granted a charter of incorporation in 1868, the mayor and the new council were able to reorganise the whole area upon a more rational basis, take over and extend the powers, assets, and responsibilities of the Waterworks Commissioners, buy out the Gas Company, and promote a new Improvement Act which was passed in 1871. The expanded town, like other large towns, followed the Private Bill road.

[47] *HC* 12 May 1866, 6de.
[48] Mr Batley, addressing the incorporation inquiry, ibid., 21 Dec. 1867, 7a–f, 8a–c.
[49] Meeting of Commissioners with deputations from surrounding townships, ibid., 18 May 1867, 6cde.
[50] Ibid. 21 Dec. 1867, 7a–f, 8a–c.
[51] Ibid. 18 May 1867, 6 cde.
[52] Ibid. 21 Dec. 1867, 7a–f, 8a–c.

5. THE PUBLIC HEALTH ACT OF 1848 AND THE
LOCAL GOVERNMENT ACT OF 1858:
THE IMPORTANCE OF BEING MOLDGREEN

Moldgreen is a suburb of Huddersfield, straddling the road to Wakefield, whose growth in the 1850s and 1860s owed much to events in Huddersfield itself. In the 1830s, under the lax management of Sir John Ramsden, it cost 1s. 9d. to 2s. 3d. to rent a cottage in Huddersfield, and even less of course, 1s. 3d. to 1s. 6d., to rent a cellar. Rented accommodation was said to be 'within reach of the working class'.[1] In the 1840s large numbers of men, living in the town, were able to secure a yearly tenancy upon a plot of land, and build on it. In 1845 Joseph Kaye told the Health of Large Towns Commission how it was 'the practice in this town for working men to put into what is sometimes called a building club; sometimes a money club.' When they had accumulated £50 they would go and build a house 'that costs perhaps seventy or eighty'.[2] There was 'a peculiarity observable in Huddersfield that workmen pride themselves in being able to build and have a house of their own.' 'More cottages', it was observed, 'belong to workmen than in any other town.'[3]

This state of affairs began to change about 1850. The lower end of the market was transformed when the Improvement Commissioners resolved to control lodging-houses, and the Improvement Commissioners and the trustees, acting together, prohibited cellar dwellings and forbade the construction of back-to-back houses.[4] The upper end was thrown into confusion in 1859, when Sir John William Ramsden put an end to tenancies at will. There were, at that time, forty-one building societies in Huddersfield with 1,794 members who were forced either to abandon their plans, or to build more expensive houses upon the leasehold land which was still available from the

---

[1] Springett, 'Landowners and Urban Development', p. 135.
[2] *PP* 1844 XVII, p. 705, *Appendix to SLT1*, p. 177.
[3] Springett, 'Landowners and Urban Development', p. 135.
[4] Springett, 'Urban Land Development in Huddersfield', p. 163.

estate.[5] Those who could not support the additional expenditure joined the tide of less well-paid workmen who
were obliged to move out of the town altogether and take
up residence in the suburbs. Moldgreen, which lay just
across the river Colne, within easy walking distance of
Huddersfield, was one of the obvious places to go.
Although the term 'Moldgreen' must have been understood by contemporaries, the district had at that time no
defined boundary. It lay mainly in the township of Dalton,
partly in the parish of Almondbury, and partly in the
parish of Kirkheaton. For this reason statistics for
Moldgreen itself are difficult to come by. But by the late
1850s it was said to have a population of between 4,000
and 5,000,[6] and people were pouring into Moldgreen and
Dalton, where they could still dwell in cellars, and where
the lodging-houses were uncontrolled.

This, in turn, meant that Moldgreen was beginning to
have a public health problem, and in 1857 a group of residents, led by Mr Gelder, resolved to invoke the Public
Health Act of 1848, and employed a local solicitor, Mr
Jacomb, to petition the General Board of Health to send an
Inspector and carry out a Preliminary Inquiry. The inquiry
was held in May, and was conducted by Mr A. L. Dickens.
The Inspector heard a good deal about the need to lay
proper sewers, and to light the streets with gas. But the
principal reason why the petitioners wanted to bring
Moldgreen within the operation of the Public Health Act,
was that they believed this would help them to obtain a
regular supply of fresh water. The present source, the Calf
Well, was inadequate, and in summer the poorer people
crowded round it 'during the whole of the night, waiting
to obtain water as it sprung into the well'. 'Parties rose at
all times during the night to fetch water',[7] while others,
the inquiry was told, preferred to walk one and a quarter
miles to obtain water fit for cooking.[8] Those who could
afford to bought water, but at one source, the pump

---

[5] Springett, 'Landowners and Urban Development', p. 135.
[6] *HE* 9 May 1857, 7f, Mr Jacomb.
[7] *HC* 9 May 1857, 5f, Mr Sykes.
[8] Idem, Mr Gelder.

belonging to Mr Tolson, situated close to his factory, water was sold to the public for one hour a week on Saturday morning, and 'what was obtained then, had to be stored up for use during the whole of the following week'. At another, Mr Kaye's pump, the water was 'not fit for culinary purposes'.[9] So great were the difficulties that 'the owners of property complained that their tenants left because of the want of good water'.[10] No mention was made of the death-rate, but a medical practitioner testified to the prevalence of fever 'of a gastric type which, in many cases, went through a whole family, and dyspeptic cases together with loss of teeth', which he said could be attributed 'in a great measure, to the quality of the water'.[11]

By the time Mr Dickens's report became available in November, there was an opposition. At a meeting of ratepayers, complaints were made that 'the report . . . was too expensive for working men to purchase',[12] that the introduction of the Act would be for the advantage of the landlords rather than the cottagers,[13] and that, if the Act were to be applied, the property qualification for the members of the Local Board would be so high that they would not have 'many persons in Moldgreen who could sit at the Board . . . (a voice: "That's what us poor devils are kept down with")'.[14] Many ratepayers, not least the poorer ones, were afraid that a Local Board would be extravagant, and run up huge debts, like the Improvement Commissioners in Huddersfield. For their part, proponents of the Act admitted that the Improvement Commissioners 'had done wrong, and spent their money wrong', but went on to argue that that was no reason why 'they should do so at Moldgreen'.[15] Opponents preferred not to take the risk. Common sense suggested that here in Moldgreen they could make do with cheaper alternatives. Granted that 'the drainage and sewerage of the district was defective to a certain extent', 'it was the duty of the owners of property to drain it'.[16] When it came to lighting the streets, the fact

[9] Idem, Mr Sykes.
[10] *HE* 9 May 1857, 7f, Mr Gelder.
[11] Idem, Dr Gardiner.
[12] Ibid. 7 Nov. 1857, 3cde.
[13] Idem, Mr Watson.
[14] Idem, Mr Chapman.
[15] Idem, Mr R. Brook.
[16] *HC* 7 Nov. 1857, 8de, Mr Samuel Day.

was that the houses were supplied with gas already, and anyone who came home at a reasonable hour could find plenty of light to see by. They could obtain water without the expense of Commissioners and surveyors—in short 'they wanted to go on honestly and straightforwardly as their forefathers did'.[17]

No decision had been reached when the General Board of Health was wound up by the Local Government Act of 1858. The public health party was obliged to begin again, and lost no time in forwarding a petition with 167 signatures to the Home Secretary asking him to instruct the Local Government Act Office to send an Inspector down to Moldgreen to hold another inquiry and determine the boundaries of a Local Board district. In November 1858 Mr Dickens returned to Moldgreen. The meeting, which was to take place at the Kaye's Arms, was crowded out and had to be adjourned to the school-room. Mr Gelder's party, who thought of themselves as struggling to win independence for Moldgreen, were represented by Mr Wasney. Dalton township and Almondbury parish, from which they were trying to detach themselves, had briefed Mr Floyd and Mr Sykes. Much time was taken up with a squabble over the means employed to secure signatures to the petition, before the inquiry could move on to consider the point at issue. Mr Wasney reminded the inquiry that

The district proposed to be brought within the act seemed to be just the sort of district contemplated by the act. It was densely populated, and was likely to become more so. Huddersfield belonged to only one proprietor, so that no freeholds could be bought within the precincts; but on this side of the water [the Colne], freeholds could be purchased, so that the increase of population was likely to go on . . . if the district did not call for the Local Government Act, he could not conceive what sort of a district would require it.

Mr Floyd put the case for the people living in those parts of Dalton which did not wish to become involved with the proposed Local Board, and Mr Sykes explained why the inhabitants of Almondbury believed that the proposed

[17] *HE* 7 Nov. 1857, 3cde, Mr Samuel Day.

boundary would transfer too much of the valuable property in the parish to Moldgreen and leave too little in the hands of their own overseers and highway surveyors. As one of the witnesses, Mr John D——, put it, 'it would be a curse to Almondbury, entailed from generation to generation'. The Inspector, Mr Dickens heard all the evidence, made a tour round the proposed boundaries, and returned to London to make out his recommendations.[18]

Six weeks later when the boundaries were settled, the time arrived, under the procedures laid down in the Local Government Act, for the owners and ratepayers living within the boundaries of the new district to meet and decide whether they wished to adopt the Act. The meeting was held in the school-room, which is said, upon this occasion, to have been no more than two-thirds full.[19] Mr Gelder was elected to the Chair. He announced that he had been in communication with the Secretary of State, and that it had been made clear to him that the only people who were entitled to attend were the owners and rate-payers of the new district. Mr Jacomb, the solicitor for the proponents, had accordingly withdrawn, and he asked Mr Sykes and Mr Roebuck, from Almondbury, to leave. Mr Sykes made a scene, and refused to depart. Mr Jebson then rose to propose the adoption of the Act. He ran over the main headings of the case in favour: lighting was needed, and sewering, too, for 'all the medical men who have been in Moldgreen have given evidence . . . that the sanitary condition of the place is such that none of us are safe'. But, above all, like everyone before him, he stressed the need for water.

Does any gentleman . . . undertake to say that there is a supply of water for twelve months in the year, and during every day in the month, for every inhabitant of Moldgreen? . . . if you cannot gain a supply by night and by day by watching every spring and every pump, and drawing upon the resources of every trades-man and every individual who has a quart of water to spare—if you cannot even find water for the culinary and domestic pur-poses of your present population, what must you do if the

---

[18] *HE* 6 Nov. 1858, 3g, 4ab: this account is fuller than *HC* 6 Nov. 1858, 8bc.
[19] *HC* 24 Dec. 1858, 6ef.

population goes on increasing . . . an inadequate supply of water is preventing people from laying out their money here, and is preventing people from coming to live here.

He stigmatised those who opposed the adoption as the parties 'who wish to snuff out Moldgreen from the map of the nation'.[20']

The motion was seconded, the chairman refused, in accordance with the rules laid down in the Act, to accept an amendment, and put the motion to the meeting.[21] Mr Bird asked him not to go so fast, and Mr Watson, as he later deposed, demanded a poll.[22] The chairman took no notice, and the show of hands on both sides appeared to be close. When the chairman ruled that the motion had been carried, there was uproar. In the middle of the confusion Mr Fitton moved that the number of Commissioners under the Act should be twelve. The chairman declared the meeting over, and Mr Sykes 'then sprang to his feet and shrieked—This is the most abominable—(deafening confusion) . . . the most abominable transaction that ever took place.' He denounced the chairman for misconduct,[23] and an appeal was lodged with the Home Secretary. Towards the end of January Mr Henry Austin, the Inspector appointed by the Secretary of State, arrived in Moldgreen to hold an inquiry into the conduct of the late meeting by the chairman, Mr Gelder. The school-room was 'crowded to excess, and the most intense excitement prevailed'.[24] The appellants put their case, the Inspector retired to London, and at the beginning of March it became known that the Secretary of State was going to rule that the meeting had been properly conducted, and that the adoption was valid.[25]

Even then, that was not the last that was heard from the opposition. In April a meeting of ratepayers at Dalton empowered a committee to take any measures they could to frustrate the adoption of the Act, and Mr Sykes applied to the Court of Queen's Bench for a writ of mandamus to

[20] *HE* 24 Dec. 1858, 2e.
[21] Idem.
[22] *HE* 29 Jan. 1859, 4abc.
[23] Ibid. 24 Dec. 1858, 2e.
[24] Ibid. 29 Jan. 1859, 4abc.
[25] Ibid. 12 Mar. 1859, 3a.

compel the Secretary of State to take a poll. The promoters thereupon instructed Mr Jacomb to oppose the application, and guaranteed to pay his expenses out of their own pockets.[26] Another month passed before the mandamus was refused, and the election of the first Commissioners took place. Both sides fielded twelve candidates. But the public health party swept the board, their candidates receiving votes ranging from 261 to 323, while the opposition candidates received between 98 and 180.[27] After over two years of vigorous politicking Moldgreen finally became a locality in its own right, and the reformers found themselves in a position of responsibility.

No Local Board can ever have taken office with a clearer idea of what it intended to achieve, and with higher hopes of carrying its intentions into effect. From the first the business was carefully prepared, and the meetings ran like clockwork. On 14 June 1859 the officers were elected, and Mr Gelder became chairman and Mr Jacomb, clerk. Copies of the relevant Acts of parliament were made available to every member of the Board, and the clerk was instructed to have the by-laws ready before the next meeting in a fortnight's time.[28] This was not quite so onerous as it might sound. The Local Government Act Office furnished draft by-laws to every locality which adopted the 1858 Act,[29] and the localities combed through the draft in much the same way that they went through the sections of the Act, deciding for themselves how many they wished to adopt. In a single evening on 4 July the Local Board at Moldgreen adopted 124 by-laws regulating the conduct of the Board and the duties of its officers, five relating to the sweeping of footways, the disposal of refuse, and the cleansing of privies and ashpits, ten to the removal of nuisances like snow, dirt, and dust, four to the width, sewerage, and construction of new streets, five to the structure of house walls, eleven to the free circulation of air in rooms, and twenty to the drainage of new buildings and the closure of

[26] Ibid. 16 Apr. 1859, 3d.
[27] Ibid. 11 June 1859, 2g.
[28] MLBMB 14 June 1859.
[29] HPL/KHT/17/1 Bradley LBMB, 2 Apr. 1862.

buildings unfit for human habitation, eighteen to the regulation of common lodging-houses, and fifteen to the regulation of slaughter-houses.[30]

The list furnishes a statement of the priorities of the reformers. The by-laws appear to have been enforced, standards of construction were raised to the level of good practice, and the Board borrowed money to enable it to carry out the necessary improvements—first a small sum of £126 for the installation of the first street-lights, which were turned on in October, and then, in 1865–7 much larger sums of £1,000 and £3,000 to enable it to lay sewers.[31] The Board was a busy one, and in 1866 it adopted the Public House Closing Act.[32] But it was also litigious, or had litigation forced upon it. The dispute which had hampered its formation continued after it came into being, and led in 1862 to the secession of a part of the district lying in Almondbury,[33] leaving the Local Board with a reduced area of 597 acres.[34] The clerk fell out with the Commissioners, resigned, and threatened, for over two years, to sue them for his fees.[35] The collector was clumsy, and was unable to account for the rates he had collected, and had to be replaced.[36]

All these mishaps, however, paled into insignificance compared with another failure, which was more fundamental. At every stage of their campaign the reformers had argued that the establishment of a Local Board would assist the inhabitants to secure bountiful supplies of pure water, and it was by their success or failure in this respect that they would be judged in the end. No sooner had they taken up office than they approached the Huddersfield Waterworks for a supply.[37] But the Waterworks could not oblige them—it had, the Water Commissioners said, no

[30] MLBMB 4 July 1859.
[31] *PP* 1860 XXXI, p. 623; 1866 XX, p. 515; 1867–8 XXI, p. 153, *Local Government Act, 1858, Second Annual Report*, p. 7, *Eighth Annual Report*, p. 9, *Tenth Annual Report*, p. 9.
[32] MLBMB 1 Oct. 1866.
[33] Ibid. 3, 24 Feb., 3, 24, 28 Mar., 5 May, and 2, 16 June 1862.
[34] *HC* 21 Dec. 1867, 7 a–f, 8a–c.
[35] MLBMB 18 June, 8 Dec. 1862; 25 Apr., 13 June 1864.
[36] Ibid. 6, 20 Mar. 1865.
[37] Ibid. 14 June 1859.

power to provide water outside Huddersfield itself (although it did, in fact, supply the whole of Marsh).[38] Next, they cast eyes upon the water at Penny Spring, but Messrs Day made stipulations which the Board was unable to accept.[39] In 1860 they inquired upon what terms Sir John William Ramsden would allow them to construct a reservoir at New Laiths Shrog. For eleven months the negotiation appeared to have some prospect of success, and there was talk of a sixty-year lease. Then Sir John William Ramsden backed out.[40] In 1861 they sought water from the Holme Valley reservoirs.[41] When this scheme, too, came to nothing, they went back to the Ramsden estate, but Sir John William's terms were now 'such as the Board could not entertain'.[42] In 1862 they approached the Water Company at Dewsbury—the Company was willing to supply water, but the cost of bringing it to Moldgreen would be prohibitive.[43] For a third time they attempted to negotiate with Sir John William, and he agreed to let them have two acres to impound the Channel Dyke, at a rental of £50 p.a. on a lease of 99 years. This time the scheme failed because the Board laid it before a meeting of the ratepayers, who refused to let them proceed unless Sir John William would sell them the freehold of the land.[44] In 1863 and 1864 the Board joined forces with the Local Board at Lockwood, which was also in need of water.[45] A new source was identified in a cutting on the branch railway which was being constructed to Meltham,[46] and there was talk of forming a company.[47] Then there was an offer from Messrs Oldham of Old Moll Mill, Honley.[48] Next, the

[38] HPL/KHT/15/1 Marsh LBMB, 1 May 1861, 'Resolved that we accept the Offer of the Warter works Commissioners of using their warter for highway Purposes.'
[39] MLBMB 10 Oct. 1859.
[40] Ibid. 2 Apr. 1860; 13 Mar. 1861.
[41] Ibid. 4 Nov. 1861.
[42] Ibid. 2 Dec. 1861.
[43] Ibid. 7 July 1862.
[44] Ibid. 5 Sept., 6 Oct. 1862; 2 Mar., 1 June 1863.
[45] Ibid. 3 Aug., 7 Sept., 5 Oct. 1863.
[46] Ibid. 7 Sept. 1863.
[47] Ibid. 7 Dec. 1863; 4 Apr. 1864.
[48] Ibid. 7 Mar. 1864.

members of the two Boards went out to inspect Harden Moss.[49] Every project turned out to be a non-starter, and before the end of 1864, Lockwood and Moldgreen seemed to be left with no alternative but to try and secure the good offices of the Improvement Commissioners in Huddersfield, to bring pressure to bear upon the Waterworks Commissioners to obtain a new Act which would enable them to supply the whole district.[50] In 1866 Moldgreen petitioned the House of Lords in favour of the Huddersfield Waterworks Bill,[51] and Mr John Day, 'a member of the Local Board of Moldgreen', was the first witness called to give evidence in its support.[52] Moldgreen was probably more grievously affected than any other locality when the Bill was thrown out. The rejection meant that the Board would have to continue to resort to expedients to improve the existing supplies which Mr Kaye, Mr Crosland, and Mr Tolson made available out of what was surplus to the requirements of their mills.[53]

The story of Moldgreen Local Board is a tale of thwarted endeavour. By the beginning of 1867, when the population had risen to 6,960 and the rateable value to £12,224,[54] the Commissioners themselves seem to have realised that there was only one thing left to do, which was to throw in their lot with Huddersfield, and support the movement for incorporation, hoping that when this was achieved the enlarged unit with its enhanced status would be able to reorganise the water supplies for the whole district. It must have been a bitter pill to swallow. One of the objects which the proponents of a Local Board had hoped to achieve in 1857–9, had been to assert and preserve their independence of the big town with the heavy burden of debt. Fortunately, by 1867, Huddersfield's borrowings had been reduced, and in May the Moldgreen Commissioners called a public meeting at which they recommended the

[49] Ibid. 4 Apr. 1864.
[50] Ibid. 7 Nov. 1864.
[51] Ibid. 19 Apr. 1866.
[52] *HC* 5 May 1866, 8e.
[53] MLBMB 13 Mar., 3, 24 June, 1, 25 July, 2 Sept., 7 Oct. 1861; 6 Jan., 6 Oct. 1862 etc.
[54] *HC* 21 Dec. 1867, 7a–f, 8a–c.

locality to combine with Huddersfield. The crucial speech came from Mr Hirst, a Waterworks Commissioner, who said he spoke 'as a Moldgreen, and not as a Huddersfield man'. 'There was no other way possible for them to obtain water, except through Huddersfield. . . . His candid opinion was that they would never be able to get a supply of water until they were merged with a large town and become a great people.'[55] Incorporation would bring them votes at the parliamentary elections for the borough,[56] which would then shake off its 'anomalous position', and 'take its proper place which its commercial importance demanded'.[57] The union was approved unanimously and with loud cheering, the Board joined its best endeavours to those of the Improvement Commissioners in Huddersfield, and in 1868, when incorporation was achieved, the Moldgreen district Board, which had been such an active one, and had deserved something better, ceased to exist, after a short life of nine years.

6. THE LOCAL GOVERNMENT ACT OF 1858: THE NAMED SUBURBS

Moldgreen was the first locality in the Huddersfield area (and one of the first places in the country) to adopt the Local Government Act. It was followed, within the next few years, by a rush of others. These can be divided into three groups, the first consisting of the four townships named in the Huddersfield Act of 1848 which lived under the immediate threat of being brought, upon application to the Privy Council, within the jurisdiction of the Improvement Commissioners, the second of the places, lying, in perception if not in distance, just a little way further outside the town, which were also incorporated with it in 1868, and the third of the more remote towns and villages which were in no danger of being absorbed by Huddersfield in the nineteenth century.

[55] Ibid. 18 May 1867, 6e.
[56] Idem Mr Robson.
[57] Ibid. 11 May 1867, 7f, Mr Day.

In the four townships, Marsh, Fartown, Deighton, and Bradley, which lay in the shadow of the Huddersfield Improvement Act of 1848, people expected to be swallowed up at any moment. The Local Government Act appears to have offered a forlorn hope of maintaining their independence. It was adopted in Deighton on 8 August 1859,[1] in Marsh early in 1861,[2] and in Bradley on 27 February 1862.[3] In these three places the inhabitants discovered in themselves just enough will to adopt the Act, and not enough to make it worth their while spending money to implement it afterwards.

Deighton was a small hamlet of 367 acres, with a population of 1,150 and a rateable value of £2,000. It was semi-agricultural, and the motives of the inhabitants, when they adopted the Act, were said to have been to protect themselves from the expansionism of the Improvement Commissioners, and to retain in their own hands their 'local government'. The first attempt at adoption failed, because the Secretary of State denied that Deighton had a defined boundary. When the citizens demonstrated that there was one, marked with stones all the way round, he relented, and authorised them to call another meeting. This time the Improvement Commissioners in Huddersfield themselves objected to the adoption, presumably upon the ground that Deighton was, indeed, earmarked by Act of parliament for absorption into Huddersfield town. Deighton 'placed the matter in the hands of the clerk to the Board at Moldgreen, Mr. Fredk. William Jacomb', and he persuaded the Secretary of State to accept the adoption as valid.[4] It is a pity the ratepayers did not make more use of the opportunity afforded to them. Only three Commissioners were appointed, and eight years after the inhabitants had attempted to safeguard their right to govern themselves, they had carried out no sanitary works of any kind, and borrowed no money.[5]

[1] *HE* 13 Aug. 1859, 2f.
[2] HPL/KHT/15/1 Marsh LBMB, the first entry is dated 3 Apr.
[3] HPL/KHT/17/1 Bradley LBMB, preface.
[4] *HE* 13 Aug. 1859, 2f.
[5] *HC* 21 Dec. 1867, 7a–f, 8a–c.

Marsh was more culpable still. It was a small place of 433 acres, with a dense population approaching 7,000. It was said, moreover, to contain every variety of urban property, 'mills, cottages, middle-class houses, and the first class villas of suburban residents',[6] and it ought, therefore, to have been blessed with a fair share of public-spirited citizens. But the first clerk to the Local Board in Marsh was the only one in the whole area, who was clearly not fit for the post. The minutes of the second meeting of the Board read, in their entirety, 'Nothing to do particular and only 6 Member present',[7] while those for July 24 ran 'All Present Except Thomas Dean and Wm. Calverley. Not much going on at present.' The entries did become more informative as time went by, but even then, no money was borrowed and no public works of any importance were undertaken.[8] Unlike Moldgreen, the place received water from the town, and evidently did not care about anything else.[9]

Bradley managed, in some ways, an even more dismal record. It was a large hamlet of 1,288 acres. The land surface was devoted mainly to agriculture, and the population of 781 was small, but there were extensive mills at the eastern end which brought the rateable value for the whole district up to £5,106. The mills belonged to Messrs Haigh, who exercised 'great influence and control over the other ratepayers, who are chiefly the operatives employed by them'. The Haighs, it was said, 'rule and govern the district',[10] and the proposal to adopt the Local Government Act was motivated, as the petitioners informed the Local Government Act Office, by the hope of being allowed 'the same priviledge' of escaping—or appearing to escape—from the clutches of Huddersfield, that had been extended to Deighton.[11] That granted, the Local Board knew what was

[6] Idem.
[7] HPL/KHT/15/1 Marsh LBMB, 17 Apr. 1861.
[8] *HC* 21 Dec. 1867, 7a–f, 8a–c.
[9] Ibid. 18 May 1867, 6cde.
[10] Ibid. 21 Dec. 1867, 7a–f, 8a–c.
[11] HPL/KHT/17/1 Bradley LBMB, preface, copy of letter to Tom Taylor at the Local Government Act Office, 22 Mar. 1862.

expected, or not expected, of it, and here, too, no public works of any kind had been executed by 1867.[12]

In this competitive display of civic inertia, the prize was won by Fartown, an important suburb of 1,268 acres with a population, like Marsh, of nearly 7,000, and a high rateable value—£15,000. Here there was a Board of Highway Surveyors, but no Local Board.[13] No attempt appears to have been made to adopt the Local Government Act until 1867, when there was an appeal and the adoption was declared invalid.[14] In December, when Captain Donnelly arrived in Huddersfield to conduct the inquiry into the town's petition for incorporation, Fartown was still without a Local Board.[15]

In these four cases, then, it appears as though proximity to Huddersfield, and the constant fear of being taken over, inhibited or distorted the development of local government, and deprived the inhabitants of the will to help themselves, even when the Local Government Act furnished them with the means of doing so. Paradoxically, but perhaps also understandably, when the time came for them to be merged with Huddersfield, three out of four of these districts put up a show of resistance. In May 1867, when the first consultations about incorporation took place, Deighton, Marsh, and Bradley all expressed hostility.[16] Both Marsh and Bradley petitioned against it. Marsh later withdrew its petition, but Bradley held out to the end, arguing that it was being asked to surrender its independence in order that it might be turned into the outfall for the sewage of the whole area. But Bradley had already been accepted into the parliamentary boundaries of Huddersfield, and looked at from the town's point of view, the fact that it held 'the key of the sewerage of the entire district', meant that there could be no question of letting it escape.[17]

---

[12] *HC* 21 Dec. 1867, 7a–f, 8a–c.
[13] Idem.
[14] *PP* 1867 XIX, 675, *Local Government Act, 1858, Ninth Annual Report*, p. 5.
[15] *HC* 21 Dec. 1867, 7a–f, 8a–c.
[16] Ibid. 18 May 1867, 6cde.
[17] Ibid. 21 Dec. 1867, 7a–f, 8a–c.

7. THE LOCAL GOVERNMENT ACT OF 1858:
THE REMAINING SUBURBS

A second group of localities which had not been named in
the 1848 Improvement Act, but which were joined to
Huddersfield in 1868, consisted of Moldgreen, which has
been dealt with already, Longwood, which adopted the
Local Government Act on 27 February 1860, followed
by Lindley cum Quarmby, 16 March 1860, Newsome,
14 August 1862, Almondbury, 30 October 1862, and
Lockwood, 5 February 1863.[1]

At Longwood the meeting to adopt the Local Government Act was called 'in order that they might take measures
to avoid being brought under the operation of the Highway
Bill at present passing through the House of Commons'.[2]
Mr Henry Brook explained that the Bill would empower
the Magistrates at quarter sessions, 'without ever consult-
ing the ratepayers', to form the townships into unions 'the
same as under the Poor-law Act'.[3] The mention of this
dreaded word 'union' galvanised the inhabitants into
action. The only way in which they could escape was to
adopt the Local Government Act, and 'the spirit of the
meeting was evidently in favour of the adoption . . . the
great inducement appearing to be the desirability of
having the management of their own affairs in their own
hands, and not leaving their money to be expended by
other people.'[4] Unlike the four districts named in the
Improvement Act of 1848, Longwood did make some use
of its independence. In addition to looking after the highways, the Local Board borrowed £2,000 for drainage, street
improvement, and lighting, and adopted the Public House
Closing Act.[5]

In Lindley cum Quarmby the Thornhill estate was being developed in this period, and there was a lot of

[1] HPL/KH File, preface.
[2] *HC* 3 Mar. 1860, 8de.
[3] *HE* 3 Mar. 1860, 3b.
[4] *HC* 3 Mar. 1860, 8de.
[5] *PP* 1866 XX, p. 514, and 1867 XIX, p. 679, *Local Government Act, 1858, Eighth Annual Report*, p. 8, *Ninth Annual Report*, p. 9.

middle-class housing. The adoption appears to have been a quiet one, and the Board proceeded cautiously, attending to the highways, and ordering the removal of a nuisance from time to time. It can scarcely be said to have given the district a lead, and the evidence suggests that it took its colour from the elections. In 1862 the ratepayers 'were determined to elect gentlemen that would carry out their economical views'.[6] Two years later so little was going on that a deputation waited upon the Board to demand street-lights. The reason given was not that darkness favoured crime, but that it facilitated sin. 'Immoral practices' were alleged to be rife,[7] and ten months later, when there were still no lights, the vicar himself headed a second deputation which urged 'the necessity of lighting the streets with Gas and providing a better supply of Water for the Township'.[8] This Board, too, adopted the Public House Closing Act.[9] The locality would have benefited considerably had the Huddersfield Waterworks Bill of 1866 passed the House of Lords, and in 1867 ten out of the eleven members of the Board who attended the meeting voted in favour of incorporation.[10]

Newsome consisted to some extent of that part of Almondbury parish which was included, in 1858, within the boundaries of the Moldgreen Local Board, and seceded in 1862. The separation was engineered from Almondbury, where the inhabitants had never forgiven Moldgreen for poaching,[11] and it must have come as a shock to Almondbury when the inhabitants of Berry Brow, Newsome, Salford, and Taylor Hill, decided to adopt the Act for themselves, and formed the Newsome district.[12] All that then remained of Almondbury was a rump, called Almondbury village, which adopted the Act without much enthusiasm two months later.[13] Newsome set out with

[6] *HE* 31 May 1862, 4f.
[7] HPL/KHT/14/1 Lindley cum Quarmby LBMB, 21 Dec. 1864.
[8] Ibid. 11 Oct. 1865.
[9] *PP* 1866 XX, p. 513, *Local Government Act, 1858, Eighth Annual Report*, p. 7.
[10] *HC* 18 May 1867, 6cde.
[11] Ibid. 6 Nov. 1858, 8bc.
[12] *HE* 16 Aug. 1862, 5d.
[13] HPL/KHT/19/1 Almondbury LBMB, preface.

good intentions, hoping that it might 'become a pattern to the neighbourhood for cleanliness, sanitary improvement, good roads, and every other local convenience which the act they had adopted would give, if properly managed',[14] but it conformed more to the pattern set by Deighton, Marsh, Fartown, and Bradley. It had an area of 880 acres, and a population of about 6,000. The housing density was high, but the rateable value, which was £7,200, was unusually low. It had some excuse, therefore, for its failure to undertake any public works of importance,[15] and in May 1867 it declined the Huddersfield Improvement Commissioners' invitation to take part in exploratory talks about incorporation.[16] Almondbury village, on the other hand, was very different. There, the few surviving weavers were engaged in making only 'those low descriptions of goods that were almost out of demand', and the place was becoming a slightly superior, clean, residential area, which contained a population of 4,500, and had a rateable value of £7,750.[17] The villagers were brought up to believe that many centuries ago, before Huddersfield came into existence, Almondbury, with its castle, was a thriving community. They cherished a kind of rhetorical resentment against the modern town, and living at an altitude of 800 ft., above the level of the Huddersfield reservoirs, they had little prospect of being able to join in the water bonanza which incorporation was expected to bring.[18] The Local Board erected gas-lamps, and cleared an obstruction or two.[19] So far as the inhabitants were concerned that was sufficient. A public meeting voted by a majority not to join up with Huddersfield,[20] and in the two Local Board districts of Newsome and Almondbury taken together, 927 people signed the petitions against incorporation, and only 240

---

[14] *HE* 16 Aug. 1862, 5d.
[15] *HC* 21 Dec. 1867, 7a–f, 8a–c.
[16] Ibid. 18 May 1867, 6cde.
[17] *PP* 1835 XIII, p. 101, *Report from the Select Committee on Handloom Weavers' Petitions, Minutes of Evidence*, p. 79, Qn. 856, Mr Joseph Milner; *HC* 21 Dec. 1867, 7a–f, 8a–c.
[18] *HC* 1 June 1867, 7e.
[19] HPL/KHT/19/1 Almondbury LBMB.
[20] *HC* 1 June 1867, 7e.

signed those in favour.[21] In the circumstances the majority were, perhaps, unlucky to be overruled.

After Moldgreen, Lockwood was the most active show-piece Local Board of the entire area. The district covered 860 acres,[22] and the first proposal to adopt the Act came, in 1859, from the owners of house property and was opposed by the millowners. The Lockwood estates were not, by the standards of the Ramsdens and the Thornhills, extensive, but they were owned by shareholders, managed professionally, and intensively developed.[23] Here, as in so many other places, the problem was water. For several years the proprietors had been considering the possibility of obtaining water by means of a private Act. Now, the Local Government Act, they believed, would enable them to achieve their object without incurring a great expense. It was dreadful that they had been obliged to wait so long. As Mr Etchells said, 'if it had been a mill or a steam engine that had been in want of water, it would have been supplied long ago.' One of the proprietors of houses, Mr Ashton, accused the millowners of being the sort of men

who, residing in Huddersfield, have all the benefit of water-works and gas-works, and all the improvements which an Improvement Bill can give them. They come to Lockwood to erect mills in order that they may have long leases free from Sir John, and that they may have an easement on their rates, and yet they tell us politely that they will not assist the inhabitants of Lockwood to obtain water.

The opposition was 'Simply rates against health'.[24] In reply the millowners denounced the proprietors for seeking to rate other people in order to put up the value of their own land and cottage property. A little unwisely, perhaps, Mr T. P. Crosland said that he would rather be thought of as a man who, while he was drinking good water in Huddersfield, did not care what the inhabitants of Lockwood drank, than be compelled 'to supply water for the enhance-

[21] Ibid. 21 Dec. 1867, 7a–f, 8a–c.
[22] Idem.
[23] Springett, 'Urban Land Development in Huddersfield', p. 126 and map at p. 130.
[24] *HE* 3 Dec. 1859, 3cd.

ment of the value of other people's property'. He pointed out that 'by adopting the Local Government Act, they would tax the best interests of the district', the employers, and argued that they would rue it 'all the days of their lives'. He offered to supply all the water Lockwood needed from his own well.[25] Upon this occasion the ratepayers appear to have been impressed by the arguments advanced by the millowners, and the motion to adopt the Act was lost.

The inhabitants continued, therefore, like those at Mold-green, to depend for their water upon the surplus made available to them from the mills. But there had always been a second argument in favour of adopting the Local Government Act, which was that it would prove to be the only way of ensuring that Lockwood was not incorporated into Huddersfield. Huddersfield was burdened with £40,000 of debt, and as Mr Ashton said, 'it is our duty . . . to prevent ourselves from being united with Huddersfield or anybody else. We can govern ourselves much better than any other body. We don't want a mayor, and a mace and gold chain. We simply want good water and good health.'[26] When the second proposal for adoption was made in February 1863, Mr Ashton repeated that 'His object . . . was to save Lockwood from being incorporated with Huddersfield', and then clinched his argument with a reference to something which would be even 'worse than that—the operation of the Highway Act'. Opponents made a last desperate attempt to show that Lockwood would have nothing to fear from a Highway Union. What township, Mr Gledhill asked, could Lockwood possibly be forced to combine with? All the other localities round about had already put themselves under the operation of the Local Government Act. The argument backfired, as it deserved to do, and this time the resolution to adopt was carried by a majority of about five or six to one.[27]

The first elections produced a Board consisting of six woollen manufacturers, one engineer, one machine-maker,

[25] *HC* 25 Feb. 1860, 8de.
[26] *HE* 3 Dec. 1859, 3cd.
[27] Ibid. 14 Feb. 1863, 8c.

one timber merchant, one farmer, one innkeeper, and one gentleman.[28] The minute-book of the Lockwood Local Board has disappeared, but we do know that the Board enjoyed the reputation of being 'an exceedingly active and effective' one. Within four years it had spent £2,400 upon sewering a part of the district, and £900 on large and conveniently arranged offices. In 1867 the population had reached 8,445, the rateable value was £20,709, and the Board was preparing to borrow another £3,000 for the execution of public works.[29] The details of the Board's borrowings survive and are shown in Table 1.

All the money borrowed by the Board appears, then, to have been raised locally, and none from the Public Works Loan Commissioners in London. All the loans were contracted at 5 per cent (the rate charged by the PWLC), except for nos. 5, 8, and 9, where the Board was to pay 4½ per cent. The periods varied from three years (no. 3), to five years (nos. 2, 8, 9), six years (no. 1), seven years (no. 5), ten years (no. 4), twelve years (no. 6), and twenty-nine years (no. 7). It is worth noticing that Crosland's opposition to the adoption of the Act did not prevent him lending money to the Local Board, that the money came from places as far afield as Shelley, that lenders were able to pool their resources, and that those with money to spare included a labourer, and the surveyor (J. H. Abbey) employed by the Huddersfield Improvement Commissioners. Unfortunately, for all its enterprise in borrowing money and undertaking capital works the Board was still unable to secure a supply of water, and in 1867 Lockwood, like Moldgreen, decided to throw in its lot with Huddersfield. It was a sad moment for the members when Mr Haigh asked whether in that case their expensive, purpose-built offices would become redundant, and the clerk said they would.[30]

In this second group of localities, then, Newsome achieved little, Lindley cum Quarmby was easy-going, and Almondbury was proud. In Longwood and Lockwood,

[28] Ibid. 13 June 1863, 5d.
[29] *HC* 21 Dec. 1867, 7a–f, 8a–c.
[30] *HC* 11 May 1867, 6ef, Special Meeting of Lockwood Local Board.

TABLE III.1. *Borrowings by Lockwood Local Board*

No.	Date	Amount	Name, address, and occupation or status of lender
1	1865	£500	Joseph Roberts, Meltham Mills
2	1865	£400	John Hinchliffe, of Neeleys in Honley
3	1865	£300	James Boothroyd of Newsome, pattern-weaver Tom Shaw, Lockwood, cloth-finisher Hiram Wrigley, Marsh, engineer
4	1865	£500	Elizabeth Crosland, Huddersfield, spinster
5	1865	£300	Benjamin Haigh, of Healey in Shelley, farmer Eli Jessop, of Shepley, designer David Addy, of Shelley, farmer John Crawshaw, of Cumberworth, weaver Thomas Dyson, of Shelley, labourer
6	1866	£1,000	Edward Parkin, Castle Hill, Almondbury, clothier
7	1866	£500	Bentley Shaw, Woodfield Ho., Lockwood, Esq. John Shaw, Lockwood, gentleman Thomas Pearson Crosland, [of] Gledholt, Esq. Henry Brown, Lockwood, farmer and innkeeper Robert Robinson, Lockwood, druggist Timothy Tate, Lockwood, gentleman Henry Crowther, Lockwood, manufacturer Josiah Berry, Lockwood, manufacturer John Henry Abbey, Lockwood, land surveyor John Dow, Lockwood, surgeon William Whiteley, Lockwood, machinist
8	1867	£500	John Shaw, Berry Brow, grocer Thomas Shaw, Berry Brow, draper
9	1867	£500	Joseph Haigh, Newhouse, Lingards, clothier[31]

[31] HPL/KHT/20/3 Lockwood Local Board Register Book, recording loans to the Board.

however, where anxiety about being united with other townships in a union under the Highway Act provided an additional stimulus to the adoption of the Local Government Act, fear of incorporation with Huddersfield induced exertion not paralysis. Much was achieved before the water-imperative led to a voluntary surrender.

8. THE LOCAL GOVERNMENT ACT OF 1858: THE TOWNS AND VILLAGES OF THE DISTRICT ROUND HUDDERSFIELD

Lying at a distance, beyond Moldgreen and Almondbury, Lockwood and Longwood, a score of communities connected to Huddersfield by trade and business lived without fear of being absorbed by the town. The annual reports submitted to parliament by the Local Government Act Office show that, already by August 1860, Kirkheaton, Kirkburton, Shepley, Austonley, Holme, Meltham, and Marsden in Almondbury had passed resolutions adopting the Act. Within the year they were joined by Cartworth, Upperthong, Golcar, and Linthwaite. Many more townships followed when it became clear that the only way of escaping the threat of being forced into a Highway Union by the Justices was to adopt the Local Government Act. By August 1862, Shelley, Thurstonland, Fulstone, Scholes, Netherthong, Scammonden, Slaithwaite, and Marsden in Huddersfield had adopted the Act,[1] and in the following year, before the Justices made any move to implement the Highways Act, Wooldale followed suit.[2] Last to adopt the Act was Honley, which had adopted the Lighting and Watching Act of 1833 in December 1859, and blithely supposed it was safe from the operation of the Highways Act because it boasted surveyors and a population of over 5,000.[3] This was an error of judgement, the population in

[1] The adoptions can be followed in the annual reports of the Local Government Act Office, *PP* 1859 sess. 2, XI, p. 117; 1860, XXXI, p. 617; 1861 XXXIII, p. 43; 1862 XXVIII, p. 317.

[2] *HE* 27 Dec. 1862, 4f, reports the passing of the resolution. The first meeting of the Local Board took place on 7 Mar. 1863, HPL/UHO/W, Wooldale LBMB.

[3] *HC* 10 Mar. 1860, 8a, and 19 May 1860, 8a.

1861 was 4,626,[4] and the town exchanged the Lighting and Watching Act for the Local Government Act in great haste in June 1864 after the Overseers of the Poor had received a letter from the Clerk of the Peace at Wakefield to say that a proposal would be made at the ensuing quarter sessions, to be held at Bradford, to divide the West Riding into Highway Districts.[5]

Meltham and Honley, with over 4,000 inhabitants apiece, were substantial towns. But most of the townships which adopted the Local Government Act in order to avoid the Highway Act were small, and in many of these little places which had once been the strongholds of the independent clothiers of the eighteenth century, the population had levelled off, and was now declining as people moved away to find work among the suburbs of Huddersfield. This applied to places like Thurstonland with 1,116 inhabitants in 1861 and 1,001 in 1871, Holme with 807 and 724, Netherthong with 1,097 and 1,092, and Scammonden with 1,012 and 803. But similar shifts in population could be observed even in moderate-sized places like Kirkheaton with 3,011 inhabitants in 1861 and 2,646 ten years later, and Upperthong, with figures of 2,690 and 2,419.[6] All over the West Riding the pattern was the same. When these declining townships took advantage of the opportunity furnished by the one Act to escape being coerced into the operation of the other, Tom Taylor, who was in charge of the Local Government Act Office, took a complaisant view.[7] But others in Whitehall and Westminster were not so indulgent. The Public Health Act of 1848 had been represented as a Health of Towns Act, and the Local Government Act, in its turn, had also, apparently, been thought of, in London, as an urban measure. Central government cried foul, and blew the whistle. In 1863 the Local Government Act was amended to prevent places

[4] *PP* 1862 L, p. 192, *Population (England and Scotland), Census of England and Wales: Population Tables; Numbers and Distribution of the People*, p. 158.

[5] HPL/UHO/HY Honley LBMB, preface.

[6] Figures from *PP* 1872 LXVI, pt. II, pp. 465–6, *Population (England and Wales), Area, Houses, and Inhabitants*, pp. 437–8.

[7] *PP* 1871 XXXV, pp. 575 and 576, *RSC2, Vol. iii, Pt. 1, Minutes of Evidence from Nov. 1869 to June 1870*, pp. 17, 18, Qn. 8721 and 8729.

with fewer than 3,000 inhabitants from carrying out an adoption unless they secured the permission of the Secretary of State. Those which had already adopted the Act were allowed to continue provided they appointed a surveyor, and the Yorkshire townships spurned the incentives offered to them in this amending Act to give the Local Government Act up again.[8]

Hatred of the New Poor Law had been burned deep into the consciousness of the population of the Huddersfield area, and the ratepayers disliked a centralised Union almost as much as the poor detested the regime in the workhouse. The feeling that the new Highway Union would be as objectionable as the Poor Law Union of 1834 appears to have been universal. At Meltham the ratepayers accepted Mr Jacomb's advice that there was 'no time to lose' if they wished to escape the operation of the Highway Bill;[9] in Golcar they were impressed by the argument that 'it was now or never';[10] in Cartworth they held a meeting to consider the desirability of adopting the Act in order 'to evade the Highway Bill';[11] and at Kirkheaton they admitted that there would have been 'no idea of adopting the Local Government Act' had they not thought that it was the only way open to them to escape the Highway Bill.[12] The strength of the motivation cannot be denied. But that does not mean that it was disreputable or un-British. Nearly two generations earlier the ratepayers of the Isle of Wight had been formed into a Highway Union, and many of the most able and energetic of them had already, as at Ryde,[13] or now wished, as at Ventnor,[14] to escape from it. The behaviour of the West Riding townships can be presented in a more favourable light than that in which it was exhibited in London.

In the first place, of course, there is the obvious point that there was no reason why the localities should not have done anything which the law allowed them to do. In

[8] 26 & 27 Vict. c. 17.
[9] *HE* 18 Feb. 1860, 3b.
[10] Ibid. 10 Mar. 1860, 3de.
[11] Ibid. 24 Mar. 1860, 3d.
[12] *HC* 17 Mar. 1860, 8de.
[13] See ch. II. 1, above.
[14] *IND* 24 Oct. 1863, 7c, says that in 1852 Ventnor paid £262 in highway rates of which only £160 was expended in the town.

the second place, the adoptions were not always carried out in a spirit of blind prejudice. In Austonley the rate-payers were summoned to a discussion 'of the relative merits of the Local Government Act and the proposed Government Highway Bill'.[15] In Kirkburton and Lingards the Highway Bill was not without its defenders. Mr Fitton thought 'there must be some beauty' in it,[16] and the Revd C. A. Hulbert made no secret of the fact that he preferred government by Justices to government by Boards.[17] In the third place it was not correct to suggest that the districts which decided to go independent were simply trying to escape their responsibilities: far from it, they were con-tracting into a duty to maintain their own roads, and declining to opt out by allowing themselves to be formed into a union where somebody else would take the decisions for them. The surviving minute-books make it clear that even the least energetic Local Board did attend to the high-ways. In the fourth place few of these Boards, even in the smaller places, failed to go any further than the mainten-ance of the highways. When Mr Parkin, at Kirkburton, said that they had 'no other intention in getting the act passed [i.e. adopted] except to repair the roads', Mr Armitage pointed to the names of 'thirteen gas proprietors' among the requisitionists who had called for the meeting, and concluded, plausibly enough, that it was 'therefore doubtful if they would confine themselves' to that object.[18]

Finally, it is worth adding that every one of these little Local Boards seems to have developed some characteristic of its own which distinguished it from all the others and formed the basis of its *esprit de corps*. At Shepley the Local Board kept an unusually close watch upon the attendance record of individual members.[19] At Wooldale the Board met regularly every fortnight, instead of once a month as required by the Act.[20] At Upperthong the Surveyor and the Inspector of Nuisances were expected, not just to make themselves available if required, but to attend every

[15] *HC* 24 Mar. 1860, 5e.
[16] *HE* 3 Mar. 1860, 3cd.
[17] Ibid. 17 Mar. 1860, 3d.
[18] Ibid. 3 Mar. 1860, 3cd.
[19] HPL/UK Shepley LBMB.
[20] HPL/UHO/W Wooldale LBMB.

meeting of the Board.[21] At Linthwaite, where members
were required to stand when speaking,[22] the Board passed,
and apparently adhered to, a resolution that anyone with
important business, should give notice at one meeting of
his intention to raise the matter at the next.[23] Distinctive
little characteristics like these might not appeal to tidy-
minded officers of state in Whitehall, but they do not
suggest that the members of Local Boards were indifferent
to their work, and all over the West Riding the Local
Boards survived to become Urban District Councils when
local government was reorganised in 1893.

What the surviving records do reveal is something which
Whitehall, of all places, was least likely to be able to
appreciate. Every few hundred yards, in this part of Yorkshire, there really is another locality with a strong sense of
its own identity, and an earnest desire not to be taken for a
ride by its neighbours. To an outsider it must have appeared
ridiculous that the two Marsdens, Marsden in Almondbury
with 2,027 inhabitants, and Marsden in Huddersfield with
662, were unwilling to sink their differences, and unite to
form a single district for town improvement purposes.[24]
Looked at from a distance it is astonishing that 'the enlightened views of . . . making one district for the whole of
Holmfirth' came to nothing,[25] and that the surrounding
townships, Cartworth, Upperthong, and Wooldale, which
took over much of the responsibility, were unwilling to act
together, and went their separate ways. After the Act had
been adopted the Local Board at Wooldale actually passed
a resolution that 'it is not desirable that this Board should
unite with the Local Boards of Cartworth and Upperthong

[21] HPL/UHO/U Upperthong LBMB.
[22] HPL/UCV/L Linthwaite LBMB, 23 May 1863.
[23] HPL/UCV/L Linthwaite LBMB.
[24] In Apr. 1860 Marsden in Almondbury adopted the Act and Marsden in
Huddersfield did not: *HE* 7 Apr. 1860, 3c. Marsden in Huddersfield adopted the
Act in Mar. 1862. As the *HE* commented, 'A change has come over the views of
the inhabitants of the township. Two years ago, they refused to unite with the
other township, and also declined by an overwhelming majority, to adopt the
act. It was again thrown overboard last year; while this year, the ratepayers are
all of one mind. "Time works wonders".' (15 Mar. 1862, 4f.)
[25] *HC* 3 Nov. 1860, 8b.

with respect to sanitary measures'.[26] The ordinary rate-payer was hypersensitive to the suggestion that so much as a single farthing of his 'taxes' might be spent for somebody else's benefit. At Golcar, this led to a situation in which the movement to adopt the Act nearly foundered when the inhabitants of Wellhouse suddenly discovered that they were in danger of being swamped, or brought 'under bondage', by electors with smaller properties in other parts of the town. There was an appeal against the adoption, and the Inspector who came to conduct the inquiry saved the day by dividing the town into three wards, Wellhouse which returned six members to the Board, and a north-east ward and a north-west ward which returned three members each.[27] At Kirkburton the locality was kept in a state of excitement for weeks on end while the division of the district into wards was being debated.[28] At Honley the division was accomplished more peacefully.[29] Even the division into wards, however, did not serve to solve every problem. Linthwaite, for example, was divided, from the very first, into three wards, but that did not stop the ratepayers of Lower Linthwaite attempting to achieve a separation, and in 1865 they took their demand all the way to a public inquiry.[30] The Home Secretary's decision went against them, and they must have compared themselves rather ruefully with the inhabitants of Almondbury who had organised a successful rebellion against Moldgreen.

[26] HPL/UHO/W Wooldale LBMB, 22 Apr. 1863.
[27] *HC* 7 Apr. 1860, 5e, and 27 Oct. 1860, 6d.
[28] *HE* 21 July 1860, 3a; *HC* 21 July 1860, 5f.
[29] HPL/UHO/HY Honley LBMB.
[30] HPL/UCV/L Linthwaite LBMB, 18 Apr. 1865; *PP* 1866 XX, p. 507.

IV

Local and Central Government

1. 'THIS COMPLETE AND EXCELLENT ACT', THE ISLE OF WIGHT, THE HUDDERSFIELD DISTRICT, AND THE LOCAL GOVERNMENT ACT

Edwin Chadwick and Sir John Simon favoured government by experts, the imposition of standards of engineering and hygiene by authoritarian direction, and disinterested professional administration from the centre. In the twentieth century, their biographers, sympathising with their subjects, have been tempted to write as though the local Acts passed in the late eighteenth and early nineteenth centuries were worse than useless, that progress was made under the Public Health Act of 1848 (though less than there would have been had the Act been still more rigorous), and that the passage of the Local Government Act in 1858 was a retrograde step.[1] It would be foolish to deny that the history of the Isle of Wight and of the district round Huddersfield furnishes examples of the confusion of administrative units and the mingling of private and public interests which Chadwick had in mind when he condemned local Acts. But the overall picture presented in this study is almost exactly the opposite of that painted by Chadwick, Simon, and their biographers. Local Acts did some good, least was achieved under the Public Health Act, and the passage of the Local Government Act led to a rush of adoptions and (with exceptions) improvements. Clearly

---

[1] Finer, *Edwin Chadwick*, Lewis, *Chadwick and the Public Health Movement*, and R. J. Lambert, *Sir John Simon and English Social Administration, 1816–1904* (1964). In a much more recent book, *Medicine and Society in Wakefield and Huddersfield 1780–1870* (1987), p. 18, Hilary Marland writes dismissively of a basic failure in local government in the 19th c., but this is, of course, only incidental to her own pioneering work in a new field of study.

there was another England in addition to that perceived by Chadwick and Simon.

As Professor Keith Lucas has suggested, it is really quite unhistorical, in looking at local Acts, to try and wish private Bill legislation out of the way.[2] It was an established procedure. Jane Player and Sir John Ramsden both had experience of private Bill legislation upon their own account, enabling them to make, or vary, the terms of family wills and settlements. A private Act was one of the managerial instruments by which a great estate could be kept intact and improved. Private Bill legislation was as much part of the world in which persons of property, landed or commercial, traditional or entrepreneurial, lived, as the air they breathed and the ground they trod. It was scarcely surprising that the connections between Improvement Commissioners and the proprietors of utilities were as close as they were at Ryde, West Cowes, and Huddersfield. These links were not necessarily corrupt, and some of the attempts made by the reformers to blacken the reputation of the old Commissioners at Huddersfield in 1848 appear somewhat forced.[3] It is difficult to see who else could have taken the initiative in paving, and watching and lighting, and localities which followed the private Bill road, learned from the deficiencies of their own Acts, went for a new Act in every generation, and kept their legislation up to date, as Ryde and Huddersfield itself did, derived some benefits from it.

Admittedly, private Bill legislation was expensive, but the answer to that lay in parliament, in the drafting of model clauses Acts, and the passage of permissive legislation. The creation of the General Board was a legislative anomaly. Chadwick and Simon knew—none better—that the Board aroused antagonism and was encompassed by enemies. But Chadwick lacked the local attachments needed to understand why, in the parish of Newchurch, in the Isle of Wight, the centralised Poor Law Board had been condemned as 'the incarnation of Whig iniquity', 'one of

[2] B. K. Lucas, 'Some Influences affecting the Development of Sanitary Legislation in England', *Economic History Review*, 1953–4.
[3] MPPI.

the villanous creations of Whig bureaucracy', the chief aim
of which was 'to bring about the dismal swamp of officialism'.[4] Neither Chadwick nor Simon would have been
likely to comprehend why Huddersfield, whose inhabitants had little cause to bless or rely upon central government, steered clear of the Public Health Act. Unfortunately
for the centralisers, the very existence even, of a General
Board of Health, and fears of interference and inspection,
acted to the detriment of the public health party. In Ryde,
indeed, these feelings were so strong that the reformers
never were able to secure a majority of votes in favour of
the application of the Public Health Act in a town poll. In
Moldgreen the antagonism aroused by the public health
party's attempt to invoke the 1848 Act and establish a
Local Board, was so vociferous that the application had to
be left as unfinished business when the General Board was
abolished in 1858. The subsequent attempt to adopt the
Local Government Act, although successful, was almost
certainly rendered more acrimonious than it would otherwise have been by what had gone before. Only in West
Cowes was a local Act given up, and a Local Board of
Health established under the 1848 Act, and there the old
Commissioners seized control of the new machinery, and
little was effected by the change.

The local newspapers welcomed the extinction of the
General Board. For years past, the *Huddersfield Examiner*
said, it had had occasion 'to deplore the centralising tendencies of modern English legislation', and to denounce
'the insidious attempts of our rulers to introduce contin-
ental systems'.[5] At the other end of the country the editor
of the *Isle of Wight Observer* regretted that the only means
so far employed to escape the dominance of 'broad acres
and brown tops', had been to adopt 'the Whiggish system
of centralisation and officialism'.[6] He accused the Whigs of
having tried to introduce 'French Centralisation', and
praised the Derby administration for sweeping away 'all
that mass of Centralising cobwebs which Whiggish officials

[4] *IWO* 22 June 1861, 3a.
[5] *HE* 3 July 1858, 2c.
[6] *IWO* 24 Apr. 1858, 2e.

have for the past 10 years been so busily weaving around about 300 towns, through the medium of the Public Health Act'.[7] In both the Isle of Wight and the Huddersfield district, the ratepayers had an overwhelming desire to be allowed to manage their 'own business' for themselves,[8] to 'manage their own affairs',[9] and 'to govern themselves in their own fashion' believing that they knew best what was 'good for themselves'.[10] They did not want 'the power of self-government' to be taken 'out of their own hands',[11] and they did not wish to see 'their money . . . expended by other people'.[12] They wished instead 'to take upon themselves the responsibilities of local government'.[13] The language was unmistakable, and the feelings that inspired it were to be found on both sides of the political divide and baffle attempts at easy labelling. It was astute, as the Liberal newspaper the *Isle of Wight Observer* pointed out, of the Derby government to recognise how strong it was,[14] and to pass the Local Government Act.

In 1858 the inhabitants of Ryde rejoiced that 'local government is . . . once more free of the fetters of red tape'.[15] The Local Government Act was a versatile piece of legislation. It could be adopted by any representative Council, or body of Commissioners, and places which already possessed local Acts were allowed, like Ryde, to lay them down in exchange for the general Act, or, like Ventnor, and to a lesser extent Huddersfield, to pick and choose their way through the clauses of the general Act, and the model clauses Acts which were embodied in it, taking what they judged they needed to supplement their present powers. In Honley the ratepayers laid down one permissive Act, the Lighting and Watching Act of 1833, in favour of the new, more comprehensive one. Existing bodies could

---

[7] Ibid. 22 June 1861, 3a, and 28 Aug. 1858, 3a.
[8] Mr Farrer, Holmfirth, *HC* 29 Jan. 1859, 8cde.
[9] Mr Ashton, Lockwood, ibid., 25 Feb. 1860, 8de, and Mr Littlewood, Cartworth, ibid., 31 Mar. 1860, 8a.
[10] Marsden in Huddersfield, *HE* 3 Mar. 1860, 3a.
[11] Marsden in Almondbury, idem.
[12] Longwood, *HC* 3 Mar. 1860, 8de.
[13] Cartworth, ibid. 25 May 1861, 8a.
[14] *IWO* 28 Aug. 1858, 3a.
[15] Idem.

trade in their local Acts, or obtain a retread, or exchange one permissive Act for another, just as they chose. In a place which did not already possess a representative Council or a Board, the Act could also be adopted, as it was in East Cowes, Sandown, and Shanklin, and through-out the Huddersfield area, at a meeting of the owners and ratepayers. Perhaps the most important feature of the Act was the recognition, by the legislature, of the existence, all over the country, of places like Sandown, which were unable to afford a private Act, and unwilling to subject themselves to a General Board of Health. There was still a huge unrealised potential for local self-government, and the Local Government Act promised to refresh parts of the body politic which other Acts of parliament had been unable to reach. In Huddersfield the editor of the *Examiner* thanked the government for a law 'which will greatly facil-itate the action and extension of municipal self-govern-ment'.[16] In the Isle of Wight the editor of the *Observer* pointed out that 'instead of a ruinous outlay for a private Act . . . this complete and excellent Act "may be adopted by a resolution of a majority of owners and ratepayers, at a public meeting" ', and praised the Act as 'an inestimable advantage to the community'. 'Had such a valuable Act been in existence 25 years ago—when sanitary reform com-menced—what an infinite saving of money to the nation, and of time to the Legislature, it would have effected.'[17]

Adoption was astonishingly cheap, and for people of modest means living in small communities the simplicity of the procedures opened up possibilities which had never existed before. At Kirkburton, Mr Parkin was a little too optimistic when he said that 'the expenditure would only be a penny postage-stamp, to send a letter to the Home Secretary'.[18] But at Longwood the cost was expected to be about £20,[19] and at Lockwood, which had been toying with the possibility of obtaining a local Act, the cost would be 'comparatively nothing'.[20] As the editor of the *Isle of Wight Observer*, who might almost have had Yorkshire in mind,

[16] *HE* 7 Aug. 1858, 2d.
[17] *IWO* 28 Aug. 1858, 3a.
[18] *HC* 3 Mar. 1860, 8cd.
[19] Ibid. 3 Mar. 1860, 8de.
[20] *HE* 3 Dec. 1859, 3cd.

put it, 'no town in England—no aggregate of houses even, not yet having acquired the name and legal character of a town' could any longer 'plead the cost of a local act as a reason for remaining without powers for its own government and improvement'.[21] The local newspapers hailed the Act's passage, familiarised their readers with its contents, and exhorted them to avail themselves of the opportunities it created. Editors regarded adoptions as news, and the high level of excitement which attached to them proves that they were right.

Whether the Act was to be adopted by a Council or Local Board, or by a meeting of owners and ratepayers, the localities generally seem to have held preliminary, deliberative meetings of the constituencies. At Meltham a meeting was held where the provisions of the Act were 'carefully considered', and the text was later 'read by many most deeply interested'.[22] At Holmfirth, a special meeting was held in Hoyle's Temperance House, when the Act 'was read and discussed'.[23] At Lingards copies of the Act were made available.[24] Mr Jacomb, a solicitor, and the clerk to the first Local Board established at Moldgreen, became, like George Butler of Ryde, a localitarian evangelist, and addressed audiences at Austonley, Deighton, Golcar, Kirkheaton, Linthwaite, and Meltham.[25] Ventnor was an exception, and here the Commissioners' failure to consult the ratepayers was adversely commented upon.[26]

The preliminary meetings held to study the Act appear to have raised the level of popular interest shown in the adoption meetings themselves. In Lockwood the duly requisitioned meeting had to be adjourned from the town's small school-room to the Red Lion Inn.[27] In Golcar the owners and ratepayers were summoned to meet in the vestry of St John's Church. Being unable to fit in there,

[21] *IWO* 15 Jan. 1859, 3ab.
[22] *HE* 3 Mar. 1860, 3a.
[23] Ibid. 15 Jan. 1859, 3a.
[24] *HE* 17 Mar. 1860, 3d.
[25] *HC* 24 Mar. 1860, 5e; *HE* 13 Aug. 1859, 2f; ibid. 10 Mar. 1860, 3de; ibid. 10 Mar. 1860, 3c; ibid. 10 Mar. 1860, 3b; *HC* 18 Feb. 1860, 8c.
[26] *IND* 24 Oct. 1863, 7cd.
[27] *HE* 25 Feb. 1860, 3efg.

they adjourned to the Rose and Crown Inn, and when that
in turn proved too small they trooped across to the National
School.[28] In Kirkheaton they adjourned from the vestry of
St John's Church to the Beaumont Arms Inn, in Cartworth
from the vestry to the Shoulder of Mutton, in Austonley
from the vestry of St David's Church to the National
School, in Slaithwaite from the church to the National
School-room, and in Almondbury from the vestry to the
Woolpack Inn.[29] Everywhere, it seems, the organisers
underestimated the number of people who would want to
attend a meeting.

In many localities a crowded meeting meant that there
was an opposition. The difference between the Public
Health Act and the Local Government Act was not that
one was universally hated and the other loved. The distinction lay in the point at which the opposition found
expression and the manner in which it was heard and the
decision taken. Under the Public Health Act there was no
way in which opponents could prevent one-tenth of the
ratepayers from approaching the General Board, and the
first opportunity offered to them to argue their case was in
front of an Inspector from London. Under the Local Government Act opponents could make themselves heard at
every stage of the proceedings, and they debated the case
with their neighbours, before, if necessary, presenting it to
an Inspector, who came from London, but whose guise
was less that of a dictator and more that of an umpire. In
these circumstances the discussions preceding the adoption of the Act were, in many localities, the first stirrings of
political life.

It was, therefore, one of the virtues of the Local Government Act that it furnished opponents with many opportunities of making themselves felt. In the first place they could
challenge the means used to obtain signatures to the original requisition. It was alleged that at Moldgreen the promoters had employed an agent who was paid by the hour.[30]

[28] Ibid. 10 Mar. 1860, 3de.
[29] *HC* 17 Mar. 1860, 8de; *HE* 24 Mar. 1860, 3d; ibid. 31 Mar. 1860, 3e; ibid.
12 Apr. 1862, 5a; ibid. 11 Oct. 1862, 4f.
[30] The accusation was made at Holmfirth, *HC* 29 Jan. 1859, 5cd.

At Holmfirth 'some of the more knowing' objectors 'recollected that some time ago, two young men . . . had called at a few homes with a paper' without making it clear to the inhabitants that it was the Local Government Act that their support was being solicited for.[31] Benjamin Broadbent received a round of applause when he said that: 'He was told nout but what they were now baan to have a leet or two, that was all! (Laughter.) If he had knoawn they were coming wi' a petition tu't government, he would a' ordered them a' at u' t doour. (Laughter.)'[32] In these circumstances, much time was spent both at Moldgreen and at Holmfirth in contesting and proving the validity of the signatures.

At the adoption meeting, opponents could put up a rival candidate of their own to take the chair, as happened at Kirkburton, where 'after a great deal of personal bickering, uproar, and confusion, Mr Samuel Rhodes was appointed to the chair by a small majority, in preference to Mr Joseph Cook'.[33] If this manœuvre failed, they could challenge the conduct of the chairman, as Mr Bird did at Moldgreen, when he said 'Stop a bit, Mr Chairman. You are chairman, but you are not altogether master.'[34] They could, if they thought they might win it, demand a poll, as happened in Almondbury, Cartworth, Upperthong, and many other places.[35] The campaign which preceded a poll might be fiercely contested, and at Golcar there were three weeks or more of agitation, and the opposition was accused of personating five or six dead men.[36] If defeated at the poll, opponents might, as they did at Cartworth, complain of irregularity in the counting of the votes, and secure a second election.[37] At any stage in the process opponents could appeal to the Secretary of State, and ask him to conduct an inquiry into the conduct of the chairman of the adoption meeting, as he did at Moldgreen,[38] and at

[31] *HE* 15 Jan. 1859, 3a.
[32] *HC* 29 Jan. 1859, 8cde.
[33] Ibid. 3 Mar. 1860, 8cd.
[34] *HE* 24 Dec. 1858, 2e.
[35] Ibid. 12 July 1862, 5b; *HC* 21 Apr. 1860, 5f; ibid. 2 Mar. 1861, 8b.
[36] Ibid. 7 Apr. 1860, 5e.
[37] *HE* 28 Apr. 1860, 3c.
[38] Ibid. 29 Jan. 1859, 4abc.

Kirkburton, where the successive stages of the disputed and protracted adoption process kept the place in a turmoil for months on end while 'the excitement' continued 'as great as ever'.[39] Every step taken by the opponents of the Act added, it has to be admitted, to the (originally small) costs of obtaining it, and raised the stakes. At both Moldgreen and Holmfirth, opponents proposed resolutions authorising the payment of their own expenses out of the Highway rates.[40] This would have been illegal, and was prevented, but proponents themselves had to be prepared, if there was a struggle, public-spiritedly to subscribe to the costs of the battle.[41]

The grounds of opposition varied, but three main ones can be identified. In the first place there was still, even under the new regime, a strong disposition to mistrust the central government. At Ryde, in the days of the controversy over the Public Health Act, Mr J. H. Hearn had denounced all connection with a *'central* Board'. 'His local patriotism' had been applauded, and 'his burning eloquence' had melted 'the tender sympathies of the Muckabites'.[42] Once aroused, these sentiments were not easily laid to rest, and even after the abolition of the General Board, ratepayers frequently said that they were unable to distinguish between the Act of 1848 and that of 1858. The point was made by a witness addressing the public inquiry held to determine the boundaries of the new Moldgreen district. The Inspector demurred, and the following dialogue took place.

Inspector. 'You have not seen the Local Government Act in operation.'
Witness. 'Board of Health—'
Inspector. 'Ay, but this is a new act altogether.'
A Voice. 'Not so very different though.'[43]

At Holmfirth, Mr Wimpenny professed to believe that the two Acts, 'Health of Towns or Local Government . . .

---

[39] *HC* 5 May 1860, 8cd, 7 July 1860, 5f, 8 Sept. 1860, 5e.
[40] *HE* 16 Apr. 1859, 3d; *HC* 24 Mar. 1860, 8a.
[41] As at Moldgreen, *HE* 16 Apr. 1859, 3d.
[42] *IWO* 16 Jan. 1858, 2e.
[43] *HE* 6 Nov. 1858, 3g, 4ab.

were both alike' in their arbitrary and centralising character.[44] Two years later, he reappeared at Upperthong to
argue against the adoption of the Act. 'They would be
astonished at the powers of the Secretary of State. . . . He
contended that it was *not* a Local Government Act; all the
power being in his hands.'[45] Over 200 miles away his
words were echoed at Ventnor, where Sir Raymond Jervis
professed to believe that the Local Government Act would
place all the power in the hands of 'those connected with
Government'.[46] He was supported by Mr Jewell, who
declared that 'he did not like arbitrary acts', and prophesied
that 'if they adopted this Local Government Act, they
would be having a Government Inspector down, and
whatever he said would be law'.[47] In Newport, too, when
the timid burghers did eventually decide to fall into line
with their neighbours living in the cleansed towns of the
sunshine belt in the south-east of the island, they still
needed to be reassured that 'by the adoption of the Act,
the Council will not subject itself to any Government
control'.[48]

In the second place there were objections from the ratepayers to any increase in taxation. Here, the remonstrances
did not come from the very bottom of society, for it was
the universal practice at this period for those living in
poverty to be excused payment of the rates, and the
minutes of the Local Board at Shepley, for example, include detailed exemption lists.[49] Observers slipped easily
into the assumption that wealthy owners and employers
were enlightened, that lesser men were not, and that resistance came from the smaller ratepayers. The *Hampshire
Independent* drew a distinction between the large owners at
Ryde, who were said to be intelligent, and the small ratepayers who were reluctant improvers.[50] When a poll was
taken at Cartworth, 115 small occupiers voted against
adoption, while the owners and the larger ratepayers all
voted in favour.[51] But it was not always so. At Ventnor

[44] HC 29 Jan. 1859, 5cd.
[45] Ibid. 26 Jan. 1861, 8b.
[46] IWO 11 Aug. 1860, 4bcd.
[47] IND 24 Oct. 1863, 7cd.
[48] IWO 26 Jan. 1867, 3f.
[49] HPL/UK Shepley LBMB.
[50] IND 21 Mar. 1863, 7d.
[51] HE 5 May 1860, 3c.

public pressure had to be brought to bear upon the Commissioners, all of whom were large owners, to adopt the Act, by smaller ratepayers from the outside.[52] At Kirkheaton, Mr Tolson contended that 'so far from giving an ascendancy to the wealthy ratepayers', the Local Government Act would 'rather act against them'.[53] In the Huddersfield area the millowners at Lockwood were not the only ones to believe that adoption would enable people of modest means to filch money out of the pockets of the rich and transfer it to their own.[54] Similar fears surfaced at Honley, where positions were taken up and attitudes hardened while the town was still being governed under the Lighting and Watching Act. The millowners asked why the mills should be rated to light Honley, and again, 'What would Honley be, but for the mills?' They were met with the smart retort, 'What would the mills be but for Honley?', there was 'Great cheering', and the speaker continued

it would conduce to the comfort of workers, and the advantage of the employers, if the poor children of Honley and the immediate neighbourhood, who have to go plodding to the mills at five o' clock on dark, wet winter mornings, could get there without being up to the ancles in dirt and water, and losing half an hour in drying their clothes, while the power in the mills was running for nothing. (Hear.)[55]

The millowners of Honley had to keep an eye on their costs, but even so they got the worse of the argument. Happily, not all millowners in the district took a gloomy view of their prospects in the international market, and at Meltham it was said that the larger ones were 'universally in favour'.[56]

The third objection was related to the second. The *Hampshire Independent* had welcomed the election clauses contained in the Public Health Act of 1848 as 'a move in the right direction', away from the situation in which the rich obtained local Acts and governed through self-perpetuating

---

[52] *IWO* 22 Oct. 1859, 3c.
[54] Ibid. 25 Feb. 1860, 8de.
[56] *HE* 3 Mar. 1860, 3a.

[53] *HC* 17 Mar. 1860, 8de.
[55] Ibid. 14 Apr. 1860, 7d.

bodies of Commissioners. It was a step 'from the petty despotism of a few, towards the influence of the many; from local feodality to individual representation'.[57] The newspaper had a point. But it was not the only one that could be made, and the fact was that both the high qualifications demanded of those submitting themselves for election, and the weighted scale of voting, left the whole system biased heavily in favour of the rich. In Ryde complaints were made that, under the 1854 Act, which followed the formula laid down in the Public Health Act of 1848, 'the plurality of votes completely swamped individuals'.[58] In Ventnor critics of the town's Act pointed out that the qualification for the Commissioners was so high that 'it is impossible to elect but one class of persons over and over again'.[59] Adopting the Local Government Act, with its £500 property qualification, and its unchanged weighted scale, did nothing to ameliorate this state of affairs, and as the movement to adopt the Act swept through the Huddersfield area, where it was still the custom to hold open vestries, the criticisms were forthright and pungent. At Holmfirth, Mr Wimpenny argued that what he called 'the "disfranchising clauses" were particularly obnoxious, so much so that, in some of the townships included in the proposed district, the popular element would be almost annihilated'.[60] At Upperthong he calculated that anything up to three-quarters of the inhabitants would be disqualified.[61] At Kirkburton, Mr Armitage alleged that 'the real object of the promoters . . . was to take the power entirely out of the hands of the small ratepayers'. If they adopted the Act, he warned them, 'that would be the last town's meeting they would ever have'.[62] At Moldgreen, Kirkheaton, and Newsome, the point was made that, after taking into account the high property qualification, 'they had not many persons . . . who could sit at the Board'.[63] Objectors thought that everyone should have 'a voice in all public business', and that 'the working class should be

---

[57] *IND* 26 Mar. 1853, 6b.
[58] *IWO* 12 Feb. 1859, 3b.
[59] Ibid. 9 July 1859, 3d.
[60] *HC* 29 Jan. 1859, 5cd.
[61] Ibid. 26 Jan. 1861, 8b.
[62] Ibid. 3 Mar. 1860, 8cd.
[63] *HE* 7 Nov. 1857, 3cde; *HC* 17 Mar. 1860, 8de; *HE* 16 Aug. 1862, 5d.

oftener appealed to', 'which would be better than setting class against class'.[64] But they were overridden. At adoption meeting after adoption meeting the chairman ruled, correctly, that it was only owners and ratepayers who were entitled to be present. If it came to a poll, then the votes cast counted for anything between one and twelve according to the wealth of the person casting them. The results were, in the language of the day, described as having been 'summed'.

Expressive as the opposition was, everywhere, in the districts studied here, the friends of the 1858 Act prevailed, and even places like Cartworth and Lockwood, which rejected the Act, changed their minds and adopted it at the second proposal. Clearly there were strong feelings in favour as well as noisy calls against. In the Isle of Wight every town that could reasonably have been expected to adopt the Act, with the possible exception of Yarmouth (which, after 1863, would have been held too small), did so, and in the district round Huddersfield adoptions spread rapidly until the whole area, almost, was covered.

The positive reasons for wanting to adopt the Local Government Act were stronger than the negative ones against it, and the high property qualification and the weighted voting, which lasted until 1894, appealed to the middle classes. For thirty or forty years, ever since the days of Sturges Bourne, intelligent and self-made men of property had been engaged in a war upon two fronts, to break down the exclusivity of the aristocracy above them, and to insulate themselves from the working classes below. Now they were in charge, local government was where the action was, and they controlled the media. The *Isle of Wight Observer* used the language of 'educated worth' to describe the sort of persons now coming forward and offering themselves for election to the Local Boards. The Local Government Act was bringing the hitherto 'disfranchised intelligence of the country' into administration.[65] Around the Solent, then, the rhetoric of emancipation attached to the 1858 Act. In the Huddersfield area people

[64] *HC* 29 Jan. 1859, 5cd.
[65] *IWO* 7 Feb. 1863, 3a, in a leader noticing the death of Lord Lansdowne.

were less demonstrative, perhaps, but at Kirkburton the inhabitants were aware that with the adoption of the Act 'the old dynasty' had fallen,[66] and at Slaithwaite the ratepayers were promised that in the 'vigorous and judicious hands into which power was then passing', the Act would 'conduce to the development and improvement of an already thriving village'.[67]

From the point of view of Palmerston and Lord Derby, the advantage of the Local Government Act was that it solved the two most intractable problems faced by successive administrations ever since the beginning of the nineteenth century—those of agency, and of the choice of boundaries and units of administration. The way the Act worked, it was left to the localities to start sorting these matters out. Towns were *free to adopt it or not, at the will of their representative bodies, or their owners and ratepayers*.[68] Once adopted, it was to be carried out by the established bodies and boards, and where these did not already exist the owners and ratepayers themselves were to decide how many Commissioners would be needed, to nominate candidates, and to carry out elections. The Act stipulated only that, whatever number of Commissioners they settled upon it must be divisible by three, in order that one-third of the Commissioners might retire each year, and new elections be held, just as they were under the Act of 1835 among the Municipal Corporations. The central government did not attempt to identify individuals, and was able to evade making a choice between administration by magistrates, which was out of keeping with the spirit of the times, and by parish officers, too many of whom were chaotic and ineffectual.

When it came to units and boundaries, once again the people in the localities were to decide for themselves what townships they belonged to, and how widely their common identity of feelings extended. If the unit they chose was a new one, without an established boundary, then the proceedings had to be suspended to allow the Home

[66] *HC* 21 July 1860, 5f.
[67] *HE* 17 May 1862, 5a.
[68] *IWO* 15 Jan. 1859, 3ab.

Secretary to send an Inspector to decide where the boundary should run. If adjacent localities fell out, and were unable to agree where the line between them should be drawn, then the dispute between them was of their own, and not of Whitehall's, making. In both cases the Inspector sent down from London appeared in the locality not as a commander handing down orders, but as an arbiter. This in turn appears to have made it easier for disputants in the localities to appeal to higher authority and to forward points at issue to the Department for resolution. At Moldgreen, Mr Sykes, who was infuriated by the chairman's conduct, appealed 'to Government to protect the people',[69] and at Cartworth 'the chairman of the meeting . . . wrote to head-quarters'[70] for advice.

Relations between central and local government were much more relaxed in the early 1860s than they had been in the 1850s, and all through the early 1860s parliament, which had established the permissive system, was continually adding to it. In 1860 a new Nuisances Removal Act gave local authorities in England the power to provide ambulances.[71] In the same year, Lord Ashley, who was seeking to extend the benefits of the permissive system as widely as possible, beyond the areas already covered by the Local Boards, promoted a Public Improvement Act, which allowed any parish in England with a population of over 500 to construct public walks, exercise grounds and playgrounds, and to levy a rate for their maintenance.[72] In 1864 parliament passed the Public House Closing Act. This was a modest little gesture towards temperance, applying to England and Wales, which enabled a body of Improvement Commissioners, or the owners and ratepayers assembled, to prevent the sale of intoxicating liquors in their district between 1 a.m. and 4 a.m.[73] It was adopted, as we have seen, in Huddersfield and in some of the surrounding places.[74] Two years later the Sanitary Act of 1866 gave local authorities power to cleanse houses, to disinfect bedding and clothing, and to provide mortuaries and save families

[69] *HE* 24 Dec. 1858, 2e.
[70] *HC* 21 Apr. 1860, 5f.
[71] 23 & 24 Vict. c. 77, s. xii.
[72] 23 & 24 Vict. c. 30.
[73] 27 & 28 Vict. c. 64.
[74] See ch. III. 4, 7, above.

from having to live with their dead in the house while they were waiting for burial.[75]

Parliament, which emptied this cornucopia of opportunities over the localities, became increasingly interested in ascertaining whether they were being used. There had been no provision included in the Lighting and Watching Act of 1833 for parishes which adopted the Act to inform the Secretary of State that they had done so. But a parish which adopted Ashley's Bath-houses Act of 1846 had to secure the approval of the Secretary of State, while a town, which did not have to seek his consent, did have to submit the by-laws which it made for the good conduct of the bath-house to him for his inspection.[76] The Public Health Act of 1848 could not be put into operation at all without his co-operation, and places which adopted the Local Government Act were obliged to notify him of their decision. In 1860, two years after the localities had vindicated their right to self-government, the Home Secretary introduced a measure called the Local Taxation Returns Bill.[77] The preamble to this statute, which applied to England and Wales, said that 'Rates, Taxes, Tolls, and Dues to a large Amount are levied for Purposes of Local Government and Improvements', and went on to declare that it was desirable parliament 'should be informed annually of all Sums so levied'. The returns were published every year from 1862, and provide a more or less complete record of all the rates levied under each Act throughout the country.

Gradually, as the statistics accumulated, it was possible to form an impression of the extent to which the localities were taking advantage of the opportunities afforded to them by a benevolent parliament. Ashley's Bath-houses and Wash-houses Act had been adopted in eight of the large London parishes by 1865, and by twenty-four places ranging from Birmingham to Maidstone.[78] But that,

[75] 29 & 30 Vict. c. 90.
[76] 9 & 10 Vict. c. 74.
[77] 23 & 24 Vict. c. 51.
[78] This was a separate inquiry: *PP* 1865 XLVII, pp. 279–84, *Baths and Wash-houses Acts, A Return of all Places wherein the Baths and Washhouses Acts have been adopted.*

somewhat surprisingly, since the Victorian ratepayer liked his working classes clean, appeared to be all. The Public Libraries Acts, too, had been taken up but slowly. Here the opposition came from the middle classes themselves. Booksellers, proprietors of subscription libraries, and publicans all opposed adoption. Ratepayers alleged that reading-rooms would be crowded by errand boys and tramps using them as havens from the rain, and that a lecture room, if one was provided, would be taken over by subversives.[79] Three libraries were opened between 1847 and 1850, and twenty-three more, including one in Scotland, between 1851 and 1862. In the next four years one more town, only, adopted the Public Library Acts.[80] But the prize for non-achievement was thought to lie elsewhere: Ashley's admirable Lodging House Act of 1851 appeared, according to the returns, not to have been adopted at all, and its author himself accepted that it had been 'a dead letter'. But this we know to have been wrong, because the Act had been adopted in Huddersfield.[81] The town was not levying a separate rate for the lodging-house, whose existence was masked by a return identified as a general district rate, and one wonders whether there were other omissions of this kind.

Turning from what might be called the extra-curricular parts of the permissive system to the core syllabus the situation was much more encouraging. Following the passage of the Public Health Act of 1848, 219 places had been brought within the scope of its provisions in ten years. By August 1864 another 268 localities had adopted the Local Government Act and, thirty-one more had adopted parts of it in order 'to complete Local Acts and to meet local requirements'.[82] The Act 'had sufficient clauses in it for

[79] T. Greenwood, *Public Libraries* (4th edn. 1894), p. 85; T. Kelly, *A History of Public Libraries in Great Britain, 1845–1975* (2nd edn. 1977), p. 30.

[80] Kelly, *Public Libraries in Great Britain*, p. 23.

[81] *PP* 1884–5 XXX, p. 91, *Minutes of Evidence taken before the Royal Commission on the Housing of the Working Classes*, p. 1, Qn. 5; G. B. A. M. Finlayson, *The Seventh Earl of Shaftesbury* (1981), pp. 348, 589.

[82] *PP* 1865 XLVII, pp. 433–40, *A Return of the Towns . . . that have acquired New Powers under the Local Government Act*. Annual reports at *PP* 1859, sess. 2, XI, p. 117; 1860 XXXI, p. 617; 1861 XXXIII, p. 43; 1862 XXVIII, p. 317; 1863 XXVI, p. 739; 1864 XXX, p. 563.

any city in England, and yet it was simple enough for the smallest village'.[83] Liverpool adopted it, in part, to complete its local Acts, and Nottingham adopted the whole Act. From Shropshire to Sussex, and from Durham to Devonshire, medium-sized and small towns took advantage of the opportunities parliament had created for them. At the end of the decade Basingstoke, Chichester, Seaford, Stafford, and Tiverton had still not adopted the Act, and in Basingstoke 'the more intelligent inhabitants' were always overborne 'by the cottage rate-payers, or by the failure of getting the required majority of two-thirds of the Town Council'.[84] But these were the exceptions. Everywhere, as Tom Taylor, the Secretary to the Local Government Act Office, put it, 'the country is being gradually covered by those powers'.[85]

As more and more localities adopted the Local Government Act, the number of places governed under the Lighting and Watching Act declined, from 316 parishes in 1861 to 271 in 1867.[86] All over the country localities were abandoning the Act of 1833 in favour of the Act of 1858, and graduating from smaller responsibilities to greater ones. In the late 1860s notes were printed with official returns of rates levied under the Lighting and Watching Act to indicate which entries were to be the last, because the places making them had adopted the larger Act.[87] For the localities, changing from one Act to the other was political education indeed, a maturational milestone, and while many localities were moving on, year by year others were embarking upon their careers in local self-government by adopting the Lighting and Watching Act. The measure was ideal for a new residential district like Castelnau Villas

[83]   Said at Kirkburton, HE 3 Mar. 1860, 3cd.
[84]   PP 1871 XXXV, p. 379, RSC2, Vol. ii, Arrangement of Sanitary Statutes, Analysis of Evidence, Precis of Oral Evidence, p. 185, Mr Soper.
[85]   Ibid. p. 576, Vol. iii, Minutes of Evidence from November 1869 to June 1870, p. 18, Qn. 8729.
[86]   PP 1863 XXX, pp. 355–72, Local Taxation Returns, Abstract of the Returns transmitted to the Secretary of State for the Home Department, pursuant to the Local Taxation Returns Act, pp. 351–68, and 1868–9 LII, pp. 318–28, Local Taxation Returns, pp. 294–304.
[87]   e.g. PP 1867 LVIII, pp. 355–66, Local Taxation Returns, pp. 291–302.

in Barnes, which adopted it in 1863,[88] and a new railway junction like Malvern Link (1867).[89]

At the inquiry held in Huddersfield in December 1867 to examine the town's petition for incorporation, the yard-stick used to measure the worth of the various Local Boards was borrowing.[90] In the early nineteenth century parliament had been cautious or even grudging about the localities' need to borrow. The breakthrough came in 1848, when section 107 of the Public Health Act permitted the Local Boards to mortgage the rates for up to thirty years, and section 108 allowed the Public Works Loan Commissioners (a body whose history needs to be written) to make advances for the purposes of the Act. Henceforward, the great engine of borrowing, which had enabled eighteenth-century Britain to mobilise her resources and engage in a century-long cycle of transoceanic wars, was to be employed in the benign cause of town improvement and public health. In England and Wales borrowing increased from £2,956,178 in ten years under the Act of 1848, to £7,208,507 in thirteen years between 1858 and 1871 under the Act of 1858.[91] Compared with the amounts spent during the French wars, these sums were small. But in the 1860s, while central government avoided intervening in European wars, and reduced its share of public spending as a proportion of gross national product, local government increased its share of public borrowing and expenditure dramatically. By the end of the decade it was estimated that in England and Wales local authorities of all kinds, including those responsible for the poor law, were borrowing £5,450,000 a year, paying back about £1,750,000, and adding £3,700,000 a year to their liabilities. Expenditure by central government in England and Wales increased by 5 per cent between 1826 and 1868. Over the same period local taxation increased by 83.7 per cent. Before the end of the decade the annual expenditure by local authorities in

---

[88] *PP* 1865 XLVI, p. 320, *Local Taxation Returns*, p. 320.

[89] *PP* 1868–9 LII, p. 322, *Local Taxation Returns*, p. 298.

[90] See *HC* 21 Dec. 1867, 7a–f, 8a–c.

[91] *PP* 1872 XXVIII, 1, pp. 45–6, *First Report of the Local Government Board*, xliii–xliv.

England and Wales was estimated at £30,240,000, that in Scotland was put at £3,000,000, and that in Ireland at £3,050,000, making a grand total equal to half that required by the government of the United Kingdom itself.[92] The money was not all finding its way into measures of town improvement and public health, but much of it was, and the construction of an urban environment fit for human beings to live in was the supreme achievement of the Victorian age.

Rightly or wrongly, in the mid-century the localities appear always to have felt that their quarrels were with governments, ministers, and the departments of state, rather than with parliament itself. Parliamentary representation was the distinguishing characteristic of the British nation, the debates in parliament were reported at many columns length, and almost verbatim, in the local newspapers. They were read with avidity because, as Bagehot pointed out, parliament was a theatre where the actors played real parts.[93] Time and again, in this period, the life of a ministry turned upon the outcome of a debate. People taking part in local affairs thought, in their turn, in parliamentary images, and members of Town Councils and Commissioners sitting upon Local Boards were inclined to think of those bodies as miniature parliaments.

In the course of the adoption meeting at Moldgreen, Mr Jebson referred to 'gentlemen on the other side of the house'.[94] At Fulstone, Mr Littlewood, and at Lockwood, 'an operative', moved that 'the meeting should be adjourned to that day twelve months'.[95] When it came to a show of hands, and the outcome was in doubt, meetings moved almost as if by instinct to a parliamentary division. At Cartworth it was suggested that 'those for should go to one side of the room, and those against to the other. Ultimately "the house divided" to that effect . . . the "goats" were on the left of the chairman, and the "sheep" to the

---

[92] PP 1870 LV, pp. 187–8, Report by Rt. Hon. G. J. Goschen, President of the Poor Law Board, on the Progressive Increase of Local Taxation &c., pp. 5–6.
[93] W. Bagehot, The English Constitution (World's Classics edn. 1928), pp. 17–19.
[94] HE 24 Dec. 1858, 2e.
[95] Ibid. 12 Apr. 1862, 4f; 14 Feb. 1863, 8c.

right.'[96] At Golcar the room was cleared, tables were placed down the middle, and those in favour of the motion came back into the room to the chairman's right, while those against it returned to his left.[97]

At Ryde, when the newly elected Commissioners took their seats under the provisions of the local Act of 1854, 'some of them declared their policy', a course of action which the *Observer*'s reporter thought 'worthy of being followed by a much higher House'.[98] In Cowes it was reported that 'the bills before the house had moved a stage'.[99] From Newport, information came that, 'Our Local Legislators meet again on Tuesday next . . . when the new member for the south ward will take the oaths and his seat. Our Chancellor of the Exchequer, the Town Clerk, will then . . . read his financial statement.'[100]

These examples can be paralleled almost exactly from the West Riding. There, the *Huddersfield Examiner* referred to 'the parliament of Marsden-in-Almondbury',[101] and the *Chronicle*'s reporter waxed lyrical about a meeting of the 'House of Uncommons' (the Lighting and Watching Commissioners) at Honley. His account stated how 'After a long interval the "house" met on Tuesday.' 'On taking the chair, the Speaker . . . said he was glad to meet hon. members on the present occasion', and welcomed two new members, 'the hon. member for Buxton-road', and 'the hon. member for New Paradise', before going on to report that, as the result of an adverse vote taken at a public meeting, the ' "prime minister" ' had resigned.[102] Some of this can no doubt be attributed to whimsy among journalists, and even more, perhaps, to a kind of pretentiousness among the members of Local Boards. But reporters knew that the public was familiar with parliamentary terms and parliamentary procedures, and that a local newspaper's readers would like to think of a Town Council or a Local Board as a parliament in miniature.

In the 1850s parliament gave central government a rough

[96] *HC* 7 July 1860, 5f.   [97] *HE* 10 Mar. 1860, 3de.
[98] *IWO* 3 Apr. 1858, 2d.   [99] Ibid. 23 Jan. 1858, 3c.
[100] *IND* 4 Feb. 1854, 5c.   [101] *HE* 4 Aug. 1860, 3c.
[102] *HC* 7 Apr. 1860, 8a.

ride, and dismissed no fewer than six ministries in the space of eight years. In that decade people in the localities seem to have thought of themselves and parliament as fellow sufferers from the pretensions of central government, and as comrades-in-arms in a struggle against the centralising policies beloved of Whigs and Peelites alike. In the early 1860s, the view from the localities, after the General Board of Health had been abolished, showed central government, parliament, and the localities in harmony for the first time for many years. Looked at from the standpoint of the first three-quarters of the twentieth century, the parliament which abolished the General Board of Health and passed the Local Government Act appeared to have abdicated its responsibilities. In the eyes of many contemporaries it had done its duty. Central government had been returned to its proper sphere. In the new era of permissive legislation the townships could forge ahead on their own, and the great parliament of the nation seemed to have smiled upon the little parliaments of the localities. In turn, the Members elected by the localities to serve in the parliament at Westminster were able to take to heart Disraeli's reminder that they were a parliament and not a vestry,[103] to raise their eyes to the far horizons, and to concentrate upon the larger issues of the day, the future government of India, free trade with France and fortifications along the Channel coast, President Lincoln's struggle to preserve the Union, the Schleswig-Holstein question, a second Reform Act, and the needs of British North America. Debates in parliament soared to new heights of sublime excellence, and an MP who was called upon to address a dinner or a rally in his constituency was able, without distraction, to direct the attention of his audience to the role of Britain in the world.

[103] P. Smith, *Disraelian Conservatism and Social Reform* (1967), p. 267.

2. SCOTLAND: THE GENERAL POLICE ACTS, FIFE

In 1833 England and Wales with their little Lighting and
Watching Act had been left far behind by Scotland where
the General Police Act was more comprehensive, and conveyed powers of lighting, watching, paving, cleansing,
and watering.[1] The Scottish Act of 1833, however, was not
very widely adopted,[2] and, in Scotland as in England,
many of the larger towns preferred to work through
private Bill legislation. The Act had applied to royal
burghs, burghs of regality, and burghs of barony, but not
to new parliamentary burghs created by the Scottish
Municipal Corporations Reform Act of 1833.[3] In 1847 the
Act was amended in such a way as to permit the new
parliamentary burghs to adopt it, and to allow existing
representative bodies to take the initiative and call a meeting of the householders to consider the adoption of the
Act.[4] Three years later, in 1850, both the 1833 and 1847
Acts were repealed (this meant that they ceased to be available for adoption—where they had already been adopted
they remained in force), and a new Act was substituted for
them.[5]

The second General Police Act (often referred to as
Rutherfurd's Act) was a great advance upon the first: it
could be applied to more places, it could be adopted more
easily, and it contained the more extensive range of
powers which time had shown to be necessary. The Act
introduced the concept of the 'populous Place', an
administrative unit whose boundaries were to be determined by the Sheriff. This inspired move meant that in
future any locality with more than 1,200 inhabitants could
adopt the Act, or appoint a committee to study it and
report back to a later meeting.[6] Voting remained in the

[1] 3 & 4 Will. IV c. 46.
[2] See ch. I.4, above.
[3] 3 & 4 Will. IV c. 77. Mr Urquhart tells me that in practice the only burgh
affected by the restriction was Portobello.
[4] 10 & 11 Vict. c. 39.
[5] 13 & 14 Vict. c. 33.
[6] Ibid. s. xiii.

hands of the £10-householders, but the three-quarters majority in favour of adoption required by the 1833 Act was dropped in favour of a simple majority.[7] In royal burghs and in parliamentary burghs the Magistrates and Council were to be *ex officio* the Commissioners of police, and in burghs of regality or of barony the Act allowed the £10 householders to take an irrevocable decision that the Town Council should become the Commissioners, thus ridding many burghs of the dual system of government.[8] The 391 clauses of the Act, which were arranged in sections, contained almost the whole range of provisions for 'police', in the broad Scottish sense, and town improvement, which were now embodied in the model clauses Acts. Existing powers were enlarged and refined in the light of experience, and the police were given new powers to deal with fires, public bathing, and lodging-houses, for example;[9] and in addition to the provisions relating to the supply of water, the laying out of streets, the construction of sewers, and the drainage of houses, fresh air was now added to the list of qualities to be desired in an urban residence.[10]

The Scots, in short, were given the kind of provision for town improvement and public health which the English and Welsh might have expected. The 1850 Act upgraded the model clauses Acts into a piece of fully-fledged permissive legislation, and allowed Scotland to do for itself, on the voluntary principle, what seemed to many people in the localities to have been forced upon England and Wales by the Public Health Act of 1848 and the operations of the General Board. There was apparently, during the twelve years that elapsed before the 1850 Act was repealed and replaced, no return made to parliament of the number of burghs and populous places which adopted this second General Police Act. But Mr Urquhart has discovered fifty-two adoptions, eleven of which were carried out by burghs

---

[7] Ibid. s. xix.
[8] Ibid. ss. xxxviii, xxxix. See ch. I.2, above.
[9] 13 & 14 Vict. c. 33, ss. xcviii–ci, cxxxvi, clxvii–clxxi.
[10] Ibid. ss. cclxxxviii–ccxciii.

which were trading in the first General Police Act for the Second.[11]

Once again, this was a respectable but not a spectacular number, and after 1858, when the Local Government Act was passed and towns in England and Wales found themselves, for the first time, in possession of even greater opportunities and powers than Scottish towns did, the feeling seems to have grown that further legislation was necessary. In 1860 parliament passed an Act to enable Scottish burghs to carry out sanitary measures and to make improvements without going to the expense of setting up and maintaining a police force. This was a stopgap measure, and it was repealed two years later when parliament passed yet another General Police Act for Scotland.[12] The new Act, which was known as Lindsay's Act, after Provost William Lindsay, a solicitor and businessman of Leith, who drafted it, contained 449 clauses, and was even more clearly divided into sections covering every aspect of town improvement and public health than its predecessor. Like the Local Government Act, the General Police Act of 1862 took account of the different circumstances of the various burghs. Some towns possessed private Acts. Some had adopted previous general Acts. Others had omitted to do anything at all. In royal and parliamentary burghs where there were no police Commissioners at all, the Town Councils were empowered to adopt the Act: in others where there were dual arrangements, the Commissioners under either a local Act or a general Act were empowered to adopt it. Places being neither royal nor parliamentary burghs, which had adopted the second General Police Act of 1850, were empowered to adopt the third through their Commissioners. Elsewhere, in populous places, which were now defined as localities with over 700 inhabitants, the Act could be adopted by householders. The Act covered all cases, and like its equivalent in England, it was widely taken up.

A return made in 1870 showed that ninety-six towns in Scotland had adopted the General Police Act of 1862 in

[11] Urquhart (1987), Table 2, pp. 246–9.
[12] 23 & 24 Vict. c. 96, and 25 & 26 Vict. c. 101.

whole or in part.[13] From Coldstream to Oban, and from Dalbeattie to Nairn, the beneficial effects of the Act were being felt. Thirty-seven years after the passage of the first General Police Act 136 burghs and populous places had taken advantage of the opportunities made available to them under the three permissive Acts of 1833, 1850, and 1862. The adoption experience of the Scottish burghs and the categories into which they fell can be summarised as follows:

16 burghs which had adopted the 1833 Act were still content with it

4 burghs which had adopted the 1833 Act had subsequently adopted the 1850 Act and were still content with that

7 burghs which had adopted the 1833 Act and had subsequently adopted the 1850 Act had adopted the 1862 Act

14 burghs which had adopted the 1833 Act and which had not adopted the 1850 Act had adopted the 1862 Act

20 burghs which had embarked upon the course of self-government by adopting the 1850 Act were still content with it

21 burghs which had embarked upon the course of self-government by adopting the 1850 Act had subsequently adopted the 1862 Act

54 burghs had embarked upon the course of self-government by adopting the 1862 Act[14]

The accounts of the adoption meetings held in Fife in the 1860s, to take just a single Scottish county as an example,

[13] *PP* 1870 LV pp. 763–74.
[14] Compiled from Urquhart (1985) and (1987) and *PP* 1870 LV, pp. 763–74, *General Police and Improvement (Scotland) Act (1862), Return of Burghs or Populous Places . . . where the . . . Act . . . is in Whole or in Part in force.* The categories are sound, but the figure given for the number of burghs and populous places in each category should be treated with caution. Some burghs which were apparently still soldiering on under the 1833 Act may have given it up, and some burghs and populous places which had adopted the Act of 1862 may have been omitted from the parliamentary return. *PP* 1871 LVIII, pp. 599–604, *Police (Scotland), Returns of all Burghs, Towns and Populous Places in Scotland in which . . .*

bear many resemblances to those held in the Isle of Wight and in the district round Huddersfield. Fife was a county with agriculture, market towns, a very important fishery, ports, and seaside resorts, and, at the western end round Kirkcaldy, collieries and ironworks. In June 1862, the *East of Fife Record* reported that the House of Commons had been occupied 'an entire morning sitting discussing in Committee the clauses of the new Police Bill for Scotland'. The paper praised the measure for 'the multiplicity of topics which it embraces', and promised its readers that the new legislation would be 'the means of saving a great amount of expenditure to burghs . . . by freeing them from the necessity of applying to parliament for local police bills'.[15] The *Fife Herald* agreed, saying that, 'All who had anything to do with the old Police Act had found it so deficient that they would have been obliged to have petitioned for a private one, had not this general Act fortunately passed, and saved them a great deal of trouble and expense.'[16]

In Scotland as in England, study groups were formed to go through the Act. At St Andrews the Provost was anxious to have the subject 'fully considered', and asked his brother Magistrates to join him 'in going over the whole of the clauses'.[17] At Pittenweem the Town Council appointed a committee to peruse the Act.[18] At Inverkeithing the householders set up a committee which recommended 'the adoption of the several clauses of the Act having reference principally to the water supply'.[19] What one misses, however, in Fife, even in towns like Inverkeithing, where the school-room in which the adoption meeting took place was 'crowded',[20] is the feeling of excitement that pervaded the public meetings in England. The ingredients were lacking. In the first place the novelty had worn off, for the Act was not the first but the third of its kind. In the second place, feelings against the Board of Supervision, which

the Police is regulated under the Act 13 & 14 Vict. c. 33 . . . and . . . under the Act 3 & 4 Will. IV. c. 46 is defective.

[15] *EFR* 28 June 1862, 2a.   [16] *FH* 15 Jan. 1863, 3f.
[17] *FJ* 5 Feb. 1863, 6ef.   [18] *EFR* 21 Sept. 1866, 3ab.
[19] *FH* 9 May 1867, 3de.   [20] Idem.

had been formed in 1845 to oversee the working of the Scottish Poor Law, did not run high, and the Scots had not been subjected to a General Board of Health. In an abrasive moment, the *Fife Herald* pronounced the clause which required a locality (in the case at issue, Dunfermline) to obtain the assent of the Sheriff 'to legalise the adoption of this General Police Act',

a rather formidable objection to the adoption of the Act at all by a free and independent burgh, as it gives the Sheriff, who is a functionary of the central government, a casting vote in one of the most important movements which a burgh can make, an organic change, and points the way to a further enlargement and extension of his power.[21]

But this was an alarmist view, and in Elie and Leslie the Sheriff's part in the procedure appears to have been welcomed.[22] Finally it is worth noticing that Scotland had escaped the divisive weighted-voting system favoured in England and Wales (though there were plural votes for business premises). Divisions between rich and poor rate-payers were less evident than they were in England, the householders were in control, and few people either hoped or feared that the Act would bring about a change in the personnel of local government.

Notwithstanding this slightly lower level of expectation, the Act was adopted, in the one county, in the course of eight years at a number of places (see Table 2). The most newsworthy of these adoptions appear to have been those where the Act was adopted in stages, and St Andrews, at least, was famous enough to be assured of extensive publicity. In 1863 Bailie Lees travelled all the way to Leith and asked Provost Lindsay whether they should take up only such clauses as they considered necessary, or adopt the whole Act. Lindsay answered that the way to proceed was 'to adopt the whole bill and select portions of it for enforcement as suited their case'.[23] His advice was probably based upon the fact that under Scottish law the Magistrates could 'exercise their own discretion in enforcing the Act by

[21] Ibid. 15 Jan. 1863, 3f.
[22] EFR 13 Jan. 1865, 3a; FH 14 Sept. 1865, 3g.
[23] FJ 5 Feb. 1863, 6ef.

TABLE IV.1. Adoption of the General Police Act

Place	Date	By whom	How much	Earlier adoptions
Dunfermline	January 1863	Commissioners	in whole	none
St Andrews	January 1863	Town Council	in part	1838, 1849
Elie	December 1864	Householders	in part	none
Elie	July 1865	Commissioners	more	1864
Leslie	September 1865	Householders	in part	none
St Andrews	January 1866	Town Council	more	1838, 1849, 1863
Pittenweem	September 1866	Town Council	in whole	1842
Elie	December 1866	Commissioners	remainder	1864, 1865
Leven	March 1867	Householders	in whole	1833
Inverkeithing	May 1867	Householders	in part	none
Leslie	November 1869	Commissioners	more	1865
Cupar	January 1870	Town Council	in part	1834, 1848, 1861[24]

[24] Compiled from PP 1867 LVI, pp. 547–56, *Police and Improvement (Scotland) Act, Returns . . . of Burghs or Populous Places in Scotland* where 'The General Police and Improvement (Scotland) Act, 1862' is 'in whole or in part' in force, and 1870 LV, pp. 763–74, *General Police and Improvement (Scotland) Act (1862), Return of Burghs or Populous Places . . . where the . . . Act . . . is in Whole or in Part in force*, and from Urquhart (1985) and (1987).

penalties and prosecutions'. All actions had to be brought before the Police Commission at the instance of the Procurator-fiscal, 'and as he is their servant, they can control him as to what acts he shall prosecute as offences'.[25]

Lindsay's counsel was not followed. At St Andrews, somewhat surprisingly in a seaside town, opponents, objecting to anything which would tend to increase the cost of lodgings, claimed to be taking the part of the visitors.[26] The first time the Town Council took a look at the Act, the following sections, according to the *Fife Herald*, were adopted:

Part 1st, section 4th, clause 40, the whole of section 6th, and also of 7th, except clauses 77 and 78; the whole of Part 2d; Part 3d, the whole of section 1st, except the 111th clause, and none of the other sections or clauses of this part; Part 4th, the whole of the clauses in sections 1 to 11 inclusive, except clauses [sic] 210 in section 9th; Part 5th, the whole of section 1st, clauses 254 and 258 in section 2d, the whole of sections 5th, 6th, and 7th, clauses 336-7-8-9 of section 9th, 344-5-6-7 of section 11th, 356-7 of section 12th, and the whole of the clauses in sections 13th and 14th; Part 6th, the whole of the clauses in sections 1st, 2d, 3d, 4th, 5th, and 6th; and the whole of Part 7th.[27]

The newspaper did not attempt to spell out what this all meant, which was that the Council resolved to constitute themselves as Commissioners under the Act, that they took power to carry out assessments and levy rates, and to appoint a Surveyor and an Inspector, that they agreed to carry out the 'ordinary' police purposes and the 'general' police regulations specified in the Act,[28] that they obtained

[25] Dr Adamson, quoting an unnamed Edinburgh advocate, *FH* 11 Jan. 1866, 2gh, 3a.

[26] *FJ* 5 Feb. 1863, 6ef.

[27] *FH* 5 Feb. 1863, 3g.

[28] The ordinary police purposes were lighting, cleansing, paving, naming streets and numbering houses, improving streets and removing obstructions, laying out new streets, looking after public sewers, the drainage of houses, and the supply of water. The general police regulations involved precautions during repairs to buildings and in relation to old and ruinous tenements, nuisances and obstructions in the streets, drunks, street shows, brokers and pawnbrokers, articles lost or stolen, the suppression of vagrants, places of public resort and disorderly houses, harbouring constables and disorderly persons, restrictions upon the sale of spirituous liquors, fires, ventilation, cleansing, slaughterhouses, and markets.

powers to make by-laws, to borrow money, to purchase lands, and execute works, and undertook to promote the public health. Can it really be that in St Andrews every ratepayer slept with a copy of the Act under his pillow, and was able to make out for himself that the Town Council was *not* taking powers to appoint a Medical Officer of Health, that it was *not* proposing to insist upon owners of houses and tenements installing water-closets, that it was *not* accepting responsibility for making shopkeepers give accurate weight, and that hackney-carriages were to be allowed to continue to ply for hire without regulation?

Upon the second occasion, the Council became involved in splitting hairs, and found itself taking legal opinion whether it could or could not adopt part of the 251st clause of the Act. This was the catch-all clause for dealing with ferocious dogs, workmen who mended casks, boys who let off fireworks, and women who beat carpets in the streets. This time it was Dr Adamson who sought the advice of Provost Lindsay, who took the view that 'the whole clause in its integrity must be adopted—that is, you cannot adopt the half of it.'[29]

Finally, the cautious approach taken by the Town Council at St Andrews can be compared to that of the rate-payers and the Commissioners at Elie, whose confidence grew with experience, and who succeeded, in three steps taken over a period of twenty-five months, in adopting the whole of the Act. Here, the outcome of the first adoption meeting was celebrated in verse. The 'fors showed pluck', the ''gainsts gaed aff in smoke', and the 'Shirra', who sat down to a celebration dinner with the promoters,[30] was praised for having 'set a' right', and 'Made brithers o' us a''.

> Is this a time to think o' wark,
>   Or e'en to play the pipes?
> Gie me my hat, I'll tae the street,
>   And see the blazing lights.

---

[29] *FH* 11 Jan. 1866, 2gh, 3a.   [30] *EFR* 27 Jan. 1865, 2d, 3a.

For there's nae place like oor wee toon—
There's nae place ava',
That's half sae licht as Elie toon,
Frae Taft to Rotten Raw.[31]

3. INTELLECTUALS AND JUDGES

In the early 1860s critics of permissive legislation fastened upon two points. The first concerned the freedom which localities enjoyed not to adopt permissive Acts, or even, having adopted them, to give them up again. The second was the failure of localities which had adopted permissive Acts to carry out their provisions.

Freedom not to adopt was fundamental to the concept of permissive legislation. If local liberty was worth having, this was the price that had to be paid, and here the localities were ill-served by the political philosophers. Of the two most widely read British philosophers of the 1860s, John Stuart Mill and Herbert Spencer, one failed to perceive that self-government in a local community was an important part of human liberty, and the other, who did at one time see it, betrayed it.[1]

Mill, who thought that 'the conduct of a large portion of the affairs of society should be left in the hands of the persons immediately interested in them',[2] was, nevertheless, too obsessed with individuals to pay much attention to localities, and the chapter on Local Government in the essay on *Representative Government* scarcely mentions permissive legislation.[3] Spencer, on the other hand, believed in a fundamental dichotomy between 'military' societies and 'industrial' societies. Centralisation appeared to him to be 'an essential trait of the militant type', and

[31] Ibid. 13 Jan. 1865, 3a.
[1] Of all the Liberal philosophers the one most likely to have appreciated local liberty was T. H. Green. But Green published little, the public knew nothing about him until he secured a kind of academic canonisation after his death in 1882, and his work upon the Oxford School Board and in favour of local option (in the licensing of public houses) has scarcely received, from his biographers, the attention which it deserves.
[2] J. S. Mill, *Principles of Political Economy* (2 vols. 1848), ii, bk. 5, ch. XI, p. 513.
[3] Ch. XV, 'Of Local Representative Bodies'.

decentralisation 'an essential trait of the industrial type'. One result of the advances made by industrial societies must be 'that the inhabitants of each locality will object to be controlled by the inhabitants of other localities'. This, he thought, would lead to 'the carrying of local rule to the greatest practicable limit'.[4] But having reached that conclusion Spencer was temperamentally unfitted to take the side of the localities in their struggle against the central government. 'Sanitary administration by the State' was wrong, not because it wounded local feelings, but because it diminished individual responsibility. It followed, therefore, that sanitary administration by local authorities was wrong too—what Spencer called 'aggression'. A local authority, Spencer concluded, was not good because it was local, but bad because it was an authority. Spencer's last word was that all measures of town improvement and public health ought to be carried out in accordance with the principles governing the conduct of an 'industrial' society.

Houses might readily be drained on the same mercantile principle that they are now supplied with water. . . . Paving and lighting would properly fall to the management of house-owners. Were there no public provision for such conveniences, houseowners would quickly find it their interest to furnish them. Some speculative building society having set the example of improvement in this direction, competition would do the rest.[5]

Not for Spencer the distinctions which his contemporaries drew between public ownership, public management, and public supervision and inspection. This passage also shows an astonishing degree of unawareness of the extent to which, in an 'industrial' society, business, or private enterprise, itself constructs authoritarian structures, and coerces individuals. It is bad sociology, and it is also remarkable in another way. With his preference for voluntary actions, Spencer might have been expected to observe that the alternative to compulsory rating was not so much

[4] H. Spencer, *Political Institutions* (1882 edn.), pp. 743–4.
[5] H. Spencer, *Social Statics* (1892), pp. 214–15.

entrepreneurial provision, as town improvement by public subscription. There were examples which he might have noticed. At Newport a street beside the parish church was widened by subscription.[6] In Moldgreen there had at one time been talk of 'a subscription to be made to supply water and gas to the village'.[7] The practice was not, then, unknown in England, and was apparently common in Scotland. In West Anstruther, the inhabitants refused to adopt the Lindsay Act, and were condemned by the *East of Fife Record* for striking a better dirty than taxed attitude.[8] For many years their reply to this was to continue to judge for themselves what was necessary, and do it their own way, which was by voluntary subscription. As late as 1893 they held a concert to raise money for the paving fund,[9] and the following year, in August, the town held 'a grand bazaar to raise funds to reduce the debt of, and to effect some improvements in, the burgh of Anstruther-Wester'. Opening the bazaar, Mr Scott-Davidson said, 'Roads and streets, and other improvements for burghs, towns, villages, and county places were all very much needed. They were all interested in these improvements . . . it was universally admitted that a bazaar was the best medium for collecting money for all improvements.'

'The success of bazaars', he continued, 'was largely due to the great interest that the ladies took in them', and the Provost himself thanked the 'thousand fingers' which had been busy preparing for the event, and announced that the local MP had contributed 'generously to their funds'.[10] The sale raised £180 9s. 10d., and with a delightful touch of social irony, the goods that remained unsold in well-to-do Anstruther-Wester were disposed of four months later at knock-down prices in East Anstruther, a poorer community which had accepted responsibility for cleansing itself, and levied an improvement rate, ever since it adopted the first General Police Act in 1841.[11]

Liberty not to adopt a permissive Act was fundamental. So, too, the localities might have been heard to murmur,

[6] *IND* 15 Oct. 1853, 5d. [7] *HC* 7 Nov. 1857, 8de.
[8] *EFR* 10 Mar. 1876, 2bc. [9] Ibid. 17 Nov. 1893, 2f.
[10] Ibid. 24 Aug. 1894, 2de. [11] Ibid. 21 Dec. 1894, 2c.

was the freedom to give one up again. The Lighting and Watching Act of 1833 contained clauses setting out a formal procedure for de-adoption, and in his handbook to the Act, J. Tidd Pratt warned Inspectors elected under the Act that 'it would not be advisable . . . to enter into any contract for a longer time than they themselves are to continue in office'.[12] Lawyers are paid to warn their clients to be cautious, but the language Pratt used did not suggest that he thought a decision to abandon the Act was an unlikely eventuality. The County Constabulary Act of 1839 was actually amended in 1840 to allow the Justices, if they were 'of opinion that the Constables . . . are no longer needed in their County', to inform the Secretary of State, and with his permission to abandon the Act.[13] No formal machinery to enable Local Boards to relieve themselves of their responsibilities, or householders to terminate the existence of their Local Board, was included in the Public Health Act of 1848, the Local Government Act of 1858, and the General Police Act of 1862, and the point did not pass without notice in the localities. At Kirkburton, John Carter asked according to one newspaper whether if they adopted the Act they could get out of it,[14] and according to another whether they could take the Act on a year's trial.[15] At Mirfield, when Mr Chadwick informed the ratepayers that it was like taking a wife, if they adopted the Act they would have it for ever, a voice popped up 'Can we have a divorce?'[16] The lack of a statutory de-adoption procedure tempted the members of Boards who wanted to give up, just to stop attending meetings and to disappear. R. A. Lewis has called attention to the case of Bromyard, where the Local Board elected under the 1848 Act refused to meet, and so 'committed suicide'.[17] Hitchin, too, which had adopted the 1858 Act, subsequently allowed it to fall into abeyance: 'no elections are held, and a receiver has

[12] J. T. Pratt, *The Law relating to Lighting and Watching of Parishes, 3 & 4 Will. IV c. 90* (1856), p. 46.
[13] 3 & 4 Vict. c. 88, s. xxiv.
[14] *HE* 3 Mar. 1860, 3cd.
[15] *HC* 3 Mar. 1860, 8cd.
[16] *HE* 21 Mar. 1863, 8d.
[17] Lewis, *Chadwick and the Public Health Movement*, p. 302.

been appointed to receive the rates and pay the expenses of the works carried out.'[18] In Scotland critics referred to Beith, where the Commissioners resigned in May 1869, and the burgh became defunct, and to Lossiemouth and Branderburgh, where, at the annual meeting for the election of new Commissioners in June 1869, no new Commissioners were elected and the Act was allowed to fall into abeyance.[19]

The cases of towns which sought to escape from a permissive Act after they had adopted it were notorious. But there were not many of them, and it was much more common for the Commissioners in a locality which had purchased a local Act of its own or adopted a general Act, to fail to carry out its provisions. As the second Report of the Sanitary Commission put it in 1871, 'The powers of the local Act being granted to the locality on application to Parliament come to be regarded as weapons to be used or laid aside at the pleasure of the Authority on whose petition they were granted, rather than as powers accompanied by a duty to put them into force.'[20] Much the same consideration applied to places which adopted the Local Government Act, or the General Police Act. At Newport, as we have seen, the Town Council sought reassurance that they would not be 'compelled to carry out any of its provisions' not suited to their requirements, before they would adopt the Act.[21] At Marsden in Almondbury the Local Board, according to the *Huddersfield Examiner*, when first elected, had 'no intention of spending any money in new local improvements'.[22] In Scotland the Lindsay doctrine was that burghs should adopt the 1862 Act *in toto* and then pick and choose which parts to enforce and neglect the remainder.[23]

The crucial defect about permissive legislation was the

[18] *PP* 1871 XXXV, p. 36, *RSC2, Vol. i, Report*, p. 30.
[19] *PP* 1870 LV, pp. 764, 767, *General Police and Improvement (Scotland) Act (1862), Return of Burghs or Populous Places . . . where the . . . Act . . . is in Whole or in Part in force*, pp. 2, 5.
[20] *PP* 1871 XXXV, p. 42, *RSC2, Vol. i, Report*, p. 36.
[21] *IWO* 26 Jan. 1867, 3f.
[22] *HE* 4 Aug. 1860, 3c.
[23] See ch. IV.2, above.

inability or unwillingness of the Courts to provide a remedy. In English law everything turned upon the meaning attributed to the word 'may' in a statute. Far back in 1832 Mr Justice Tindal had ruled that 'where the object and intent of the statute manifestly requires it, words that appear to be permissive only, shall be construed as obligatory'.[24] In the early 1850s Judges handed down conflicting decisions. In the case of *Jones* v. *Harrison*, which came before the Court of Exchequer in April 1851, Chief Baron Pollock recognised that 'the question depends upon the meaning of the word "may"', and taking as his guide the rule that 'we ought to construe statutes according to the plain and obvious meaning of the language used', he concluded that the word, 'may' meant that the person named had the power to do the specified act or not to do it at his discretion.[25]

Eight months later, in *Macdougall* v. *Paterson*, Chief Justice Jervis, in the Court of Common Pleas, saw 'very cogent reasons for differing' from the construction delivered in the Court of Exchequer. The word 'may' in this instance was not used 'to give a discretion, but to confer a power . . . and the exercise of such power depends, not upon . . . the discretion . . . but upon the proof of the particular case'.[26] Two months later still, in February 1852 a third case came before the Chief Justice of the Court of Queen's Bench. Lord Campbell referred to the advantage he enjoyed and the embarrassment he felt at finding that this question had 'already been decided by the Court of the Exchequer and the Court of Common Pleas, and decided different ways'. 'Having . . . considered very attentively the words of the statute and the reasons given by the learned Judges of the two Courts, we agree with those of the Common Pleas, which exhaust the subject . . .'.[27]

The question at issue in these cases related to the recovery of a debt. Had the same interpretation been carried over into the sphere of town improvement and public health, it

[24] *Crisp* v. *Bunbury, English Reports* 131, p. 448.
[25] *Jones* v. *Harrison*, ibid. 155, p. 569.
[26] *Macdougall* v. *Paterson*, ibid. 138, pp. 672–80.
[27] *Crake* v. *Powell*, ibid. 118, pp. 747–8.

might have been possible to arrive at a situation in which a clause saying that the local authority 'may' remove refuse from the street, would have been interpreted to mean that, if there was refuse in the street (which there might not be), the local authority had a duty to remove it. Alas, this was not what happened, and the crucial decision appears to have been taken by Lord Campbell himself in *ex parte* Bassett in January 1857.

The case involved a drain belonging to John Parsons in Ham, Surrey, which needed cleansing. The Sanitary Inspector appointed by the Local Board of Health applied to the Justices for an order to compel Parsons to cleanse the drain within fourteen days, and if this was not done to authorise him to enter the premises, carry out the work, and recover the costs. The Justices granted the order, and the Sanitary Inspector then omitted to serve it on Parsons (the reports do not explain why, and we can only guess, but perhaps because Parsons was himself a member of the Local Board and his employer). Bassett, who lived downstream from the offensive drain, was aggrieved by this failure on the part of the Inspector. He went to the Justices, and at his request the clerk to the Justices caused a copy of the order to be served on Parsons. Nothing happened, and Bassett served notices on the Inspector and chairman of the Local Board. After another fortnight had passed, he served more notices, and added that 'in default of your compliance with this request . . . I shall apply to the Court of Queen's Bench for a writ of *mandamus*'.[28] When the application came before the court, Mr Bovill argued that there must be some means of enforcing the Act on behalf of an aggrieved party. The statute enacted that any person not obeying the order for abatement to the satisfaction of the Justices should be liable to a fine of 10*s*. a day, and that 'the local authority may . . . enter the premises to which the order relates, and remove or abate the nuisance'. At this point Lord Campbell pounced, 'The word is "may", not "shall".' Mr Bovill started to contend that this section of the Act imposed a duty which the

[28] Ibid. 119, pp. 1251–2.

Board was bound to perform for the benefit of the public. But Lord Campbell repeated that this was not obligatory, and could not be made the ground for a mandamus. Bassett could not compel the Inspector or the Local Board to act, though, if they chose, the Justices could fine Parsons 10s. a day for committing an offence.[29] It turned out, then, as one barrister put it, that in any case where the provisions of the Act were permissive, 'there can be, since the cases will be cases of discretion, no legal "default in enforcing the provisions" '.[30] That being so, it is astonishing that the politicians charged with the responsibility for piloting the Local Government Act to the statute-book did not attempt to provide a remedy.

In Scotland aggrieved parties did not experience quite the same difficulty with the word 'may'. Even so, the Scottish courts do not, in the mid-century, appear to have been much more successful than the English ones in coming to the assistance of towns which fell into the procedural traps lying in wait among the clauses of permissive general Acts. In 1850 Galashiels was anxious to adopt the first General Police Act. But the Act called for the minutes of the adoption meeting to be reported to 'the Sheriff of the County within which such burgh shall be situated'. It was Galashiels's misfortune that the area which was to be included within the district of the new Commissioners lay in two counties, Selkirkshire and Roxburghshire. The minutes had been carried to the Sheriff of Selkirkshire. The legality of the adoption was challenged, and the conclusion reached by Lord Mackenzie was that in this instance 'the Act can be worked neither by one nor two Sheriffs, that is to say, it cannot be worked at all'. His fellow Judges concurred, though they had the grace to add that they did so with reluctance.[31] Fortunately for the householders of Galashiels the Judges' decision made little difference, because the second General Police Act of 1850 provided for the case of burghs lying in two counties, and

[29] *The Times*, 28 Jan. 1857, 8ef.
[30] E. Jenkins, 'The Legal Aspects of Sanitary Reform', *Transactions of the National Association for the Promotion of Social Science* 1866, p. 487.
[31] *Session Cases*, 2 ser. XII, pp. 476–81.

Galashiels, which had a busy year, adopted the new Act in October 1850.[32]

The best known of all the cases which came before the Scottish courts were those of *Anderson* v. *Widnell* and *Tod* v. *Anderson*, which were heard in November 1868 and January 1869. Both concerned the adoption of the General Police Act of 1862 at Lasswade. The Act stipulated that the householders attending the adoption meeting must at once proceed to decide the number of Commissioners needed to put it into execution. This formal requirement had been overlooked. The promoters failed to persuade the Sheriff to call a second meeting to determine the number of Commissioners, but did later prevail upon him to call another meeting at which six householders were declared to have been elected. The new Commissioners' standing was challenged, and in *Anderson* v. *Widnell* it was decided that the Act had been validly adopted but that a subsequent meeting had no power to fix the number of Commissioners. The elections which had taken place, and all the proceedings of the 'Commissioners' thereafter were set aside. This left Lasswade in a deadlock, because the Act could not be operated without Commissioners, and having once been declared a populous place by the Sheriff, Lasswade no longer fell into the category of places which could adopt the Act. But there was still a ray of hope. In giving judgement, the Lord Justice Clerk, Lord Glenalmond, had added that there might be 'a power resident in the court to direct that a meeting be called to remedy the error'. He did, to be fair, add that he saw formidable objections to that course, but he thought there were 'some plausible grounds on which such an exercise of our praetorian power might be vindicated'.[33] This was an open invitation to the disappointed parties to come back to the court, which they did. They might have spared the effort. The Lord Justice Clerk now took the view that it was no part of his proper province to dispense parties from the formal obligations contained in a statute, and indignantly delivered his opinion that before interfering

[32] Urquhart (1987), Table 2, p. 248.
[33] *Session Cases*, 3 ser. VII, Court of Session, pp. 81–6.

in any case in the exercise of our *nobile officium*, we must be satisfied of two things, viz. (1) that there is a necessity which requires the remedy of an evil, and (2) that there is a cure direct and palpable for the evil experienced. Now I am of opinion that the circumstances here are not such as to raise a case of necessity . . . I confess that on reading the General Police Act it does not appear to me that it is all-important or a matter of public concern that this burgh, or any burgh, should have police commissioners.

For his part Lord Cowan pointed to the length of time which had elapsed since the adoption. He did not 'by any means say that we might not have interfered had this petition been presented within a week or two after the date of the blunder'. But in the meantime a new Act amending the General Police Act of 1862 had lowered the franchise from £10 to £4 and changed the constituency,[34] and he agreed with the Lord Justice Clerk's conclusion. He went on, however, to suggest that there was nothing to prevent the parties from beginning the proceedings for the adoption of the statute *de novo*. Lord Benholme distanced himself from Lord Cowan, and in effect took much the same line as the Lord Justice Clerk. Lord Neaves in turn differed from Lord Benholme, and agreed pretty well with Lord Cowan.[35]

Lasswade's experience suggests that the Scottish Judges, fearful lest they be accused of taking sides between the parties in a town, were not likely to go out of their way to assist a burgh caught in the snares of permissive legislation. Turriff was more fortunate. Here, the Commissioners of Police elected under the second General Police Act of 1850 unanimously resolved, on 24 November 1873, to adopt the Lindsay Act in whole. The resolution was reported to the Sheriff who issued the necessary deliverance. It then transpired that in adopting the new Act the Commissioners under the old Act had abolished themselves, and that new elections would have to be held. At this point accusations were made that the correct procedures for the

[34] 31 & 32 Vict. c. 102.
[35] *Session Cases*, 3 ser. VII, pp. 412–15. I am indebted to R. M. Urquhart for drawing my attention to a similar case involving the same Sheriff at Penicuik which was, in effect, determined by what took place in *Anderson* v. *Widnell* and *Tod* v. *Anderson*.

adoption had not, in every respect, been followed. The Sheriff heard the complainants, agreed that they had a case, and (despite his former deliverance) suspended the proceedings. The burgh was then in a quandary. As a consequence of their attempt to transfer from the Second General Police Act to the Third the Commissioners now found themselves unable either to move forward to the new Act or to resume operations under the old one. Their predicament was brought before the courts in the case of *Stirling and Ferguson* v. *Hutcheon and others* (Commissioners of Police for the burgh of Turriff). Lord Mackenzie's judgement that the law did not allow him to get behind the Sheriff's deliverance left the burgh in a state of paralysis. But upon appeal to the Inner House of the Court of Session, the Lord President, Lord Glencorse, and his three colleagues ruled that the Sheriff's deliverance need not be held to be final unless the Police Commissioners' resolutions themselves had been good. The Judges gave their decision in May 1874. The Turriff Commissioners resumed work under the 1850 Act, and four months later, after observing the formalities and avoiding all the pitfalls, they adopted the Lindsay Act.[36]

Burghs which had run into difficulties were offered new ways of escape in 1877, when an Act was passed to allow the Court of Session to make any order which might be necessary to enable a burgh to recover from an error or a lapse in the adoption of the General Police Act.[37] Beith was never revived, but in 1878 the court permitted Dunblane to emerge from a situation in which it had been left without any Commissioners.[38] Three years later, in 1881, the court enabled the Commissioners at Lasswade to be reconstituted.[39] Finally, in 1890, more than 20 years after their Commissioners had ceased to meet, the householders of Lossiemouth and Branderburgh, who had adopted the Act and then allowed it to fall into abeyance, and 'were now

[36] *Session Cases*, 4 ser. I, pp. 935–43, 25 May 1874, and Urquhart (1987), pp. 239–42.
[37] 40 & 41 Vict. c. 22.
[38] Information from R. M. Urquhart.
[39] Idem.

desirous that the proceedings for the carrying out of the said Police Act within the burgh should be continued', petitioned the Court to allow them to hold new elections 'as nearly as possible, as if the failure . . . had not taken place', and this was granted.[40] Nothing could indicate more clearly than these cases the supremacy, throughout the United Kingdom, of statute law. Responsibility for deciding who was to carry out running repairs to legislation, like the responsibility for legislation itself, lay with parliament.

4. 1866–1875: CENTRAL AND LOCAL GOVERNMENT

It is difficult to discern much method about the way in which parliament handled the problems of central–local government relations in the middle of the nineteenth century. But one general principle which does seem to have been observed was that of encouraging the spread of ratepayers' and representative institutions. After 1828 parliament frowned upon the creation of new self-perpetuating bodies of Commissioners (those at Ryde must have been among the last), and increasingly insisted, in both public general and in private Bill legislation, upon the elective principle. Finally, in 1858, parliament passed the Local Government Act, which placed 'before the inhabitants of every locality, for the first time in the history of our civilisation, the power to do all for themselves'.[1] Unfortunately some localities were slow to adopt the Acts which parliament passed for their benefit, and others which did adopt them failed to operate them efficiently. For a short while, perhaps, MPs were inclined to sit back and take the view that with patience everything would come out right in the end. A good example would prove contagious. Localities where it was possible to walk of an evening to a permissive public bath-house or a permissive public library along streets laid out under an adopted Act and lit by permissively installed gas-lamps would attract residents.

[40] *Session Cases*, 4 ser. XVII, 18 July 1890.
[1] Lambert, 'Central and Local Relations' (1962), p. 123.

House values would rise, and other towns would want to follow suit. Certainly, this was the view taken by Tom Taylor, the Head of the Local Government Act Office, who thought that

all that government can properly be called upon to do is to place the means of local improvement as cheaply and simply as possible within reach of the population. . . . The good sense which can appreciate the advantages of cleanliness and health, the intelligence which can determine the means by which these advantages may best be secured . . . must be contributed by the public. . . . Better, in all matters of local concern, a real progress of local opinion, however slow, than the premature and delusive action of the central authority.[2]

For a few years, then, Whitehall and Westminster were in harmony. But the argument was reminiscent of the views of Herbert Spencer, and was open to the same objections.

Those who sought a ready remedy for the deficiencies of permissive legislation returned to the idea of compulsion. In 1865 a new Sewage Utilisation Act was passed which applied to the whole of Great Britain, even though it had to reach down, in an old-fashioned way, to the unit of the parish to do it.[3] Then, in 1866, parliament turned to the question of enforcement. Since the courts were unwilling to compel local authorities to carry out the provisions of the Acts which they had adopted, parliament began, once again, to look more favourably upon schemes to enable the executive departments of state to do so. According to Sir John Simon, who had been Medical Officer to the General Board of Health from 1855 to 1858, and who was now Medical Officer to the Privy Council, the breakthrough came with the Sanitary Act of 1866.[4] Clause 49, whose wording was altered to make it more effective after the change of government at the end of June, enabled anybody, whose health was endangered by the failure of a local authority to provide or to maintain sufficient sewers, to provide or to maintain a supply of wholesome fresh water, or (where it had been adopted) to enforce 'the Provisions of the Local Government Act', to make a

---

[2] Ibid. p. 128.   [3] 28 & 29 Vict. c. 75.   [4] 29 & 30 Vict. c. 90.

complaint to the Secretary of State. The Secretary of State could then conduct an inquiry, issue an order requiring the defaulting authority to put things right, and, if the local authority refused to move, appoint a contractor to carry out the work, and recover the cost through the Court of Queen's Bench. A contemporary, A. P. Stewart, writing 'On the Results of Permissive Sanitary Legislation', rejoiced 'that Parliament, which at first prescribed no remedy for the obstructiveness of local authorities', had at last provided that 'a single complainant may call a recusant corporation to account'.[5] In his memoir Sir John Simon recalled how 'the grammar of common sanitary legislation acquired the novel virtue of an imperative mood'.[6] In 1961 Dr Gutchen adjudged that 'a stroke of the pen' had 'transformed the permissive powers of the local authorities into compulsory ones',[7] and identified this clause as the turning-point in central–local government relations. The clause was used, people did complain, and R. J. Lambert, the historian of the Local Government Act Office, found that at least 115 inquiries took place in five years.[8] In seven instances the Secretary of State made use of the full powers granted to him to carry out the works which a stubborn local authority refused to undertake. But it may be as well to remember that this clause, which would, indeed, have been of assistance to Bassett, could not be enforced in Scotland, because the only way of putting it into operation lay through the Court of Queen's Bench, whose writ did not run north of the border.[9] Parliamentary draughtsmen were still clumsy when asked to prepare legislation covering the whole of Great Britain.

The passage of clause 49 put new heart into the centralists. Adoptive legislation began to be reinterpreted as a compromise forced upon the legislature by the strength and obduracy of local interests. To a sanitary reformer

[5] A. P. Stewart, 'On the Results of Permissive Sanitary Legislation', *Transactions of the National Association for the Promotion of Social Science* 1866, p. 500.
[6] Sir John Simon, *English Sanitary Institutions* (1890), p. 299.
[7] R. M. Gutchen, 'Local Improvements and Centralization in Nineteenth Century England', *Historical Journal*, 1961, pp. 91–2.
[8] Lambert, 'Central and Local Relations', p. 140.
[9] T. C. Smout, *A Century of the Scottish People, 1830–1950* (1986), p. 42.

there was 'no greater bugbear than a permissive enactment', because 'the wise and beneficent intentions of the
legislature are defeated by the passive resistance or dogged
opposition of the local authorities, who will not avail themselves of the ample permissive powers which the law gives
them.'[10] In the *Transactions* of the National Association for
the Promotion of Social Science, a barrister, E. Jenkins,
said that 'the complaint now is, that unless the statutes
specifically ordain that certain things shall be done, the
authorities will not do them.'[11] From every side the criticisms poured in. One critic who admitted that 'many of
our Local Boards . . . have done much for the improvement of their towns',[12] remained convinced that 'so long
as the adoption of a Public Health Act is optional with the
inhabitants . . . strong efforts will be made by a parish-
vestry party to exempt their little sphere of petty authority
from legal responsibility.' The remedy was to divide the
whole of Great Britain into sanitary districts.

All analogy is against restricting laws of general benefit to
particular places . . . what would have been the result of limiting that great and beneficial social reform, the Poor Law Amendment Act, to parishes which petitioned for its adoption? What
would be thought of a Constabulary Act, which enabled certain
districts, avowing themselves to be particularly honest, moral,
and quiet, to claim freedom from the visits of the police?[13]

Adoptive legislation, had come about, it was now alleged,
in cases where 'Her Majesty's government had not the
courage' to pass a compulsory measure.[14]

Everything now began to move in the same direction.
Paradoxically, both what had been achieved under adoptive legislation and what had not now told in favour of
compulsion. So many localities in England and Wales had
adopted the Act of 1858, so many places in Scotland had

[10] A. P. Stewart, 'Permissive Sanitary Legislation', pp. 491, 487.
[11] Ibid. p. 489.
[12] H. W. Rumsey, 'On Sanitary Legislation and Administration', a paper parts
of which were read to the Public Health section of the National Association for
the Promotion of Social Science in Oct. 1857 (1858), p. 13.
[13] Ibid. p. 9.
[14] Knatchbull-Hugessen, *PD* CCXXV, 460, 24 June 1875.

adopted the Act of 1862, that it ceased to be impossible to think in terms of coercing the remainder. So many of the authorities which had adopted the Acts did not take full advantage of the powers they had obtained that it became practical politics to talk in terms of replacing them under some form of central supervision. In parliament, after the second Reform Act, a new man, Knatchbull-Hugessen, announced that his generation was ready 'to knock down the wall of permissive legislation'.[15] In the localities, too, there appears to have been a change of mood, and in the early 1870s towns which had stood out against the General Board and taken the permissive road, looked on complacently while government prepared to deal with the remainder.[16]

Revived centralism scored its next major success in Scotland, where an Act of 1867 turned the Board of Supervision, which had hitherto been concerned simply with the poor law, into the authority with responsibility for sanitary matters.[17] The Board was given power to compel defaulting authorities to act, and the Act provided for the commands of the Board to be approved by the Court of Session before they were issued.[18] This was presented as a citizens' guarantee against the abuse of power, and so in a way it was. But such an involvement of the judiciary in the certification of an executive order, meaning that there could be no appeal against it, finds no parallel in England and Wales, and may not have been the best way of preserving the liberty of the citizen.[19]

In England and Wales the campaign to substitute compulsory for permissive legislation resulted in the appointment of the Sanitary Commission, with C. B. Adderley as Chairman, in 1869. The members of the Commission listened politely to Tom Taylor, representing the Local Government Act Office, as he argued in favour of continuing to trust the localities and leaving the adoption of the

[15] *PD* CCXXV, 466, 24 June 1875.
[16] Lambert, 'Central and Local Relations' (1962), p. 144.
[17] 30 & 31 Vict. c. 101.
[18] Ibid. ss. 96–8.
[19] *PP* 1871 XXXV, p. 697, *RSC2, Vol. iii, Minutes of Evidence from November 1869 to June 1870*, p. 139, Qns. 11,118–20.

1858 Act to circumstances 'which are tending in that direction'.[20] Taylor's evidence does not seem to have carried much weight. It was known that he wrote comedies, was art critic of *The Times*, and contributed to *Punch*, and he was suspected of being a dilettante. The Commission was more impressed by evidence showing that, even with weighted voting, the small ratepayers managed to outvote the 'intelligent inhabitants'. At Biggleswade 'a mass came to the meeting who refused to pass the resolution for introducing the Local Government Act'. At Dorking 'efforts . . . at adoption were long outvoted by a vast number of small proprietors of cottages.' In Lincoln there was much difficulty in inducing the Corporation to adopt the Act, 'the opposition chiefly arising from the owners of small tenements', and when the Act was adopted all those members of the Corporation who had voted in favour 'were expelled' upon seeking re-election.[21] In many cases, the Commission concluded, sanitary reforms were 'rendered impossible by the hostility of inhabitants of the poorest class'.[22] The fact that the Local Government Acts took effect only by the voluntary adoption of ratepayers or their representatives, was alone enough 'to account for the very partial operation of the law'.[23] Having heard so much evidence unfavourable to the poorer ratepayers, the members of the Commission concluded that in England and Wales the numerical value of the votes cast must at all costs continue to rise 'according to property, as is now the case under the Public Health and Local Government Acts'.[24]

The members of the Commission took care, however, to distance themselves from the arbitrary governments of Europe, which furnished examples of 'simpler plans, more uniform practice, and more systematic codification of law'. Under the French system, 'the symmetry of the plan seems to be perfect', but the Commission warned that it

[20] *PP* 1868–9 XXXII, p. 314, *RSC1, with the Minutes of Evidence up to 5 August 1869*, p. 14, Qn. 98.
[21] *PP* 1871 XXXV, p. 379, *RSC2, Vol. ii, Arrangement of Sanitary Statutes, Analysis of Evidence, Precis of Oral Evidence &c.*, p. 185.
[22] Ibid. p. 36, *RSC2* p. 30.
[23] Ibid. p. 27, *RSC2* p. 21.
[24] Ibid. p. 36, *RSC2* p. 30.

rested 'on the central power only', and was 'wholly wanting in that pervading spirit in which consist local energy and national life'.[25] In England, on the other hand, 'the principle of local self-government has been generally recognized as of the essence of our national vigour.'[26] 'So completely is self government the habit and quality of Englishmen, that the country would resent any Central Authority undertaking the duties of the local executive.'[27]

Having delivered themselves of these meaningful but perhaps somewhat ritual sentiments, the Commissioners advised the nation that local government for purposes of public health and town improvement was so important that every locality, without exception, ought to have it. Drawing courage from the success of Gladstone's first ministry in establishing elective local education boards throughout the country, they recommended a new law, whose provisions should apply to every locality in the land. Consequently, as they said, 'the whole principle of "adoption" as found in the existing Statutes, will fall to the ground'.[28] But, then, 'the Central Authority . . . must . . . avoid taking to itself the actual work of local government.' Everything must be done to confine the role of the central government to that of supervision only. A new department should be set up, but it 'must steer clear of the rock on which the General Board was wrecked'. 'The knowledge that power is in reserve together with a natural reluctance to be superseded in the management of their own affairs' would be a sufficient stimulus to the local authorities.[29]

In England and Wales these recommendations resulted in three Acts. The first, in 1871, established a Local Government Board, which took over responsibility for the supervision both of the Poor Law, and of all measures of town improvement and public health, just as the Board of Supervision in Scotland had done.[30] The Bill was introduced by Stansfeld, who denied that it 'was an effort to

[25] Ibid. pp. 22, 24, *RSC2* pp. 16, 18.
[26] Ibid. p. 22, *RSC2* p. 16.
[27] Ibid. p. 42, *RSC2* p. 36.
[28] Ibid. p. 83, *RSC2* p. 77.
[29] Ibid. pp. 41–2, *RSC2* pp. 35–6.
[30] 34 & 35 Vict. c. 70.

introduce the thin end of the wedge of a centralising system'.[31] He was seconded by Sir Charles Adderley, as he had now become, who declared that the object of the Bill, like that of the Sanitary Commission, was 'to perfect and develop local government', which had 'been made a matter of option' by previous statutes. Under the permissive system the country had become a patchwork of cleansed and unclean places, and in order to set local government 'at work throughout the country', and to spread and universalise the benefits, it was necessary to charge a government department with the responsibility for ensuring that local authorities were active and that the standards they enforced were 'uniform'.[32]

A second Act in 1872 divided the whole of England and Wales into Urban Sanitary Authorities (USAs) and Rural Sanitary Authorities (RSAs).[33] Local Boards established under the Public Health Act of 1848 and the Local Government Act of 1858 became USAs. In the country districts, the Sanitary Commission had recognised that 'the Justices of the Peace, not being representative, cannot properly execute a Statute which will involve considerable expenditure of a fund derived from local rates.[34] The parishes charged with carrying out the Sewage Utilisation Act of 1865 and the Sanitary Act of 1866 were too small. That being so, there was no alternative but to grasp the nettle, and turn to the Poor Law Unions. By 1872 they had begun to live down 'the exclusive object of their original institution', which had unfitted them 'for wider social duties and responsibilities'.[35] Once again, Stansfeld proclaimed his belief that 'our legislation should cease to be so much as it had been permissive', and announced that he intended to lay 'defined responsibility' upon the new authorities,[36] or, as Professor Lyon Playfair put it, to substitute 'positive instead of a *laissez-faire* legislation'.[37] Stansfeld denied that

[31] *PD* CCVIII, 79, 20 July 1871.
[32] Ibid. 79–80, 20 July 1871.
[33] 35 & 36 Vict. c. 79.
[34] *PP* 1871 XXXV, p. 30, *RSC2* p. 24.
[35] Rumsey, 'Sanitary Legislation and Administration', p. 11.
[36] *PD* CCIX, 598, 16 Feb. 1872.
[37] *PD* CCX, 860–1, 5 Apr. 1872.

'the clauses of this measure' were framed in a 'spirit of distrust of local government', and found stirring words in which to describe his faith in the 'intelligent, independent, and public-spirited men' who must be found to undertake such important duties if they were to be performed at all.[38]

Thirty-eight years after they were invented, the Poor Law Unions became RSAs. Chadwick, who was still alive, could have been forgiven had he supposed that his ambition to rationalise the administrative machinery of the country was beginning to be realised at last. Finally, in 1875, Chadwick's former chief at the General Board of Health, Lord Shaftesbury, introduced a new Public Health Act which completed central government's implementation of the recommendations of the Sanitary Commission,[39] and appeared, to many, to have brought half a century of adoptive and permissive legislation to an end. A balanced judgement upon this point would require another book, but the indications are that the truth is much more complicated.

In the first place the publicists for the coercive cause deceived themselves. Permissive legislation actually flourished under the new regime because permissive clauses were alive and well, lodged within the framework of supposedly compulsory Acts. The Public Health Act of 1875 itself is an example. Rhetoric might credit this with being a compulsory Act. But it contained many clauses among its 343 sections which were explicitly permissive. The Act conferred upon local authorities power to establish recreation grounds, markets, and slaughter-houses,[40] to provide ambulances and mortuaries, and to erect hospitals,[41] but it no more required them to do these things than the Nuisances Removal Act of 1860, the Sewage Utilisation Act of 1865, and the Sanitary Act of 1866 had done. Further, many of the clauses of this Act which appeared at first sight to be mandatory, proved, upon examination to be watered down in ways that returned

[38] *PD* CCIX, 600, 16 Feb. 1872.
[39] 38 & 39 Vict. c. 55.
[40] 38 & 39 Vict. c. 55, ss. 164, 166, 169.
[41] Ibid. ss. 123, 141, 131.

them to the permissive sphere. Thus the impressive-look-
ing section 120 which was summarised in the margin of the
statute with the words 'Duty of Local Authority to cause
premises to be cleansed and disinfected', only applied
when the local authority was 'of opinion' that it would be
useful for it to do so.

In the second place the whole principle of adoptive
legislation did not, as was frequently suggested, suddenly
fall to the ground. The adoption of legislation had taken
two forms, a primary, plebiscitary one according to which
the ratepayers themselves took the decision about their
own future, and a secondary, delegated one in which the
ratepayers' elected representatives took it. With the
growth of representative institutions there had been,
during the middle years of the century, some movement
among parliamentary draughtsmen, and among MPs who
debated what was drafted, away from the primary form to
the secondary one. But even primary permissive legislation
did not just disappear overnight. The Lighting and Watching Act of 1833 was not repealed, and was still being
adopted in a handful of localities in the early twentieth
century.[42] The establishment of public libraries, maintained
out of the rates, remained a plebiscitary procedure, and in
many places a fiercely contested one.[43] The temperance
movement, too, with its demand for what was upon different occasions called the Maine law, *the* permissive Bill, or
local option, took a plebiscitary approach when framing its
proposed reforms.[44] The ratepayers still had some real
opportunities to take initiatives on their own, and some
elements among them, at least, were looking for more.

As for the secondary, delegated mode of adoption by the
ratepayers' elected representatives, that was in no way

[42] There were 25 places listed in 1914, among which Thaxted (Essex), Lower
Allithwaite and Upper Holker (Lancs), Milverton (Somerset), and Startforth
(N. Riding) had adopted the Act since 1904, *PP* 1914 LXVIII, pp. 433–4, *Local
Taxation Returns (England and Wales), The Annual Local Taxation Returns, Year
1912–13, part II*, pp. 115–16.
[43] Kelly, *Public Libraries in Great Britain*, p. 30, cites Bristol and Newcastle on
Tyne as examples.
[44] B. H. Harrison, *Drink and the Victorians. The Temperance Question in England,
1815–72* (1971), pp. 198–202.

obsolescent. For fifty years after permissive legislation had become a pejorative phrase, and parliament had established a Local Government Board, the legislature continued to add, enthusiastically, to the permitted powers of the local authorities. The Artisans Dwellings Act of 1875 was to all intents and purposes permissive. 'The intervention of the Government' was 'simply to give parliamentary power and save expense.'[45] In 1878 Ashley's own Bath-houses and Wash-houses Act was amended to allow local authorities to adopt the Act and provide covered swimming-pools.[46] In 1879 Disraeli's government passed 'An Act to facilitate the control and cure of Habitual Drunkards', encouraging local authorities to license what were called 'retreats'.[47] The Act of 1888 which established County Councils allowed the new authorities to make grants in aid of emigration.[48] In 1891 the Museums Act was enlarged to allow a local authority to adopt the Act and build a gymnasium.[49] The Act could be adopted either for the one purpose, or for the other, or for both, and its provisions conjured up visions of rival parties claiming to represent *mens sana* and *corpus sanum* coming before the ratepayers to plead for their support.

In the twentieth century the last Liberal government was as productive of permissive legislation as it was of everything else. An Act of 1908, for example, allowed parish

---

[45] *PD* CCXXII, 108, 8 Feb. 1875; 38 & 39 Vict. c. 36. It was in 1875, too, that Disraeli delivered the best-known eulogy of permissive legislation, saying that it was 'the characteristic of a free people. It is easy to adopt compulsory legislation when you have to deal with those who only exist to obey; but in a free country, and especially in a country like England, you must trust to persuasion and example as the two great elements, if you wish to effect any considerable change in the manners and customs of the people' (*PD* CCXXV, 525, 24 June 1875). This was said, however, in the debate upon the Agricultural Holdings Act, and Disraeli was arguing in favour of a clause which allowed landowners to opt out of the new procedures for compensating tenants for improvements and rendered the Act a nullity. Far from being a ringing plea for citizens to be allowed to take responsibilities upon themselves, therefore, the words are a flamboyant rationalisation of the fact that one sectional interest, at least, was still too powerful for his administration to control.

[46] 41 & 42 Vict. c. 14.

[47] 42 & 43 Vict. c. 19.

[48] 51 & 52 Vict. c. 41, s. 69 (1)(d).

[49] 54 & 55 Vict. c. 22.

councils (or in a place where there was no parish council the parish meeting) to subsidise village post offices,[50] and another, of 1908, permitted County Councils to advance money to tenants wishing to purchase their smallholdings, and to 'promote the formation of . . . societies on a co-operative basis'.[51] In 1910 the Education (Choice of Employment) Act enabled local authorities to provide vocational training for school-leavers.[52] After the war of 1914–18, the Education Act of 1921 permitted any local authority with responsibility for education to provide meals at school both in term time and in the holidays, and, in cases where the parents were too poor to pay for them, to defray the cost out of the rates. Any local authority could provide school swimming-baths, centres for physical training, and holiday camps. An Urban District Council could supply, or aid the supply of, higher education, while a County Council, which was 'required to consider the educational needs' of its area, was permitted to take such steps towards the provision of higher education as it deemed desirable.[53] In 1924–5 the Royal Commission on Local Government concluded that 'it will be convenient to distinguish those functions the exercize of which is *obligatory* upon Local Authorities, that is, what the Authorities of the several types *must do*, from those functions the exercize of which by Local Authorities is *permissive*, that is, what the Authorities of the several types *may do*.'[54] The Commission listed the Parish Councils, the Rural District Councils, the Urban District Councils, and the County Councils, and tabulated the musts and the mays. The one list was as long as the other.

Right up to the twentieth century, then, permissive legislation remained built into the entire structure of local government at every level, enabling local authorities to experiment with the provision of new services, to keep the

[50] 8 Edw. VII c. 48, s. 49.
[51] 8 Edw. VII c. 36, s. 49.
[52] 10 Edw. VII and 1 Geo. V c. 37.
[53] 11 & 12 Geo. V c. 51.
[54] *PP* 1924–25 XIV, p. 540, *First Report of the Royal Commission on Local Government*, p. 34.

public-service frontier moving, and to order their priorities for themselves as they judged best for their localities. In these circumstances councillors rose above the level of mere functionaries, and careers in local government continued to be an object of ambition to able men and women. The localities' expression of feeling against the General Board of Health and in favour of the Local Government Act had not been in vain, and much of the value system embodied in the Local Government Act had survived the creation of the Local Government Board.

Index